BROWNING'S
MAJOR POETRY

BROWNING'S MAJOR POETRY

BY

IAN JACK

... the Drama—the playing of different
Natures with Joy and Sorrow.

KEATS

OXFORD
AT THE CLARENDON PRESS
1973

Oxford University Press, Ely House, London W. 1

GLASGOW NEW YORK TORONTO MELBOURNE WELLINGTON
CAPE TOWN IBADAN NAIROBI DAR ES SALAAM LUSAKA ADDIS ABABA
DELHI BOMBAY CALCUTTA MADRAS KARACHI LAHORE DACCA
KUALA LUMPUR SINGAPORE HONG KONG TOKYO

ISBN 0 19 8120486

© *Oxford University Press 1973*

*Printed in Great Britain
at the University Press, Oxford
by Vivian Ridler
Printer to the University*

FOR
HUMPHRY, WALTER
AND BELINDA

PREFACE

BROWNING'S reputation between the wars resembled that of John Donne twenty or thirty years before. A few of his poems were well known, and he had a handful of knowledgeable and enthusiastic supporters. He was—many were prepared to concede—'the first poet in the world in some things' (as Jonson had said of Donne); but against his admitted strengths were set the weaknesses which were supposed to follow from his 'optimism' and an alleged coarseness of sensibility. His mastery of the 'dramatic monologue' (a term he himself seems never to have used) was seen as a sort of special skill, and not as a development of central importance in the development of the English poetic tradition.

Yet that is what it was. While Browning is not as great a poet as Donne, he is not only one of the major English poets: he is also one of those whose writing contributes to the central tradition of our poetry. His work exerted an important influence on men as different from himself and from each other as Kipling, Hardy, Pound, and Eliot, and it is not surprising that his character and the nature of his achievement so fascinated a number of the writers of the generation that succeeded his own. 'The longer I live,' Hardy once wrote, 'the more does B[rowning]'s character seem *the* literary puzzle of the 19th Century',[1] while Henry James returned time and again to the poetry and the man. James insisted that 'the exhibition of the great constringent relation between man and woman at once at its maximum and as the relation most worth while in life for either party' forms 'quite the main substance of our author's message',[2] and he was so fascinated by the contrast between the outer Browning and the inner that he made it the theme of 'The Private Life'.

It is ironical that one of the poets whose debt to Browning is unmistakable, T. S. Eliot, was the critic who did most to depress

[1] Betty Miller, *Robert Browning: A Portrait* (1952), p. 164.
[2] 'The Novel in "The Ring and the Book" ', in *Notes on Novelists* (1914), p. 324.

Browning's critical reputation. Whereas the common reader, having read Browning at school, had no doubt that the author of 'Fra Lippo Lippi' was a major poet of some kind, too many minor and minimus critics were content to take their cue from Eliot, consigning Browning's inconveniently bulky _Poetical Works_ to the limbo of the unreadable or the merely historically interesting. That was absurd, and Eliot's mentor, Ezra Pound, always took a very different view, insisting that Browning was 'the soundest of all the Victorians' and describing _Men and Women_ as 'the most interesting poems in Victorian English'.[3] Since the publication of Langbaum's pioneering book, _The Poetry of Experience: The Dramatic Monologue in Modern Literary Tradition_, critics who had allowed themselves to be unduly swayed by Eliot's generally dismissive asides[4] have been coming round to Browning, and at the present moment his work is being read with more respect, and with a more open mind, than at any time since his death. Of course he wrote too much: of course much of the later work is inferior: but how are we to account for the greatness of his finest poems, in what terms are we to analyse them, with the work of which other poets may they best be compared?

In the present study I am not concerned with Browning's influence on subsequent writers. Perhaps the nature of my interest could best have been indicated by the use of the sub-title 'The Wood and the Trees'. That sounds facetious, but it indicates very accurately the fact that I am concerned with the shape of Browning's poetic career as well as with his individual poems. I believe that a poet's work forms a pattern, and that while that pattern can only be deduced from his individual poems, our understanding of the individual poems is enhanced and deepened by our awareness of the complete body of work of which they form a part. With some poets

---

[3] _Literary Essays of Ezra Pound_, ed. T. S. Eliot (1954), pp. 278, 419. Cf. Pound to René Taupin, May 1928: 'Und überhaupt ich stamm aus Browning. Pourquoi nier son père?': _The Selected Letters of Ezra Pound 1907–1941_, ed. D. D. Paige (1950), p. 218.

[4] Occasionally, Eliot was more favourable. In an unpublished lecture, for example, he praised Browning for being the only poet of his period 'to devise a way of speech which might be useful for others', the only one who reasserted 'the relation of poetry to speech' and demonstrated the possibility of using 'non-poetic material': see 'Browning and Modern Poetry', by G. Robert Stange, in _Browning's Mind and Art_, ed. Clarence Tracy (1968), p. 192.

the finding of the pattern in the carpet may be relatively simple: with others, as with Browning, it is extremely difficult, and the perception of the pattern may only come as a result of years of reading and reflection. What I have termed the shape of Browning's poetic career is a most unusual shape, but I believe that when one comes to perceive it one's understanding of his poetry is greatly enhanced. My aim has been to trace the successive stages in his poetic life, from his strange beginnings through his years of greatness and on to the threshold of the comparative decline of his last twenty years, and to analyse his principal poems not only in themselves but also in relation to their position in his work as a whole.

I began to plan this book more than twenty years ago. While I have tried to keep up with recent research and to record specific debts to other scholars, I have assumed that the reader would not wish the footnotes to comprise a running commentary on all my agreements and disagreements with other writers on Browning. I hope that it will not be supposed that I am unaware of the numerous books and articles which I have not had occasion to mention: I have benefited, for example, from E. D. H. Johnson's well-known study, *The Alien Vision of Victorian Poetry*, and from the remarkable chapter on Browning in *The Disappearance of God*, by J. Hillis Miller. I have of course consulted the editorial matter in the first two volumes of the Ohio edition of *The Complete Works*.

In writing this book I have once again benefited from the advice and encouragement of Jane Jack. I am grateful to Mr. J. B. Bullen for his comments on Chapter xii, and to my wife for her help in compiling the index. It should perhaps be mentioned that a few sentences have already appeared in print, principally in the Warton Lecture for 1967.

I.J.

Pembroke College
Cambridge

CONTENTS

ABBREVIATIONS

The place of publication of books is given if it is other than London or Oxford.

Brett-Smith
: *Peacock's Four Ages of Poetry: Shelley's Defence of Poetry: Browning's Essay on Shelley*, ed. H. F. B. Brett-Smith ('The Percy Reprints', 1921).

Chatterton
: *Browning's Essay on Chatterton*, ed. D. Smalley (Cambridge, Mass., 1948).

Chesterton
: *Robert Browning*, by G. K. Chesterton ('English Men of Letters', 1903).

Dearest Isa
: *Dearest Isa: Robert Browning's Letters to Isabella Blagden*, ed. E. C. McAleer (1951).

DeVane
: *A Browning Handbook*, by W. C. DeVane (2nd edn., New York, 1955). In my notes, page references to DeVane are seldom given, as *A Browning Handbook* is lucidly arranged.

DNB
: *The Dictionary of National Biography*.

Domett
: *Robert Browning and Alfred Domett*, ed. F. G. Kenyon (1906).

Drew
: *Robert Browning: A Collection of Critical Essays*, ed. P. Drew (1966).

E.B.B.
: *The Letters of Elizabeth Barrett Browning*, ed. F. G. Kenyon (2 vols., 4th edn., 1898).

ELN
: *English Literature Notes*, Boulder, Colorado.

Fuson
: *Browning and his English Predecessors in the Dramatic Monolog*, by B. W. Fuson (State University of Iowa Humanistic Studies, vol. viii, Iowa, 1948).

Gosse
: *Robert Browning: Personalia*, by Edmund Gosse (1890).

Griffin and Minchin
: *The Life of Robert Browning*, by W. Hall Griffin, completed and edited by H. C. Minchin (1910, 3rd ed., 1938).

Handbook
: *A Handbook to the Works of Robert Browning*, by Mrs. Sutherland Orr (7th edn., 1896).

Huxley
: *Elizabeth Barrett Browning: Letters to her Sister, 1846–1859*, ed. Leonard Huxley (1929).

JEGP
: *Journal of English and Germanic Philology*.

Kintner
: *The Letters of Robert Browning and Elizabeth Barrett Barrett 1845–1846*, ed. E. Kintner (2 vols., Cambridge,

Kintner (*cont.*)	Mass., 1969). As E. B. B. frequently used two dots as a mode of punctuation, it should be noted that whereas '. . .' indicates an omission, in quotations from her letters, '. .' is her own punctuation. R. B. occasionally used the same device.
Langbaum	*The Poetry of Experience: The Dramatic Monologue in Modern Literary Tradition*, by R. Langbaum (1957).
Letters	*Letters of Robert Browning Collected by Thomas J. Wise*, ed. T. L. Hood (1933).
Letters of Keats	*The Letters of John Keats 1814–1821*, ed. H. E. Rollins (2 vols., 1958).
Letters of Rossetti	*Letters of Dante Gabriel Rossetti*, ed. O. Doughty and J. R. Wahl (4 vols., 1965–).
Letters of Shelley	*The Letters of Percy Bysshe Shelley*, ed. F. L. Jones (2 vols., 1964).
Life and Letters	*Life and Letters of Robert Browning*, by Mrs. Sutherland Orr, new edn., revised by F. G. Kenyon (1908).
Litzinger and Knickerbocker	*The Browning Critics*, ed. B. Litzinger and K. L. Knickerbocker (Lexington, Kentucky, 1967).
Litzinger and Smalley	*Browning: The Critical Heritage*, ed. B. Litzinger and D. Smalley (Critical Heritage Series, 1970).
Melchiori	*Browning's Poetry of Reticence*, by Barbara Melchiori (1968).
Miller	*Robert Browning: A Portrait*, by Betty Miller (1952).
New Letters	*New Letters of Robert Browning*, ed. W. C. DeVane and K. L. Knickerbocker (1951).
New Poems	*New Poems by Robert Browning and Elizabeth Barrett Browning*, ed. Sir Frederic G. Kenyon (1914).
Parleyings	*Browning's Parleyings: The Autobiography of a Mind*, by W. C. DeVane (1927).
PQ	*Philological Quarterly.*
PMLA	*Publications of the Modern Language Association of America.*
Raymond	*The Infinite Moment and Other Essays in Robert Browning*, by W. O. Raymond (2nd edn., Toronto, 1965).
SEL	*Studies in English Literature 1500–1900*, Houston, Texas.
SP	*Studies in Philology.*
Story	*William Wetmore Story and his Friends*, by Henry James (2 vols., 1903).
Symons	*An Introduction to the Study of Browning*, by Arthur Symons (1886).
UTQ	*University of Toronto Quarterly.*
VP	*Victorian Poetry.*
Wedgwood	*Robert Browning and Julia Wedgwood: A Broken Friendship as revealed in their Letters*, ed. R. Curle (1937).

ERRATA

p. 14, line 2 from bottom: *for* stage; *read* stage; —
71, first line of notes: *for* 35 *read* 32
139, line 6 from bottom: *delete second comma*
143, line 2 from bottom: *for* Italyat *read* Italy at
258, line 3 from bottom: *read* Then up again

line 2 from bottom: *read* fearless

line 2 of note 29: *read* work,
302, line 19 from bottom: *for* 380–1 *read* 3, 80–1

I

INTRODUCTION: THE SHAPE OF
BROWNING'S POETIC CAREER

THERE are two kinds of poets, whole-time poets and part-time
poets. It is not a distinction of quality: some of the greatest poetry,
and in particular some of the greatest lyric poetry, has been written
by part-time poets—John Donne and Andrew Marvell, for example.
Part-time poets present less of a problem than whole-time poets
because they write less. Whole-time poets[1] write a great deal, and
as a rule much of what they write is of secondary interest. It is
one thing to read the poetry of Donne or Marvell or Hopkins,
another to confront the Collected Poems of Spenser or Dryden or
Wordsworth.

Or of Browning, who at the end of his life collected his *Poetical
Works* in sixteen volumes.[2] It is true that all poets tend to be read in
selections, and that a single volume will contain all of Browning's
major work;[3] but what such a volume denies the reader is an understanding of how Browning came to write the poetry which it contains. There is an obvious parallel with Wordsworth. It can well be
argued that a volume of selections, including key passages from *The
Prelude*, is sufficient to include all the greatest of his work; yet unless
a reader ventures further and studies the early poems and *The Excursion* and much else he will have at best an imperfect understanding of Wordsworth's mind and poetic vision. A second-rate

[1] I have avoided the term 'professional poet' because few poets have derived their
incomes directly from their poetry. Some (like Milton) have been mainly dependent
on a private income: others (like Spenser and Wordsworth) have enjoyed patronage
partly or wholly due to their eminence as poets.
[2] A seventeenth volume, including *Asolando* (a collection of short poems published
on the day of the poet's death), was added in 1894.
[3] Those who regard *The Ring and the Book* as Browning's greatest achievement will
of course dissent from this view.

poem, or even a bad poem, may well have an importance if it is the work of a great poet which it would lack if it were the work of an inferior poet. When we are sufficiently interested in a writer to wish to move from enjoyment and admiration towards a deeper understanding, then we begin to wonder how the poet who wrote 'Tintern Abbey' could also have written 'To the Spade of a Friend (An Agriculturist)', how the poet who wrote 'My Last Duchess' could also have written *Sordello*. And so we find ourselves becoming inquisitive about the shape of a poet's career, the pattern in his carpet.

Browning was a full-time poet. Perhaps the most revealing sentence he ever wrote about himself occurs in one of his early letters to Elizabeth Barrett:

it is not since yesterday, nor ten nor twenty years before, that I began to look into my own life, and study its end, and requirements, what would turn to its good or its loss. . . . My whole scheme of life, (with its wants, material wants at least, closely cut down,) was long ago calculated.[4]

The first sentence has a Miltonic ring to it. When he wrote it Browning was thirty-three: 'twenty years before' takes us back to his boyhood, to the time when he had 'completed a little volume of verses, called "Incondita", for which he endeavoured in vain to find a publisher'.[5] But we know that Browning was devoted to poetry at a still earlier age, thanks to reminiscences recorded by Edmund Gosse during the poet's last days:

[Mr. Browning] can hardly remember a time when his intention was not to be eminent in rhyme, and he began to write at least as early as Cowley. His sister remembers him, as a very little boy, walking round and round the dining-room table, and spanning out the scansion of his verses with his hand on the smooth mahogany.[6]

He told Gosse that he 'marvelled, as he looked back, at the audacious obstinacy which had made him, when a youth, determine to be a poet and nothing but a poet', and it is interesting to find him acknowledging that he thought that the fact that he had never had

[4] Kintner, i. 192–3.
[5] Edmund Gosse, *DNB*, Suppl. i (1901), 306b.   [6] Gosse, p. 20.

any ordinary employment 'had led to superabundance of production, since, on looking back, he could see that he had often, in his unfettered leisure, been afraid to do nothing'.[7]

Browning is so enigmatic a figure, and the pattern of his poetic career is so difficult to trace, that it is important to remember the simple fact that he never seems seriously to have thought of any other life than that of a poet.[8] Although his father was only moderately well off, we know of no attempt made by the son to earn money otherwise than by writing plays and poems. This gives him something in common with Tennyson, a man extraordinarily different in his temperament and gifts. It is natural that each of these men, dedicated to poetry, should have looked forward to the composition of a Long Poem in which he should embody his vision of life and his message to his time. It is no less natural that each of them should have gone through a lean period in early manhood, a period in which—after the acclamations of a few friends at his first setting out—he was condemned to watch his contemporaries carving out their careers and heading towards eminence in politics or the learned professions while he himself remained at home, the target of candid friends of the family who suggested that the young man would be none the worse for seven or eight hours' regular work a day.[9]

Browning's mother, who was of mixed German and Scottish parentage, was a deeply religious woman, and while he moved away from her religious views early in life a conception that never left him was that of the God-given nature of existence and the paramount duty of making something significant of it. He was pleased when Monckton Milnes told him that he was 'the only literary man he ever knew, *tenax propositi*, able to make out a life for himself and abide in it'.[10] A few months earlier he had written to Elizabeth

---

[7] Ibid., pp. 84–5.

[8] Cf. Gosse's account, *DNB.*, Suppl. i, particularly p. 307b: 'It has been said that the bar and painting occurred to him as possible professions. It may be so, but the statement just made was taken from his own lips'—the statement (that is) that he devoted himself single-mindedly to being a poet. Having fallen in love, he assured Elizabeth Barrett that he would devote some of his time to earning money for them both, but she at once rejected such a suggestion because it would amount to 'a sacrifice of duty & dignity as well as of ease & satisfaction': Kintner, i. 200, 203.

[9] Cf. pp. 70–1, below.   [10] Kintner, i. 512.

Barrett: 'I desire in this life . . . to live and just write out certain things which are in me, and so save my soul.'[11] The ambition is a noble one, none the less so because the language in which it is expressed recalls the Dissenting Chapel of his boyhood. Throughout his long life the parable of the talents was never far from Browning's mind: to save his soul was the principal aim of his whole existence, and it is not surprising that it is also the master-theme of all his poetry.[12] Annoyed at the idea that Browning should seek a regular occupation, Elizabeth Barrett quoted with approval a friend's remark that 'Wordsworth had given himself to the service of the temple from the beginning'.[13] 'A poet's affair is with God', Browning wrote to Ruskin in 1855.[14]

Browning's career as an adult poet begins with a poem of 1,031 lines which he suppressed shortly after publication—*Pauline*—followed by an experimental poem of more than 4,000 lines—*Paracelsus*. The next few years were devoted to a number of indifferent plays and a long narrative poem—*Sordello*—which has become a by-word for its obscurity. There is no comparing such a career with that of Milton, but there may be some point in comparing it with that of Dryden, a poet who took even longer than Browning to discover 'the true fire'.[15] Dryden's first surviving poem, the elegy 'Upon the death of the Lord Hastings', is an unsuccessful attempt in the decadent 'metaphysical' idiom, written about the time when he left Westminster for Cambridge: when he was twenty-seven he wrote *Heroique Stanza's* on Cromwell, which are much better: and then, at the age of thirty-five, he produced an ambitious 'Historical Poem', *Annus Mirabilis*, which no reader (perhaps) has ever wished longer. During the next ten or eleven years Dryden wrote plays which vary from the distinguished to the indifferent, and it was as he did so that he learned to write the resonant heroic couplets which he was to use in the majority of his major poems, beginning with *MacFlecknoe* in 1678. It was in his forties, and in particular in his

11 Ibid. i. 206.
12 The word 'soul' occurs about a thousand times in his poetry. In *Sordello* alone it occurs on fifty occasions.
13 Kintner, ii. 616.
14 *The Life and Work of John Ruskin*, by W. G. Collingwood (1893), i. 234.
15 The title of chapter iii of *The Poetry of John Dryden*, by Mark Van Doren (rev. edn., Cambridge, 1931). Cf. p. 124 n., below.

later forties, that Dryden unmistakably emerged as a major poet. His successor Pope, on the other hand, was able to write brilliantly by the age of twenty, and he was still in his twenties when he published the *Works* of 1717, a remarkable volume which includes *The Rape of the Lock*, 'Eloisa to Abelard', the 'Elegy to the Memory of an Unfortunate Lady', and *An Essay on Criticism*. While the striking contrast between Pope's career and Dryden's was partly due to differences of temperament and natural endowment, the principal cause was that whereas Dryden was a transitional poet, who had to pioneer the New Poetry, Pope was able to continue where Dryden had left off.

Browning's position was different from that of either, but closer to Dryden's than to Pope's. The 1830s, when he began to write poetry seriously, were a bad time for poets. A vivid description of the years after Byron's death in 1824 is given in Bulwer Lytton's book, *England and the English*:

When Byron passed away, the feeling he had represented craved utterance no more. With a sigh we turned to the actual and practical career of life: we awoke from the morbid, the dreaming, 'the moonlight and the dimness of the mind,' and by a natural reaction addressed ourselves to the active and daily objects which lay before us. And this with the more intenseness, because, the death of a great poet invariably produces an indifference to the art itself.[16]

Bulwer Lytton refers to 'the more than natural distaste for poetry that succeeded the death of Byron', and as if in echo of this Allan Cunningham, in a brief but favourable notice of *Pauline*, commented that 'the day is past, we fear, for either fee or fame in the service of the muse'.[17] It was during this period when poetry was at a discount that two exceptionally gifted young poets were trying to find their way, and it is not surprising that neither Tennyson nor Browning was able to advance with the astonishing surefootedness of Pope 120 years before. The contrasting faults of so much of the early poetry of the two men—the nugatory subject-matter and affected diction of many of Tennyson's early pieces: the soliloquizing obscurity of so much of Browning's early work—can

---

[16] *England and the English*, by Edward Lytton Bulwer (1833), ii. 105–6.
[17] *Athenæum*, 6 Apr. 1833, p. 216: reprinted in Litzinger and Smalley, p. 35.

equally be related to the unfavourable circumstances in which they began their poetic careers,[18] and in particular to their fear that there was no intelligent public for poetry, and that such a public as there was would only tolerate a limited range of subject-matter and expression.

As early as 1820 Peacock had announced that 'it is not the thinking and studious, and scientific and philosophical part of the community' that formed the audience for poetry, but rather

that much larger portion of the reading public, whose minds are not awakened to the desire of valuable knowledge, and who are indifferent to any thing beyond being charmed, moved, excited, affected, and exalted.[19]

In 1834, in the intelligent and thoughtful preface to *Philip Van Artevelde*, a 'Dramatic Romance' that was known to Browning and written by a man whose critical views owed a great deal to conversation with Wordsworth, Henry Taylor states that

The poetry of the day . . . consists of little more than a poetical diction, an arrangement of words implying a sensitive state of mind, and therefore more or less calculated to excite corresponding associations, though, for the most part, not pertinently to any matter in hand; a diction which addresses itself to the sentient, not the percipient, properties of the mind, and displays merely symbols or types of feelings, which might exist with equal force in a being the most barren of understanding.[20]

---

[18] Cf. Bulwer Lytton's satirical 'character' of a Young Poet: 'Of all melancholy and disappointed persons, a young poet in this day is perhaps the most. Observe that pale and discontented countenance, that air at once shy and proud. St. Malo is a poet of considerable genius; he gives himself altogether up to the Muse—he is consumed with the desire of fame; the loud celebrity of Byron yet rings in his ears: he asketh himself, why he should not be equally famous: he has no pleasure in the social world: he feels himself not sufficiently made of . . . He has no sympathy with other men's amusements, unless they either write poetry themselves or read *his* own: he expects all men to have sympathy with *him*. . . . He never read philosophy, yet he affects to write metaphysics, and gives with considerable enthusiasm into the Unintelligible. Verse-writing is the serious occupation of his life; he publishes his poems, and expects them in his heart to have an enormous sale. He cannot believe that the world has gone round; that every time has its genius; that the genius of *this* time is wholly antipoetic': *England and the English*, ii. 237–8.   [19] Brett-Smith, p. 18.

[20] *Philip Van Artevelde: A Dramatic Romance*, by Henry Taylor (2 vols., 1834), vol. i, pp. xx–xxi, x, xi–xii, and xvii–xviii.

Taylor remarks that certain of 'the popular poets of this century' were characterised by great sensibility and fervour, by a profusion of imagery, by force and beauty of language, and by a versification peculiarly easy and adroit, and abounding in that sort of melody, which, by its very obvious cadences, makes itself most pleasing to an unpractised ear.

The great fault of such poets was that

They wanted . . . subject matter. A feeling came more easily to them than a reflection, and an image was always at hand when a thought was not forthcoming. Either they did not look upon mankind with observant eyes, or they did not feel it to be any part of their vocation to turn what they saw to account. It did not belong to poetry, in their apprehension, to thread the mazes of life in all its classes and under all its circumstances, common as well as romantic, and, seeing all things, to infer and to instruct.

To a reader of Browning it is interesting to find Taylor complaining that in Byron's 'portraitures of human character' there 'is nothing . . . of the mixture and modification,—nothing of the composite fabric which Nature has assigned to Man. They exhibit rather passions personified than persons impassioned.' Byron and Shelley were the two great influences on Browning's early poetry, most of which he later destroyed; but we notice that *Pauline* has still something in common with the poetry censured by Taylor. In Browning's major poetry, on the other hand, we find 'the mixture and modification' of human character, 'the composite fabric which Nature has assigned to Man' delineated more brilliantly than in the work of any other non-dramatic poet since Chaucer.

A peculiarity in the shape of Browning's career is that neither he nor anyone else appears to have realized the importance of two short poems which he wrote as early as 1834 or 1835.[21] 'Porphyria's Lover' and 'Johannes Agricola in Meditation' are brilliant anticipations of the work of Browning's maturity, yet so far as we know he wrote only one other poem that is at all comparable—'Soliloquy

[21] Griffin and Minchin (p. 73) state that these two poems were written in St. Petersburg, to which Browning paid a brief visit in March–April 1834. As Anne (Thackeray) Ritchie states that 'Porphyria's Lover' was written in Russia (*Records of Tennyson, Ruskin and Browning*, 1893, p. 221), it is possible that Browning himself is the authority for the statement.

of the Spanish Cloister'—during the next seven or eight years. The reason for this is no doubt the very seriousness with which Browning regarded his own vocation as a poet. At this point in his career the writing of a series of short poems would have seemed trivial or even frivolous, measured against the greatness of his ambitions. The failure of *Sordello* marked a turning-point in his development. In the next five or six years he was reduced to publishing his plays in a series of inexpensive pamphlets printed in double columns reminiscent of the reprints of the works of the Elizabethan dramatists. During these years he wrote a handful of short poems of a more or less 'dramatic' kind, and one of them—'My Last Duchess' —is an undoubted masterpiece. The pamphlets in which he was persuaded to collect a number of these shorter poems, *Dramatic Lyrics* and *Dramatic Romances and Lyrics*, published in 1842 and 1845 respectively, should have announced to the world the advent of a poet of genius. In fact very few people noticed, but one of them was Elizabeth Barrett, whom Browning married in 1846.

It is important to observe that Browning had found his true direction—however little he may appear to have realized the fact— well before he met Elizabeth Barrett. It cannot be doubted that she gave him the happiest years of his life, the years which seemed to him to lend significance (humanly speaking) to all the rest. Her effect on his poetry is harder to assess. What seems certain is that the writing of the remarkable letters which he sent her throughout the twenty months of their strange courtship helped Browning to reassess his position and his aspirations, and gave him courage to advance. Obscure and sphinx-like as they are, these letters are much better than most of Browning's correspondence, and he must have benefited both from the act of writing them and from the sense that he had at last found an 'understander'. This was one of the most important things that ever happened to him. The other was the move to Italy, which was also his escape from Victorian England—one of the most unpromising settings there has ever been for a poet whose field was the exploration of the human passions. It was in Italy that Browning wrote the great majority of the poems collected in *Men and Women* in 1855, in two volumes that mark the summit of his poetic achievement.

II

PAULINE

Is it worth while to mention, that the very notion of obtaining a free way for impulses that can find vent in no other channel . . . is implied in all literary production? By this fact is explained . . . the . . . popular jealousy of allowing this privilege to the first claimant. And so instinctively does the Young Poet feel that his desire for this kind of self-enfranchisement will be resisted as a matter of course, that we will venture to say, in nine cases out of ten his first assumption of the licence will be made in a borrowed name. The first communication, to even the family circle or the trusted associate, is sure to be 'the work of a friend' . . .[1]

BROWNING began to write as a boy, as most poets do: later he destroyed his juvenile verses, as most poets should. Only a couplet or two survive from his earliest years, notably an attractive assertion that the little boy is determined to take his medicine like a man:

> Good people all who wish to see
> A boy take physic, look at me.

His precocity was so remarkable that when he was thirteen or so his parents tried to find a publisher for a collection of his poems to which it was proposed to give the title *Incondita*.[2] He once told Domett that 'in my youth (*i.e.* childhood) I wrote *only* musically',[3] and as an old man he informed Gosse that these early verses 'were servile imitations of Byron, who was at that time still alive; and that their only merit was their mellifluous smoothness'.[4] No doubt he

---

[1] *Chatterton*, p. 116.

[2] 'When I got older, perhaps at twelve or thirteen, I wrote a book of verses which Eliza [Flower] read and wrote to me about': *Letters*, p. 20. In *New Poems* Kenyon states that the two surviving poems 'were written in his fourteenth year' (p. 3). It is worth noticing that in 1808 Felicia Dorothea Browne (later Mrs. Hemans) had published a collection of *Poems* 'written between the age of eight and thirteen years': her poetry was well known to the Brownings and their friends.

[3] *Domett*, p. 96.   [4] *DNB*, Suppl. i. 307a.

was remembering his own early attempts in the passage in the *Essay on Chatterton* in which he wrote that

Genius almost invariably begins to develop itself by imitation. It has, in the short-sightedness of infancy, faith in the world; and its object is to compete with, or prove superior to, the world's already recognised idols, at their own performances and by their own methods.[5]

While the influence of recent poets may be discerned in the two poems which survived destruction (they were transcribed by Sarah Flower),[5a] neither is a 'servile imitation' of anyone, while the influence of Byron is conspicuous by its absence. 'The Dance of Death', which shows a remarkable command of metre for a boy, is more reminiscent of Shelley (whom Browning first read about 1826)[6] or of Coleridge, while 'The First-Born of Egypt', which opens with musical lines which recall Mrs. Hemans or the minor work of Tennyson, is equally un-Byronic. The most striking feature of the latter poem is the fact that it is a dramatic monologue describing a Biblical story: in this respect it anticipates two poems that Browning was to write almost thirty years later, 'An Epistle of Karshish' and 'Cleon'. The lines apparently underlined by Sarah Flower illustrate the power of this poem:

> I marked one old man with his only son
> Lifeless within his arms—his withered hand
> Wandering o'er the features of his child
> Bidding him [wake] from that long dreary sleep,
> And lead his old blind father from the crowd
> To the green meadows—but he answer'd not.

It is clear that the instinct to dramatize—to describe an incident as experienced by a person other than the poet himself—came early to Browning. While it is true that the 'dramatic monologue' was well established by this time, having been particularly popular with the minor and minimus poets of the early part of the century, we are

---

[5] p. 111.

[5a] It is possible, as Park Honan has pointed out, that these two poems were written as late as the winter of 1826–7, or the spring of 1827: *Browning's Characters: A Study in Poetic Technique* (1961), p. 9n.

[6] See Frederick A. Pottle, *Shelley and Browning: A Myth and Some Facts* (Chicago, 1923).

bound to be struck by the assurance with which he handles it, at so early a point in his own career.

Of the many strange features of that career, not the least strange was the occasion which led to the writing of his first long poem. On 22 October 1832 he went to Richmond to see Edmund Kean in Shakespeare's *Richard III*, and this, as he was later to record, inspired a 'childish scheme',

a foolish plan which occupied me mightily for a time, and which had for its object the enabling me to assume & realize I know not how many different characters;—meanwhile the world was never to guess that 'Brown, Smith, Jones & Robinson' . . . the respective authors of this poem, the other novel, such an opera, such a speech &c &c were no other than one and the same individual. The present abortion was the first work of the *Poet* of the batch, who would have been more legitimately *myself* than most of the others; but I surrounded him with all manner of (to my then notion) poetical accessories, and had planned quite a delightful life for him.

Only this crab remains of the shapely Tree of Life in this Fool's Paradise of mine.[7]

In a pencilled note in his own copy of *Pauline* Browning is inclined to think that he had made up his mind 'to *act* as well as to make verses, music, and God know[s] what'.[8] It tells us a great deal about Browning that it should have been the performance of a famous actor that stimulated this urge to writing by impersonation on the part of a young man destined to become the greatest master of the dramatic monologue, but we should also remember that the outstanding literary event of the immediate past had been the death of Sir Walter Scott, just a month before. It seems possible that the reading of obituaries of 'The Great Unknown', the author of a number of famous poems who had then become the anonymous author of a series of even more celebrated romances in prose, may also have served to stimulate Browning's ambition.

It would be as foolish to deny the marked element of autobiography in *Pauline* as it would be to read the poem as direct autobiography. As we have seen, Browning acknowledged that

---

[7] Browning's note in the copy of *Pauline* once in the possession of John Stuart Mill. I have checked DeVane's transcription against the copy itself, now in the Victoria and Albert Museum. [8] DeVane, p. 41.

there was an element of himself in 'the *Poet*', and the narrator is
not only Browning's own age (twenty) but in other demonstrable
respects a close relative of his creator. Here, for example, is the
passage where the speaker describes the experiences which have
gone to his own making:

> They came to me in my first dawn of life,
> Which passed alone with wisest ancient books,
> All halo-girt with fancies of my own,
> And I myself went with the tale—a god,
> Wandering after beauty—or a giant,
> Standing vast in the sunset—an old hunter,
> Talking with gods—or a high-crested chief,
> Sailing with troops of friends to Tenedos;—
> I tell you, nought has ever been so clear
> As the place, the time, the fashion of those lives.
> I had not seen a work of lofty art,
> Nor woman's beauty, nor sweet nature's face,
> Yet, I say, never morn broke clear as those
> On the dim clustered isles in the blue sea:
> The deep groves, and white temples, and wet caves—
> And nothing ever will surprise me now—
> Who stood beside the naked Swift-footed,
> Who bound my forehead with Proserpine's hair.[9]

As the poem remains a fragment, the nature of the 'delightful life'
that Browning had planned for his poet must remain a mystery;
but it is clear that many of the poet's experiences as recorded in the
poem bear a marked resemblance to his own. And Browning's
motive for writing this 'Fragment of a Confession' was surely
identical with that of the supposed speaker: he had thoughts in his
soul which he had to unlock before he could 'hope to sing'.

The poet is a highly intellectual young man who feels immeasur-
ably old and who is haunted by that sense of ill-defined guilt
which had long been a characteristic of the 'romantic hero':

> Still I can lay my soul bare in its fall,
> For all the wandering and all the weakness

---

[9] Lines 318–35. My quotations are from the original text of *Pauline*, as given in
Appendix A in my Oxford Standard Authors edition of *Browning: Poetical Works
1833–1864*. Unless otherwise indicated, all quotations from Browning's poems are
from this edition.

Will be a saddest comment on the song.
And if, that done, I can be young again,
I will give up all gained as willingly
As one gives up a charm which shuts him out
From hope, or part, or care, in human kind. (124–30)

He desires to confess to Pauline, and to be pardoned by her—
although he is aware that he can never again be the man he used to
be. He has been led from Pauline by 'wild dreams of beauty and of
good', but now he is half disposed to renounce 'All this gay mastery
of mind' if by so doing he can regain his old sense of security.
Throughout the poem we are aware of a conflict between the poet's
hunger for knowledge and his need to believe in God. *Pauline* is a
sort of *Discours de la méthode* written by a man with one of the least
Cartesian minds ever to have existed:

I strip my mind bare—whose first elements
I shall unveil—not as they struggled forth
In infancy, nor as they now exist,
That I am grown above them, and can rule them,
But in that middle stage, when they were full,
Yet ere I had disposed them to my will;
And then I shall show how these elements
Produced my present state, and what it is.
I am made up of an intensest life,
Of a most clear idea of consciousness
Of self—distinct from all its qualities,
From all affections, passions, feelings, powers . . .
                                          (260–71)

The poet is clearly speaking for Browning himself when he meditates
on the value of poetry and describes his own early poetic efforts:

And first I sang, as I in dream have seen,
Music wait on a lyrist for some thought,
Yet singing to herself until it came.
I turned to those old times and scenes, where all
That's beautiful had birth for me, and made
Rude verses on them all; and then I paused—
I had done nothing, so I sought to know
What mind had yet achieved. No fear was mine
As I gazed on the works of mighty bards,

In the first joy at finding my own thoughts
Recorded, and my powers exemplified,
And feeling their aspirings were my own.
And then I first explored passion and mind;
And I began afresh; I rather sought
To rival what I wondered at, than form
Creations of my own; so much was light
Lent back by others, yet much was my own. (377–93)

Reflections on the significance of poetry, and on that of 'music, my life', blend with meditations on the meaning of human existence, as exemplified by his own present state, to form the subject-matter of the poem. It is clear that Browning's own feeling of guilt at his apostasy from the stern and simple religion of his mother was one of his principal incitements to write *Pauline*, and by a curious chance we have direct evidence of his passion for aggressive metaphysical argument, a few years earlier. In November 1827 Sarah Flower, a close friend of the Browning family who lived on to compose the hymn 'Nearer, my God, to Thee', wrote to her guardian about her religious doubts:

The cloud has come over me gradually, and I did not discover the darkness in which my soul was shrouded until, in seeking to give light to others, my own gloomy state became too settled to admit of doubt. It was in answering Robert Browning that my mind refused to bring forward argument, turned recreant, and sided with the enemy.[10]

It is quite possible that Sarah's sister Eliza gave Browning the advice which Pauline gives the poet towards the end of the poem:[10a]

And then thou said'st a perfect bard was one
Who shadowed out the stages of all life,
And so thou badest me tell this my first stage;
'Tis done.   (883–6)[11]

[10] *Centenary History of the South Place Society*, by Moncure D. Conway (1894), p. 46: quoted in DeVane, p. 9.
[10a] Mrs. Sutherland Orr wrote that 'If, in spite of his denials, any woman inspired *Pauline*, it can be no other than she': *Life and Letters*, p. 35.
[11] Browning revised these lines to read:
And then thou said'st a perfect bard was one
Who chronicled the stages of all life,
And so thou bad'st me shadow this first stage.
DeVane misleadingly quotes only the first two of the three lines, and adds the

John Stuart Mill, who had come to realize the importance of poetry only a few years before (as he later described in a famous passage in his *Autobiography*), was reflecting a good deal on the condition of English poetry at this time, and a copy of *Pauline* was sent him by W. J. Fox. In January and November 1833 Mill published two remarkable essays on poetry in the *Monthly Repository*: soon he was reading Tennyson's volumes of 1830 and 1833, which he was to review two years later: and in 1833 he also made notes for a review of *Pauline*—notes which were shown to Browning, although the review was never written. Mill praises the poem for the truth and power of 'the psychological history' it contains, yet he has reservations:

The self-seeking and self-worshipping state is well described—beyond that, I should think the writer has made, as yet, only the next step, viz. into despising his own state. I even question whether part even of that self-disdain is not *assumed*. He is evidently *dissatisfied*, and feels part of the badness of his state; he does not write as if it were purged out of him.... Meanwhile he should not attempt to show how a person may be *recovered* from this morbid state,—for *he* is hardly convalescent, and 'what should we speak of but that which we know?'[12]

Mill observes that the writer is 'possessed with a more intense and morbid self-consciousness than I ever knew in any sane human being': an observation by which Browning appears not to have been offended.[13] Mill's censure of the poet's attitude to Pauline is less incisive, since (as Mill himself observes) she is 'evidently a mere phantom'.[14]

comment: 'The difference implied in the single word is great: the earlier version reveals the autobiographical and confessional poet of 1833; the later shows the "dramatic" poet which he strove to become': p. 40.

[12] DeVane, p. 46.

[13] 'I know myself', he wrote to Elizabeth Barrett in 1845, '. . . and always have done so—for is there not somewhere the little book I first printed when a boy, with John Mill, the metaphysical head, *his* marginal note that "the writer possesses a deeper self-consciousness than I ever knew in a sane human being"—So I never deceived myself much, nor called my feelings for people other than they were': Kintner, i. 28. A little later he wrote: 'I had a certain faculty of self-consciousness, years, years ago, at which John Mill wondered, and which ought to be improved by this time, if constant use helps at all . . .': Kintner, i. 75. It is worth noticing that Browning wanted Mill to review *Paracelsus*: cf. *Life and Letters*, pp. 66-7.

[14] DeVane, p. 42.

Whatever part Eliza Flower may have played in inspiring the poem, the girl whom the poet loves is in no way individualized, and she may best be regarded as one of the 'poetical accessories' with which Browning chose to surround his speaker. The most important character in *Pauline*, apart from the speaker, is not Pauline but Shelley, the 'Sun-treader' who presides throughout and who is apostrophized in the final paragraph. After the passage about his early poetry quoted above the poet describes how he looked for 'a star' to guide him in his further development:

> . . . one, whom praise of mine would not offend,
> Who was as calm as beauty—being such
> Unto mankind as thou to me, Pauline,
> Believing in them, and devoting all
> His soul's strength to their winning back to peace;
> Who sent forth hopes and longings for their sake,
> Clothed in all passion's melodies, which first
> Caught me, and set me, as to a sweet task,
> To gather every breathing of his songs.[15]   (404–12)

The *Essay on Shelley* provides an illuminating commentary on the poem. In it Browning states that 'the subjective poet' is not concerned 'with the combination of humanity in action, but with the primal elements of humanity . . . ; and he digs where he stands,— preferring to seek them in his own soul as the nearest reflex of [the] absolute Mind, according to the intuitions of which he desires to perceive and speak. . . . He is rather a seer . . . than a fashioner'.[16] This is as true of the poet of *Pauline* as it is of the poet of 'Alastor', while another aspect of the contrast between the subjective poet and the objective poet throws further light on Browning's early poem. Whereas the objective poet 'chooses to deal with the doings of men', the subjective poet, 'whose study has been himself, ap- pealing through himself to the absolute Divine mind, prefers to

---

[15] In 1868 Browning added a new line and a half to the beginning of this passage:
> And my choice fell
> Not so much on a system as a man.

In a further revision in 1888–9, the last line of the passage quoted above was dropped in favour of the words:
> To disentangle, gather sense from song.

[16] Brett-Smith, pp. 65–6.

dwell upon those external scenic appearances which strike out most abundantly and uninterruptedly his inner light and power, [and therefore] selects that silence of the earth and sea in which he can best hear the beating of his individual heart'. Several of the finest passages in *Pauline* are descriptions of external nature, and often (as in Shelley) external objects become a symbol for the feelings of the poet:

> Night, and one single ridge of narrow path
> Between the sullen river and the woods
> Waving and muttering—for the moonless night
> Has shaped them into images of life,
> Like the upraising of the giant-ghosts,
> Looking on earth to know how their sons fare. (732–7)

While *Pauline* reminds us of 'Alastor', it has also a number of points in common with *Epipsychidion*, that most characteristic of Shelley's 'esoteric'[17] poems. Like *Epipsychidion*, *Pauline* is described as a fragment, though in neither case are we given any information about the longer poem contemplated by the writer.[18] Like *Epipsychidion*, *Pauline* is addressed to a woman, who remains a shadowy presence throughout. Like *Epipsychidion*, *Pauline* is accompanied by an apparatus designed to show that the speaker is someone other than the poet himself. Shelley prefixed to his poem an Advertisement in which he stated that

The Writer of the following lines died at Florence, as he was preparing for a voyage to one of the wildest of the Sporades, which he had bought, and where he had fitted up the ruins of an old building, and where it was his hope to have realised a scheme of life, suited perhaps to that happier and better world of which he is now an inhabitant, but hardly practicable in this.

This may remind us of the note in French attributed to Pauline: as Shelley refers to 'my unfortunate friend', so she refers to 'mon pauvre ami'. Browning might well have written of *Pauline*, as Shelley did of *Epipsychidion*, that it was '. . . in a certain sense,. . . a production of a portion of me already dead': so much was implied

---

[17] *Letters of Shelley*, ii. 263.
[18] 'The present poem appears to have been intended by the Writer as the dedication to some longer one': Advertisement to *Epipsychidion*.

(indeed) by the 'extreme repugnance' which he felt when he was obliged to include it in his collected poems. He might equally have written of his poem, as Shelley did of *Epipsychidion*:

The present Poem, like the *Vita Nuova* of Dante, is sufficiently intelligible to a certain class of readers without a matter-of-fact history of the circumstances to which it relates; and to a certain other class it must ever remain incomprehensible, from a defect of a common organ of perception for the ideas of which it treats.

The reception of *Pauline* made it clear that the second class of readers greatly preponderated. Allan Cunningham afforded it a few words of praise in the *Athenæum*, while W. J. Fox reviewed it enthusiastically in the *Monthly Repository*. A writer in the *Literary Gazette*, on the other hand, described it as 'somewhat mystical, somewhat poetical, somewhat sensual, and not a little unintelligible', and his conclusion that it was 'a dreamy volume, without an object, and unfit for publication'[19] probably reflected that of such casual readers as glanced into *Pauline* in a bookseller's shop—for Browning was later to say that not a single copy was sold. He omitted *Pauline* from the selected edition of his poems which he published in 1849, and from the more comprehensive *Poetical Works* of 1863; but in 1868 he reprinted it, with the following introduction:

The first piece in the series I acknowledge and retain with extreme repugnance, indeed purely of necessity; for not long ago I inspected one, and am certified of the existence of other transcripts, intended sooner or later to be published abroad: by forestalling these, I can at least correct some misprints (no syllable is changed)[20] and introduce a boyish work by an exculpatory word. The thing was my earliest attempt at 'poetry always dramatic in principle, and so many utterances of so many imaginary persons, not mine',[21] which I have since written according to a scheme less extravagant and scale less impracticable than were ventured upon in this crude preliminary sketch —a sketch that, on reviewal, appears not altogether wide of some hint of the characteristic features of that particular *dramatis persona* it

---

[19] Litzinger and Smalley, pp. 34–6.
[20] An exaggeration.
[21] This important description of his own poetry was first published in the 'Advertisement' to *Bells and Pomegranates, No. III* ('Dramatic Lyrics') in 1842.

would fain have reproduced: good draughtsmanship, however, and right handling were far beyond the artist at that time.

Browning had been on the defensive about *Pauline* from the first. The motto from Cornelius Agrippa protests against malicious readers who will accuse the author of teaching forbidden arts: this is a book for intelligent readers, who may be able to derive benefit from it: in any case it must be remembered that it was written when the author was very young, and that he is describing something (a state of mind), not commending it. In the final collected edition Browning apologized for this apology, with the comment: 'This introduction would appear less absurdly pretentious did it apply, as was intended, to a completed structure of which the poem was meant for only a beginning and remains a fragment.'

The French note attributed to Pauline is a further self-criticism and apology, but as it happens it contains the best guidance available on the scope and intention of the poem. She admits that *Pauline* is a strange and confused fragment, but suggests that any attempt to co-ordinate it better might rob it of its only merit—that of giving a fairly precise idea of the nature which it has merely set out to sketch. The second paragraph of the note is particularly helpful, and loses nothing by being translated from Browning's French:

I believe that in what follows [lines 812–] he alludes to a certain examination of the soul, or rather of his own soul, which he undertook some time ago, in order to discover the sequence of objectives to which it would be possible for him to attain, and of which each one (once achieved) should form a sort of plateau from which it would be possible to perceive other ends, other projects, other delights which (in their turn) would have to be surmounted.[22] The conclusion was that oblivion and sleep should terminate everything. This idea, which I do not completely grasp, is perhaps no more completely intelligible to him than it is to me.

Browning's defensiveness about *Pauline* should be borne in mind when we consider the recent debate about the effect of Mill's

---

[22] The image of the ascent of the individual soul, or of mankind in general, is important in Browning's work. In the *Essay on Shelley*, for example, he writes of

criticisms on the poet's later development. Few people would now agree with DeVane's extreme statement that 'this critique changed the course of Browning's poetical career'.[23] On the other hand, nothing could be more certain than that Browning came to dislike all reference to *Pauline*, and was driven to reprint it only because this enabled him (contrary to what he claimed) to make some revisions in the text, as well as preventing a pirated reprint of the original edition. It seems clear that his dislike of the poem was due not only to dissatisfaction with the quality of the work but also— and in a very considerable measure—to the realization that he had written a poem 'so transparent in [its] meaning as to draw down upon him the ridicule of the critics'.[24] Although *Pauline* had been intended to be 'dramatic'[25] it was as obviously 'an idealized history of [Browning's] life and feelings'[26] as *Epipsychidion* had been acknowledged to be of Shelley's. Joseph Arnould accurately described it as 'a strange, wild . . . poet-biography: his own early life as it presented itself to his own soul viewed poetically: in fact, psychologically speaking, his "Sartor Resartus" '.[27] Browning was embarrassed both because he had revealed so much of himself and because (boy-like) he had exaggerated so absurdly. The young man who lived with his parents at Camberwell can have had little opportunity of leading the wild Bohemian life hinted at more than once in the poem, and this very fact must have made the description of the protagonist as 'A mortal, sin's familiar friend' all the more

a future time when 'one more degree will be apparent for a poet to climb in that mighty ladder, of which, however cloud-involved and undefined may glimmer the topmost step, the world dares no longer doubt that its gradations ascend'. A little later in the same essay he writes that 'An absolute vision is not for this world, but we are permitted a continual approximation to it, every degree of which in the individual, provided it exceed the attainment of the masses, must procure him a clear advantage. Did the poet ever attain to a higher platform than where he rested and exhibited a result? Did he know more than he spoke of?' Brett-Smith, pp. 68, 70. Cf. my discussion of 'A Grammarian's Funeral', pp. 168–74, below.

[23] DeVane, p. 47. A brilliant counter-argument has been put forward by Masao Miyoshi, in 'Mill and "Pauline": The Myth and Some Facts': *Victorian Studies* (Bloomington, Indiana), vol. ix, no. 2 (December 1965), 154–63.

[24] Clara Bloomfield-Moore, in *Lippincott's Magazine*, 45 (May 1890), 691: quoted by DeVane, p. 47.

[25] In 1867 Browning was still insisting that 'the poem was purely dramatic': he added that it was 'intended to head a series of "Men & Women" such as I have afterwards introduced to the world under somewhat better auspices': DeVane, p. 48.

[26] *Letters of Shelley*, ii. 434.   [27] *Domett*, p. 141.

embarrassing. Like another premature poem, *Endymion, Pauline* is 'a feverish attempt, rather than a deed accomplished', the product of that period of late adolescence in which 'the soul is in a ferment, the character undecided, the way of life uncertain, the ambition thick-sighted'.[28] Browning was to continue his exploration of the nature of the imaginative life and the role of the creative genius in human society; but before he could do so with any hope of success he had to find a protagonist who differed from himself much more markedly than the poet in *Pauline*, and so make his escape into that territory of dramatic poetry of which he was soon to become the supreme Victorian master.

[28] Preface to *Endymion*.

III

PARACELSUS

I still believe as devoutly as ever in 'Paracelsus', and find more wealth
of thought and poetry in it than [in] any book except Shakespeare.
The more one reads the more miraculous does that book seem as the
work of a man of five-and-twenty.   JOSEPH ARNOULD

Much of what my later writings have been about—the clash of
ability and aspirations, of will and possibility, at once the tragedy and
the comedy of mankind and the individual—is already adumbrated
here.   IBSEN[1]

ROBERT BRIDGES described 'The Wreck of the Deutschland' as
'a great dragon folded in the gate to forbid all entrance' to the poetry
of Hopkins.[2] *Pauline*, *Paracelsus*, and *Sordello* might be described
as a range of mountains lying between the reader and the great
dramatic poems which are Browning's supreme achievement.
Pauline is a hill rather than a mountain, but the extent and unusual
configuration of *Paracelsus* present difficulties to the ordinary
climber, while *Sordello* remains a forbidding peak only to be con-
quered by the most courageous and skilful of mountaineers. For the
ordinary reader, indeed, there is little need to trouble with these
early works: he may concentrate on Browning's most famous and
successful poems, almost all of which were written later. But if one
is concerned with Browning's work as a whole then the early long
poems are not only interesting in themselves but also of vital importance because of the clues which they contain to the pre-
occupations of the major poetry of Browning's middle years.

In his reminiscences of Browning Gosse remarks that it is
'interesting and curious to learn that at a time of life when almost
every poet, whatever his ultimate destination, is trying his power

---

[1] *Domett*, p. 86; Preface to second edition of Ibsen's *Catiline* (1875).
[2] *Poems of Gerard Manley Hopkins*, ed. Robert Bridges (1918), p. 106.

of wing in song, Mr. Browning, the early Byronic lilt having been thrown aside, did not attempt any lyrical exercise. He planned a series of monodramatic epics, narratives of the life of typical souls, —a gigantic scheme at which a Victor Hugo or a Lope de Vega would start back aghast.'[3] It is as true of *Paracelsus* as of *Sordello* that the 'stress' lies on 'the incidents in the development of a soul'.[4] In conception *Sordello* preceded *Paracelsus*, as we know from Browning's statement to Fox about the publication of *Paracelsus* in 1835: 'I have another affair on hand rather of a more popular nature, I conceive; but not so decisive and explicit on a point or two, so I decide on trying the question with this.'[5] It is astonishing to hear that *Sordello* was ever intended to be a 'popular' poem: one is reminded of Shelley, whose inability to gauge the reactions of the reading public was comparable to Browning's—as one is, again, by Browning's statement at the end of the preface to the first edition of *Paracelsus* that it is 'an experiment I am in no case likely to repeat' and his promise of 'other productions which may follow in a more popular, and perhaps less difficult form'.

The subject was suggested to Browning by the Comte de Ripert-Monclar, and at first sight it seems an odd one.[6] Today Paracelsus is of interest only to historians of science, and most of these assign him a very lowly position. Johnson refers to him in the *Lives of the Poets*, a book which Browning seems to have known well.[7] 'When he entered into the living world,' Johnson observes approvingly of Pope, 'it seems to have happened to him as to many others that he was less attentive to dead masters: he studied in the academy of Paracelsus, and made the universe his favourite volume.'[8] Another reference in Johnson—in which he mentions Paracelsus as one of the 'chymical enthusiasts' opposed by Boerhaave[8a]—is more

[3] Gosse, pp. 26–7.
[4] Preface to *Sordello*, in 1863 and subsequent editions.
[5] Griffin and Minchin, p. 89.
[6] 'In the course of one of their conversations, he suggested the life of Paracelsus as a possible subject for a poem; but on second thoughts pronounced it unsuitable, because it gave no room for the introduction of love: about which, he added, every young man of their age thought he had something quite new to say. Mr. Browning decided, after the necessary study, that he would write a poem on Paracelsus, but treating him in his own way': *Life and Letters*, p. 67.
[7] Cf. pp. 169–70, below.   [8] *Lives*, ed. Birkbeck Hill, iii. 216.
[8a] *The Works of Samuel Johnson* (1825), vi, 280.

representative of the eighteenth-century view of Paracelsus, but about the turn of the century we begin to find a marked difference of emphasis, no doubt due to the renewed interest in magic and the occult, as well as to the steadily growing interest in the history of science. In one of his early letters to Godwin, Shelley told him that as a boy he had 'pored over the reveries of Albertus Magnus, & Paracelsus'.[9] In a discussion of 'The Witch of Atlas' a modern scholar has admirably brought out the importance of Paracelsus to the young Shelley:

It is, however, in Paracelsus that the imagination as a creative power is most glorified. Thus 'The astral currents produced by the imagination and will of man produce certain states in external Nature, and these currents reach very far, because the power of the imagination reaches as far as thought can go'. It is faith and imagination, says Paracelsus, which are the bases of magic processes and by them 'we can accomplish whatever we desire. The true power of faith overcomes all the spirits of Nature, because it is a spiritual power, and spirit is higher than Nature.' The 'imagination is not *fancy*, which latter is the corner-stone of superstition and foolishness. The imagination of man becomes pregnant through desire, and gives birth to deed. . . . During sleep the sidereal man may by the power of the imagination be sent out of the physical form, at a distance to act for some purpose'. . . . 'The great world is only a product of the imagination of the universal mind, and man is a little world of its own that imagines and creates by the power of imagination'. And, as a concluding instance, 'If we only knew all the powers of the human heart, nothing would be impossible for us. The imagination is fortified and perfected through faith. . . . Faith must confirm the imagination, because it perfects the will.'[10]

De Quincey refers to Paracelsus as an 'extraordinary man', adding: 'for such, amidst all his follies, he must ever be accounted in the annals of the human mind'.[11] In October 1829, not long before Browning began work on the poem, a writer in the *Edinburgh Review* emphasized the curious historical position of Paracelsus in the following terms:

[9] *Letters of Shelley*, i. 303.
[10] Carl Grabo, *The Meaning of 'The Witch of Atlas'* (Chapel Hill, 1935), pp. 103–4.
[11] *Collected Writings*, ed. Masson, xiii (1890), 401.

The prodigious activity of Paracelsus, the arrogance of his style, the scurrility of his invectives, and even his reveries and absurdities, contributed to procure him a reputation, which was altogether un-rivalled during his own lifetime. And as he was a zealous cultivator of Chemistry, . . . he threw a lustre upon the science of which it was before destitute. . . . The invectives of Paracelsus against Galen and Avicenna, and their adherents and disciples, scurrilous and absurd as they are, were probably necessary to arouse the attention of mankind, and to induce medical men to abandon the jargon of the schools, and to apply themselves to anatomy and chemistry; the only true foun-dations on which a rational medical practice can be built.[12]

Browning had to go no further than his father's library to find the works of Paracelsus, and we know from his own evidence that his father was in the habit of talking about him, as he 'seemed to have known Paracelsus, Faustus, and even Talmudic personages, personally'.[13]

We have only to read the First Part of *Paracelsus* to see why Browning was so anxious to state, in the preface to the first edition, that he had 'endeavoured to write a poem, not a drama'. It contains no action whatever, and consists of a conversation between Paracelsus and two friends which is mainly a monologue spoken by the protagonist. All the interest centres in one man, and even the briefest outline of the work will serve to show that Browning had not yet found a suitable medium for exploring the 'development of a soul'. Such an outline will also serve as an opportunity for displaying the quality of the verse that Browning was capable of writing at this early point in his poetic career.

---

[12] Vol. I, p. 258.

[13] William Sharp, *Life of Robert Browning* (1890), p. 19.—Thomas Lovell Beddoes (whose father, Thomas Beddoes, M.D., is certain to have been interested in Para-celsus) refers to Paracelsus in one of the projected mottoes for *Death's Jest Book*, and at one time planned some sort of comedy in which Paracelsus was to figure. A letter written by Beddoes in November 1844, however, explicitly differentiates his view of Paracelsus—'the historical P., a complete charlatan, seldom sober, clever and cun-ning, living on the appetite of his contemporaneous public for the philosopher's stone and the universal medicine'—from 'Mr. Browning's' interpretation of him. Beddoes mentions that Paracelsus 'burnt Galen's works openly as professor of the university [of Basel], beginning the medical reform so, as Luther did that in religion by his public conflagration of the bull launched against him,' and concedes that Paracelsus 'was a poetical fellow in his way': *The Works of Thomas Lovell Beddoes*, ed. H. W. Donner (1935), p. 673.

In Part I, 'Paracelsus Aspires', we learn that Paracelsus is consumed by a great ambition, the desire to discover

> . . . the secret of the world—
> Of man, and man's true purpose, path, and fate.
>
> (p. 15, ll. 276–7)[14]

He likes to think of Festus and his wife Michal as leading a happy, ordinary life, while he sets off on his lonely and ambitious voyage of intellectual exploration. We notice that he conceives of this ambition in religious terms:

> Dear Festus, hear me. What is it you wish?
> That I should lay aside my heart's pursuit,
> Abandon the sole ends for which I live,
> Reject God's great commission—and so die!
>
> (p. 8, ll. 140–3)

He finds an admirable image for his task:

> . . . Be sure that God
> Ne'er dooms to waste the strength he deigns impart.
> Ask the gier-eagle why she stoops at once
> Into the vast and unexplored abyss!
> What fullgrown power informs her from the first!
> Why she not marvels, strenuously beating
> The silent boundless regions of the sky!
>
> (p. 19, ll. 345–51)

Paracelsus rejects as intolerable any ordinary destiny:

> A station with the brightest of the crowd;
> A portion with the proudest of them all!
> And from the tumult in my breast, this only
> Could I collect—that I must thenceforth die,
> Or elevate myself far, far above
> The gorgeous spectacle; what seem'd a longing
> To trample on yet save mankind at once.
>
> (p. 23, ll. 455–61)

---

[14] I quote from the first edition, in which the lines are not numbered, giving first the page reference to that edition, and then the line reference to the corresponding passage in the O.S.A. edition.

While he might be described as an exceptional man, 'deluded by [a] generous error, instigated by [a] sacred thirst of doubtful knowledge', Paracelsus is a less simple and admirable man than the protagonist of Shelley's *Alastor*, who is 'a youth of uncorrupted feelings and adventurous genius led forth by an imagination inflamed and purified through familiarity with all that is excellent and majestic, to the contemplation of the universe'.[15] While he is impelled by a Messianic complex

> To make some unexampled sacrifice
> In their behalf, (p. 23, ll. 462-3)

we notice that he has apparently little regard for ordinary men and women. In a passage that anticipates 'Childe Roland', he looks forward to behaving

> Like some knight traversing a wilderness
> (p. 24, l. 474)

who frees a 'desert-people' from a dragon and then rejects their offer of kingship and rides off towards the East. Paracelsus reminds us of *Adonais* when he confesses that he aspires 'to become a star to men for ever',[16] and at times he speaks in the true accents of the 'romantic hero':

> And when he ceased, my fate was seal'd for ever.
> If there took place no special change in me,
> How comes it all things wore a different hue
> Thenceforward? pregnant with vast consequence—
> Teeming with grand results—loaded with fate.
> (p. 27, ll. 548-52)

As a rule Paracelsus forestalls the arguments which Festus may wish to bring forward, in the manner of the speaker in a dramatic mono-logue, but at one point Festus is permitted to express his fear that if Paracelsus abjures love there will be

> A monstrous spectacle upon the earth,
> Beneath the pleasant sun, among the trees,
> A being knowing not what love is.
> (p. 33, ll. 677-9)

---

[15] Preface to *Alastor*.   [16] p. 26, l. 527.

Yet Festus is constrained to accept the view that Paracelsus is 'one
/ Of higher order—under other laws / Than bind us'.[17] Paracelsus
goes on to express his growing scorn for conventional learning—

> For men have oft grown old among their books
> And died, case-harden'd in their ignorance
>
> (p. 37, ll. 745–6)

—and to insist that the important truth is to be found within:

> There is an inmost centre in us all,
> Where truth abides in fulness; and around,
> Wall upon wall, the gross flesh hems it in,
> Perfect and true perception—which is truth.
>
> (p. 36, ll. 728–31)

In considering when man comes nearest to perceiving such truth,
Paracelsus points forwards to the moments in life which Browning
was later to choose for his most penetrating revelations:

> [For] not alone when life flows still do truth
> And power emerge, but also when strange chance
> Affects its current; in unused conjuncture,
> Where sickness breaks the body—hunger, watching,
> Excess, or languor—oftenest death's approach—
> Peril, deep joy, or woe.   (p. 38, ll. 765–70)

At the end of Part I, accordingly, the aspiring Paracelsus sets out on
his lonely quest, with the blessing of his friends, supported by the
verdict of Festus:

> You, if a man may, may aspire to KNOW.
>
> (p. 15, l. 282)

He is in a sense the embodiment of Renaissance Man, with his
boundless intellectual aspiration and his tendency to a hubristic
contempt for ordinary mortals.[17a]

In Part II we find Paracelsus fourteen years later, considering
what he has in fact achieved. He recalls how, as a boy, he had
determined 'to become / The greatest and most glorious being on

---

[17] p. 34, ll. 696–8.

[17a] 'Paracelsus was one of the great figures of the Renaissance, and one of the most
unfathomable. For us he is still an enigma': *The Collected Works of C. G. Jung*, vol.
15, trans. R. F. C. Hull (1966), p. 30.

earth', and claims that he has succeeded in making life 'consist of one idea'.[18] 'What's failure or success to me?', he asks rhetorically:

> I have subdued my life to the one purpose
> Whereto I ordain'd it; there alone I spy
> No doubt; that way I may be satisfied.
>
> (p. 47, Part II, ll. 105–8)

Looking back, however, he is constrained to admit that

> . . . there was a time
> When yet this wolfish hunger after knowledge
> Set not remorselessly [love's] claims aside.
>
> (p. 48, ll. 123–5)

It becomes more and more evident that he is bitterly unhappy, and even in fear of madness—and then with dramatic effect he hears a poet singing a strange lyric, of which the opening lines were added after the first edition:

> I hear a voice, perchance I heard
> Long ago, but all too low,
> So that scarce a care it stirred
> If the voice were real or no . . .   (ll. 281–4)

This is not the place to attempt to unravel the obscurities in the parts of the poem where Aprile appears—some of them due to the fact that Aprile refers to Paracelsus himself as a poet: for our purposes it is sufficient to note that Aprile embodies the desire for Infinite Love, as Paracelsus embodies the desire for Infinite Knowledge:

> I would love infinitely, and be loved.
> First: I would carve in stone, or cast in brass,
> The forms of earth . . .   (p. 59, ll. 420–2)

There is little or no true drama in the confrontation between the two men; indeed they are two ideas, rather than two men. Monologue does not give way, as it might have done, to the thrust and parry of true dialogue. What happens is simply that one monologue succeeds another. We notice that Aprile, the poet-artist, speaks verse that is among the most vivid in the poem:

> . . . I would contrive and paint
> Woods, valleys, rocks, and plains, dells, sands, and wastes,

---

[18] pp. 49, 48, ll. 148–9, 140.

Lakes which when morn breaks on their quivering bed
Blaze like a wyvern flying round the sun. (p. 61, ll. 450–3)

The view of the poet's task expressed by Aprile is essentially that of
the dramatic poet:

> . . . No thought which ever stirr'd
> A human breast should be untold; all passions,
> All soft emotions, from the turbulent stir
> Within a heart fed with desires like mine—
> To the last comfort, shutting the tired lids
> Of him who sleeps the sultry noon away
> Beneath the tent-tree by the way-side well:
> And this in language as the need should be,
> Now pour'd at once forth in a burning flow,
> Now piled up in a grand array of words.
>
> > (pp. 61–2, ll. 465–74)

It is more important to notice the brilliance of these lines than to
speculate on the question of how precisely Paracelsus has become
a 'king' and ill-treated Aprile, or in what sense Aprile himself has
erred in his own 'choice of life'. The final line of Part II, which
affirms, with all the emphasis of capital letters:

I HAVE ATTAIN'D, AND NOW I MAY DEPART[19]

—is clearly informed by a bitter irony. If Paracelsus has attained
the goal he set himself, it is clear that he has found that his quest
has been misconceived.

In Part III, set five years later and manifestly designed as the
centre of the poem, Paracelsus, now a celebrated professor at Basel,
is again in conversation with Festus. When Festus congratulates
him on his fame, Paracelsus replies that in the real sense he is a
failure. He describes an experience with a dying man, 'some few
weeks since', introducing it with the comment:

> Festus, strange secrets are let out by Death,
> Who blabs so oft the follies of this world:
> I, as you know, am Death's familiar oft.
>
> > (p. 77, Part III, ll. 109–11)

---

[19] The line is capitalized only in the first edition.

The dying man had been a corrupt old courtier, but at the end his thoughts had reverted to true values:

> . . . And just an hour before—
> Having lain long with blank and soulless eyes—
> He sate up suddenly, and with natural voice
> Said, that in spite of thick air and closed doors
> God told him it was June; and he knew well,
> Without such telling, hare-bells grew in June;
> And all that kings could ever give or take
> Would not be precious as those blooms to him.
>
> (p. 78, ll. 118–25)

Paracelsus confesses that he himself now finds the beauty of pansies 'much worthier argument'

> Than all fools find to wonder at in me,
> Or in my fortunes.   (p. 78, ll. 130–1)

Festus asks him why, instead of remaining in a false position which leads to his being despised as a quack, Paracelsus does not confess that the absolute knowledge which he has sought is an illusion:

> You sought not fame, nor gain, nor even love;
> No end distinct from knowledge. I repeat
> Your very words: once satisfied that knowledge
> Is a mere dream, you would announce as much
> Yourself the first.   (pp. 91–2, ll. 404–8)

The verse in which the long, casuistical reply of Paracelsus is written is markedly inferior to that spoken by Aprile in the previous Part. Paracelsus argues that by remaining as professor until he is exposed (which he now regards as inevitable) he will be doing the most good, and the least harm. He still longs for absolute knowledge—

> I cannot feed on beauty, for the sake
> Of beauty only; nor can drink in balm
> From lovely objects for their loveliness;
> My nature cannot lose her first impress;
> I still must hoard, and heap, and class all truths
> With one ulterior purpose—one intent
>
> (pp. 105–6, ll. 701–6)

—but he no longer believes that he knows God's will, and he longs for the 'youth and health and love' that he has lost. When Festus tries to console him, Paracelsus delivers a lecture on his own place in history, between the Middle Ages and the Renaissance:

> Come, I will show you where my merit lies.
>
> .   .   .   .
>
> 'T is in the advance of individual minds
> That the slow crowd should ground their expectation
> Eventually to follow—as the sea
> Waits ages in its bed, 'till some one wave
> Of all the multitudinous mass extends
> The empire of the whole, some feet perhaps,
> Over the strip of sand which could confine
> Its fellows so long time . . .   (p. 114, ll. 870–8)

When Festus asks him why he does not use the new medium of printing to diffuse his discoveries, Paracelsus replies that he possesses 'Two sorts of knowledge': the one is 'vast, shadowy', and he has now lost all faith in his ability to put it into words: the other is a certain amount of empirical knowledge—'chiefly of the over-turning sort'—which he is trying to impart to the more intelligent of his students. He knows that so much that is unsound is mixed with his true insight that it is inevitable that he will be regarded as an impostor. Paracelsus has lost 'Love, hope, fear, faith', the qualities which between them 'make humanity'. By the end of Part III his friend's faith in him has been shaken by his own sense of being a failure.

In Part IV, where Paracelsus is again talking to Festus, we find that another two years have elapsed and the expected exposure has taken place. Flushed with wine, Paracelsus tells Festus that he 'aspires' again—but in a very different way:

> I seek to KNOW and to ENJOY.[20] (p. 135, Part IV, l. 240)

'The wreck of my past self', as he describes himself, he is now determined to enjoy 'the meanest, earthliest, sensualest delight' as

---

[20] Expanded (in 1849) to:
> I seek to KNOW and to ENJOY at once,
> Not one without the other as before.

This (without the capitals) remained the text in subsequent editions.

well as the pleasures of knowledge. For almost the only time in the
whole poem Festus answers back, reproaching Paracelsus with a
lack of courage:

> . . . None
> Could trace God's will so plain as you, while yours
> Remain'd implied in it; but *now* you fail,
> And we who prate about that will are fools.
> In short, God's service must be order'd here
> As he determines fit, and not your way,
> And this you cannot brook: such discontent
> Is weak. Renounce all creatureship—affirm
> An absolute right to have and to dispose
> Your energies . . .
> . . . Set up that plea,
> That will be bold at least.   (p. 150, ll. 574–83, 586–7)

No real drama results, however, because Festus is so conscious that
Paracelsus is not as other men are, and must not be judged like
other men:

> . . . Shall one like me
> Judge hearts like yours? Though years have changed you much,
> And you have left your first love, and retain
> Its empty shade to gild your crooked ways,
> Yet I still hold that you *have* honour'd God.
>
> (pp. 151–2, ll. 604–8)

At the very end of Part IV Festus tells Paracelsus that his wife
Michal has been dead for a month. In a drama the fact that Festus
had hardly had an opportunity of mentioning this fact before would
imply a powerful ironic criticism of Paracelsus, who has (as usual)
monopolized attention; but here there is no such suggestion, and
all that happens is that Paracelsus expresses his belief that 'we do
not wholly die', before announcing his own hopes and despairs:

> As though it matter'd how the farce plays out,
> So it be quickly play'd. Away, away!
> Have your will, rabble! while we fight the prize,
> Troop you in safety to the snug back-seats,
> And leave a clear arena for the brave
> About to perish for your sport . . . Behold!
>
> (p. 156, ll. 688–93)

In Part V, which is set in Salzburg thirteen years later, Paracelsus lies dying, with Festus by his bedside. The question proposed is whether Paracelsus has been a success or a failure in his life. He acknowledges that he is now universally regarded as an impostor:

> [That] none but laughs who names me—none but spits
> Measureless scorn upon me; 'tis on *me*,
> The quack, the liar, the arch-cheat—all on *me*.
>
> (p. 164, Part V, ll. 140–2)

He explains—rather like a 'Mr. Sludge' whom Browning is defending, instead of condemning—how he came to practise 'tricks So foreign to my nature',

> To humour [men] the way they most approved.
>
> (p. 173, l. 357)

His epitaph should proclaim that he lived

> Too much advanced before his brother men:
> They kept him still in front; 'twas for their good,
> But still a dangerous station.   (p. 174, ll. 377–9)

Festus accepts this view, and proclaims that, after a period of misunderstanding, Paracelsus will be a beacon of inspiration to the men of the future. The most striking passage describes the images that succeed each other in the mind of Paracelsus as he lies—like the Bishop in Saint Praxed's—'dying by degrees':

> . . . my varied life
> Drifts by me. I am young, old, happy, sad,
> Hoping, desponding, acting, taking rest,
> And all at once: that is, those past conditions
> Flock back upon me.   (p. 180, ll. 487–91)

There is some striking verse, and one line—

> . . . thus climbs
> Pleasure its heights for ever and for ever
>
> (p. 188, ll. 651–2)

—that rivals Marlowe. The poem ends with a sort of lecture on Lamarckian evolution.[21]

---

[21] 'Browning's teleology, like that of Tennyson, is as much a development of eighteenth-century speculations about cosmic transition and change as an

Throughout *Paracelsus* Browning's insistence on the historical importance of the exceptional man, the man of genius, recalls Carlyle; and it is interesting to note that while *Heroes and Hero-Worship* had not yet appeared, Carlyle had been writing about the Hero, in one guise or another, in a good deal of his earlier work. In 'Signs of the Times', for example, the influential article which first appeared in the *Edinburgh Review* for June 1829, he had complained that

> Wonder . . . is, on all hands, dying out: it is the sign of uncultivation to wonder. Speak to any small man of a high, majestic Reformation, of a high, majestic Luther to lead it, and forthwith he sets about 'accounting' for it! how the 'circumstances of the time' called for such a character, and found him, we suppose, standing girt and road-ready, to do its errand, how the 'circumstances of the time' created, fashioned, floated him quietly along into the result; how, in short, this small man, had he been there, could have performed the like himself![22]

Browning was as inflexibly opposed as Carlyle to the levelling notion that 'it is the "force of circumstances" that does every thing; the force of one man can do nothing'. Paracelsus himself insists that

> . . . only here and there a star dispels
> The darkness—here and there a towering mind
> O'erlooks its crawling fellows.
> (p. 192, Part V, ll. 746–8)

What distinguishes Paracelsus from most heroes of romantic extraction is that he is so imperfect a hero—if he is a hero at all. From the obvious point of view he has failed, and failed partly because he has not understood

> . . . the worth of love in man's estate,
> And what proportion love should hold with power
> In his right constitution.   (p. 197, Part V, ll. 855–7)

anticipation of the modern evolutionary theory, which, in any case, Lamarck had clearly stated': Georg Roppen, *Evolution and Poetic Belief: A Study in Some Victorian and Modern Writers* (Oslo and Oxford, 1956), p. 122.

[22] Vol. xlix, pp. 453–4, reprinted (revised) in Carlyle's *Critical and Miscellaneous Essays*, Vol. II (*The Works*, 'Centenary Edition', vol. xxvii), p. 75.

It is clear that the reader is intended to accept his final judgement on himself:

> Meanwhile, I have done well, though not all well.
> As yet men cannot do without contempt—
> 'T is for their good, and therefore fit awhile
> That they reject me, and speak scorn of me;
> But after, they will know me well: I stoop
> Into a dark tremendous sea of cloud,
> But 'tis but for a time.   (p. 199, Part V, ll. 894–901)

In the light of this reading of the poem we may speculate about the reasons which led Ripert-Monclar to suggest Paracelsus to Browning as the subject for a poem. It seems likely that the two young men had been discussing the role of the man of genius in history, and possible that the difficulty of distinguishing between true genius and false became part of their discussion.[23] Martin Luther may have been mentioned: Browning's Paracelsus more than once compares himself to Luther,[24] and the historical Paracelsus had accepted or encouraged the comparison with the man whom Carlyle was to salute as one of the supreme Heroes of history. It is not surprising that Browning's friend should have decided, in the end, that the subject was unsuitable, because it gave no opportunity for the introduction of love. The historical reason for his statement was simply the tradition, recorded by Browning in his notes, that Paracelsus had been castrated. When Browning determined 'that he would write a poem on Paracelsus, but treating him in his own way', he presumably decided to make part of his theme the limitations of life without love, a theme touched on by Shelley in the preface to 'Alastor'.

One of the differences between *Paracelsus* and 'Alastor' is that Browning's poem has a historical personage as its protagonist, and

---

[23] 'In the fifty years after 1830 the worship of the hero was a major factor in English culture': Walter E. Houghton, *The Victorian Frame of Mind: 1830–1870* (1957), p. 310.—Keats was uncertain whether he himself was a genius ('Poet') or a 'Fanatic' when he wrote the introductory lines to 'The Fall of Hyperion—A Dream', and concluded that the true answer would only be known

> When this warm scribe my hand is in the grave.

[24] The most important reference occurs in Part III, lines 964–88. There are other references at III. 344, 376, and 959, and IV. 212–13.

is therefore set in a particular period of history. At the beginning of his Notes Browning writes:

The liberties I have taken with my subject are very trifling; and the reader may slip the foregoing scenes between the leaves of any memoir of Paracelsus he pleases, by way of commentary.

While the intention was clearly to escape from the transparent subjectivity of *Pauline*, in fact *Paracelsus* is much less historical than this statement suggests. Browning's theme is 'the incidents in the development of a soul', and for these he has largely to rely on his imagination. It has often been suggested (indeed) that there is a strong vein of autobiography in the poem. 'You are Paracelsus', Elizabeth Barrett was to write to Browning, while a recent biographer detects 'in the discussion between the sober Festus and the impatient, aspiring Paracelsus . . . an echo of the family conflict that preceded, at Hanover Cottage, the renunciation of a practical for a poetic career'.[25] Paracelsus has the sense that never left Browning throughout his entire life, the sense of living

As ever in my great task-Masters eye.[26]

Yet there is no point in pursuing such a parallel very far. Browning was not (after all) a eunuch, any more than he was a chemist who lived in the sixteenth century. What appealed to him about the story of Paracelsus was the opportunity of probing the character of a gifted man who may have been a genius but in whom there were unmistakable elements of a mountebank. Browning portrays his protagonist as a man who has 'aspired' further than he could 'attain'. The ultimate subject explored by the poem is the value of the life of a man of genius, however flawed by imperfections: the ultimate question posed by the poem is the question what makes success or failure in human life. That question was to recur in much of the major poetry of Browning's maturity.

The form of *Paracelsus* is as surprising as the subject, and it is understandable that Browning should have prefixed a note to the first edition expressing his anxiety 'that the reader should not, at the very outset—mistak[e] my performance for one of a class with which it has nothing in common'. This preface (later omitted) is

[25] Kintner, i. 41; Miller, pp. 4–5. [26] Milton, Sonnet vii, last line.

obscurely expressed, but the gist of its argument is that Browning has 'endeavoured to write a poem, and not a drama', and that the lack of action is therefore not to be considered as a fault. Looking for some standard of comparison, several of the original reviewers hit on Sir Henry Taylor's *Philip Van Artevelde*, an enormously long poem in dramatic form which had been published the previous year, and which had enjoyed a marked *succès d'estime*. One of them went so far as to describe *Paracelsus* as 'a dramatic poem, constructed upon the model of *Philip Van Artevelde*'.[27] More careful critics, such as Joseph Milsand, mentioned Taylor only to contrast his poem with Browning's. It is worth noticing that Taylor described his own work as 'A Dramatic Romance', while it is the concept of the 'Dramatic Poem' that Browning questions in his preface:

I do not very well understand what is called a Dramatic Poem, wherein all those restrictions [namely 'the canons of the drama' which 'have immediate regard to stage representation'] only submitted to on account of compensating good in the original scheme are scrupulously retained, as though for some special fitness in themselves.

The term 'Dramatic Poem' points away from Taylor to Byron's *Manfred* and Goethe's *Faust*, and it is worth remembering that the first complete translation of the First Part of *Faust* had been published by Moxon (the publisher to whom Browning originally submitted *Paracelsus*) two years before. Although *Paracelsus* would hardly have been written in its present form if *Faust* had never appeared, however, Browning was right to imply that it belonged to a different literary form. Metaphysical as it is, a 'Dramatic Poem' rather than a drama, *Faust* contains a good deal of action, and a good deal of personal conflict. Although Faust is primarily interested in himself, towards the end of Part I we find him seriously concerned for Margarete; while there is much greater variety of mood and tone in *Faust* than is to be found in Browning's 'Faustish' poem.[28]

Whereas *Philip Van Artevelde* was a dead end for Taylor, *Paracelsus* occupies an important position in Browning's development. It is

---

[27] Litzinger and Smalley, p. 45.
[28] Byron's adjective, describing *The Deformed Transformed: Letters and Journals*, ed. Rowland E. Prothero, v (1901), 518.

illuminating to compare it with *Endymion*, the poem which Keats had written less than twenty years before, when he was exactly Browning's age. Whereas *Endymion* is a 'Poetic Romance', an attempt to 'make 4000 Lines of one bare circumstance and fill them with Poetry', to explore 'the realm . . . Of Flora, and old Pan'[29] as a preliminary to venturing towards the more serious territory of poetry that lay beyond it, in *Paracelsus* we already find Browning engaged with his true subject matter, writing a psychological study of an isolated individual, and attempting to discover a mode of dramatic poetry quite distinct from the acting drama. Elizabeth Barrett discerned in the poem 'the expression of a new mind', while John Forster observed, with remarkable prescience, that 'Mr. Browning has the power of a great dramatic poet'.[30] What is wrong with the poem is that it is far too diffuse: in his maturity Browning would have reduced the whole to a monologue spoken by the dying Paracelsus.

[29] *Letters of Keats*, i. 170; 'Sleep and Poetry', ll. 101–2.
[30] Kintner, i. 316; Litzinger and Smalley, p. 47 (reprinted from the *New Monthly Magazine*, March 1836 (xlvi)).

IV

SORDELLO

I only wish that he would atticize a little. Few of the Athenians had such a quarry on their property, but they constructed better roads for the conveyance of the material.   LANDOR

It needs reading three times, but on the third even a school-boy of tolerable intelligence will find it luminous, if not entirely lucid. . . . The book has become a classic, and to each coming generation will in all probability present less difficulty than to the preceding one.
                                        SIR EDMUND GOSSE

Hang it all, Robert Browning,
there can be but the one 'Sordello'.
                        EZRA POUND[1]

WE know from the letter to Fox that *Sordello* was already 'on hand' when Browning wrote *Paracelsus*, and it is one of the ironies of literary history that he should have described this most obscure of poems as being 'rather of a more popular nature' than the relatively straightforward *Paracelsus*. Browning's inability to gauge the reactions of the readers of poetry comes out very clearly in a letter to Alfred Domett, who had obviously objected to the obscurity of *Sordello*:

The one point that wants correcting is where you surmise that I am 'difficult on system.' No, really—the fact is I live by myself, write with no better company, and forget that the 'lovers' you mention are part and parcel of that self, and their choosing to comprehend *my* comprehensions but an indifferent testimony to their value. . . .[2]

'I wish I had thought of this before', Browning adds—a remarkable comment on the part of a poet who had just spent the greater part of his time for seven years in writing the poem. When he first reprinted *Sordello*, in 1863, Browning claimed that he had originally

[1] *Walter Savage Landor: Last Days, Letters and Conversations*, ed. H. C. Minchin (1934), pp. 17–18; Gosse, pp. 48–9, 52; *Cantos*, II.
[2] *Domett*, pp. 28–9.

written it 'for only a few, counting even in these on somewhat
more care about its subject than they really had'—adding that he
had 'lately [given] time and pains to turn my work into what the
many might,—instead of what the few must,—like: but after all,
I imagined another thing at first, and therefore leave as I find it'.[3]
His attitude to his audience, at this point in his career, reminds
us of his idol Shelley, who commented on one of his own most
characteristic poems:

The Epipsychidion is a mystery—As to real flesh & blood, you know
that I do not deal in those articles,—you might as well go to a gin-
shop for a leg of mutton, as expect any thing human or earthly from
me. I desired Ollier not to circulate this piece except to the Σύνετοι,
and even they it seems are inclined to approximate me to the circle
of a servant girl & her sweetheart.[4]

Few poets have understood 'flesh & blood' more profoundly than
Browning, but a good deal had still to happen to him before he
could write such masterpieces of the 'human' and 'earthly' as 'Fra
Lippo Lippi' and 'The Bishop Orders his Tomb'. In *Sordello* he
is concerned with a 'soul' that is never convincingly embodied,
and which (therefore) cannot be brought into any convincing
relationship with other human beings.

Browning probably came on the story of Sordello soon after he
began Italian lessons with Angelo Cerutti at the age of sixteen.
Cary has a long note on *Purgatorio* vi, where Virgil exclaims to
Dante:

> Ma vedi là un' anima, che posta
> sola soletta, verso noi riguarda;
> quella ne insegnerà la via più tosta.[5]

[3] Dedicatory preface in 1863 and subsequent editions of *The Poetical Works*.
[4] *Letters of Shelley*, ii. 363.
[5] ll. 58–60. Cary translates the passage as follows:
> '. . . But lo! a spirit there
> Stands solitary, and toward us looks:
> It will instruct us in the speediest way'.
> We soon approached it. Oh thou Lombard spirit!
> How didst thou stand, in high abstracted mood,
> Scarce moving with slow dignity thine eyes.
> It spoke not aught, but let us onward pass,
> Eyeing us as a lion on his watch.

'The history of Sordello's life is wrapt in the obscurity of romance. That he distinguished himself by his skill in Provençal poetry is certain; and many feats of military prowess have been attributed to him. It is probable that he was born towards the end of the twelfth, and died about the middle of the succeeding century. Tiraboschi, who terms him the most illustrious of all the Provençal poets of his age, has taken much pains to sift all the notices he could collect relating to him.' It is not surprising that Sordello should have presented himself to Browning as an eligible protagonist for a poem in which he might speculate about poetry more objectively than in *Pauline*, so continuing a theme that is subordinate in *Paracelsus*. Sordello's poetry—the work of a philosophical writer who alternated between the celebration of purely spiritual passion and libertine poetry in which he boasted that every husband had reason to fear his skill in the art of love—clearly appealed to the same side of Browning's nature as the poetry of John Donne; but what may have attracted him most of all was the fact that Sordello was a poet celebrated enough to be given a position of prominence by Dante yet so obscure in his personal life that little more is known about it except his love for the beautiful Cunizza. Sordello was an eligible vehicle for Browning's characteristic meditation on the problem of what makes a human life successful, and what makes it a failure. For all the density (the unfortunate density) of the historical background of the poem, Sordello is essentially Browning's own creation. The central feature of the story—the fact that Sordello turns out to be the son of Taurello Salinguerra—is based on a very uncertain tradition. Browning's Sordello dies at the age of thirty: estimates of the age of the historical Sordello vary greatly, but they all make him old or middle-aged at the time of his death.

Unfortunately for Browning, however, he was not the only poet to take Sordello as the subject of a poem. Of the 'many singular incidents'[5a] that occurred while he was at work the most singular, and the most distressing, must have been the appearance of a poem with the same title as his own in a two-volume collection by Mrs. William Busk that was published in July 1837, *Plays and Poems*. Browning probably first heard of Mrs. Busk through a notice in

[5a] Kintner, i. 336

the *Athenæum* on the 22nd of that month which referred to her 'Sordello' with the question: 'Is this founded upon the same subject as that chosen by the author of "Paracelsus" for his announced poem?' It must have been with a sinking heart that he read Mrs. Busk's preface:

The once renowned Mantuan Troubadour, SORDELLO, probably owes the faint glimmering of celebrity that he may still enjoy, to the distinction with which he is treated by Dante, to the embrace of fraternity bestowed upon him by Virgil in the *Purgatorio*. It may, therefore, be advisable to preface the poem bearing his name by an assurance that none of the adventures here ascribed to the Poet-hero are imaginary, at least of recent imagining. Sordello's prowess and high fame in arms, as well as in the *gai science*, his chivalrous duel of emulation, not enmity, with an Apulian champion, the competition of kings and princes for the honour of possessing him at their several courts . . . and the mutual attachment that existed between him and . . . Cuniza, are all recorded by divers Italian writers.

Mrs. Busk gives an interesting reason for writing about Sordello:

It was the striking discrepancy between Sordello's career . . . and the lives of poets of more recent date, together with the impressive illustration of the ephemeral nature of literary fame exhibited in our general and utter ignorance of the writings of a poet once so celebrated,—for great must the celebrity have been which could give birth to such romance as his here versified—that awoke the desire to sketch his adventures, fictitious or real, as a picture of what a Troubadour was, or, in early times, was supposed to be.

In a poem that appeared, appropriately enough, within a month of the accession of Queen Victoria, Mrs. Busk was clearly determined to concentrate on Sordello as the poet of 'pure' and spiritual love, and to tidy up the facts of his life so that he could be presented to the readers of her day as a shining contrast to Byron and perhaps to Shelley: she points out that in her poem 'the conduct of the lovers', Sordello and Cuniza, 'has been purified from actual guilt', although she acknowledges that as a historical fact 'Their mutual passion . . . is uniformly described as of the guilty character which too often disgraced the intercourse of noble ladies with admired troubadours.' The poem itself is in six cantos of predominantly tetrameter lines in the manner that Scott had made popular a quarter of a century before. Throughout the emphasis is on romantic and chivalrous love, and the quality of the verse is more reminiscent of Mrs. Hemans than of Scott. Since Browning was so disconcerted by Mrs. Busk's 'Sordello' it is a clear inference that love was originally more prominent in his own poem than it was later to become, while we may be certain that the historical element was much less important, and the 'humanitarian' element inspired by his visit to Italy in 1838 almost entirely absent. Griffin and Minchin conjecture[6] that if *Sordello* had appeared in the summer of 1837 it would have been a poem that could have been described in the words of Tennyson describing *Maud*, as 'the history of a morbid, poetic soul . . . raised to a pure and holy love which elevates his whole nature'. In that event the relation between *Pauline* and *Sordello* would have been much more evident than it is.

The publication of Mrs. Busk's poem was only one of a number of prenatal accidents that occurred during the composition of *Sordello*. Whether or not DeVane is justified in stating that during the seven years 'there were four distinct periods of composition, and four different *Sordellos* were written',[7] there is no doubt that Browning's idea of the poem developed during these years, and no doubt that this is a principal reason for the obscurity for which *Sordello* has always been notorious. So far as the form of the poem is concerned, DeVane's conjecture that it was originally written in blank verse, like *Pauline* and *Paracelsus*, is extremely tempting. Much of the verse is so awkward—particularly when it is contrasted with the couplets of 'My Last Duchess', written only a couple of years later—that it is easy to see that many passages could well be blank verse inadequately revised to couplets. If such a revision was made, however, it can have had nothing to do with Mrs. Busk; nor can her 'Sordello' explain the fact that Browning here abandons dramatic or monologue form in favour of third-person narrative. In the preface to *Paracelsus* he had explained that he had there avoided 'an external machinery of incidents to create and evolve the crisis' in favour of a minute display of 'the mood itself in its rise and progress, [suffering] the agency by which it is influenced and determined, to be generally discernible in its effects alone'.

[6] p. 97.   [7] p. 72.

In a poem of such length this method has grave drawbacks, as was pointed out by a reviewer in the *Spectator*:

The design . . . [is] very injudicious: for the form of dialogue precludes those descriptions and digressions by which the author in a narrative poem can vary his subjects and 'interchange delights'; whilst the fundamental plan renders the whole piece a virtual soliloquy. . . . Such a poem contains in its structure the elements of tediousness, which no execution could obviate.[8]

Yet it is clear that Browning was not happy with the more usual mode of narration, since as early as the eleventh line he addresses his readers in an extraordinary aside:

> . . . Never,—I should warn you first,—
> Of my own choice had this, if not the worst
> Yet not the best expedient, served to tell
> A story I could body forth so well
> By making speak, myself kept out of view,
> The very man as he was wont to do,
> And leaving you to say the rest for him.

This is the first of three digressions with which *Sordello* begins, and between them they have probably sufficed to 'throw' many readers before the main part of the poem gets under way.[9] It is not surprising that the first of the 'elucidatory headings'[10] which Browning added in 1863, at the suggestion of Alfred Domett, should describe the poem as 'A Quixotic attempt'. But for these headings (indeed) even the following brief summary would hardly be possible.

After the digressions we are given a most confusing account of the conflict between Guelfs and Ghibellines—the partisans of the Pope and the Emperor—in twelfth-century Verona, and only then —after a brief passage about Dante—do we reach Sordello himself, more than 400 lines from the beginning of the poem. The remainder of Book I may be summarized in Browning's own headings:

His boyhood in the domain of Ecelin. How a poet's soul comes into play. What denotes such a soul's progress. How poets class at length

[8] Litzinger and Smalley, p. 40.
[9] One may compare *The Revolt of Islam*, where the first canto is an obscure allegory which has baffled many readers—yet Shelley sent it to a publisher as a specimen of the poem.   [10] *Letters*, p. 248.

—for honour, or shame—which may the gods avert from Sordello, now in childhood. The delights of his childish fancy, which could blow out a great bubble, being secure awhile from intrusion. But it comes; and new-born judgment decides that he needs sympathizers. He therefore creates such a company; each of which, leading its own life, has qualities impossible to a boy, so, only to be appropriated in fancy, and practised on till the real come. He means to be perfect—say, Apollo: and Apollo must one day find Daphne. But when will this dream turn truth? For the time is ripe, and he ready.

At the end we hear how an accident

> Opened, like any flash that cures the blind,
> The veritable business of mankind

to the still-dreaming young poet.

In Book I Sordello has 'aspired', like Paracelsus: he wishes to become a great poet, and is ready to fall in love with the beautiful Palma. In Book II we hear of his further development. The best summary is Browning's own:

This bubble of fancy, when greatest and brightest, bursts. At a court of love, a minstrel sings. Sordello, before Palma, conquers him, receives the prize, and ruminates. How had he been superior to Eglamor? This is answered by Eglamor himself: one who belonged to what he loved, loving his art and rewarded by it, ending with what had possessed him. Eglamor done with, Sordello begins. Who he really was, and why at Goito. He, so little, would fain be so much: leaves the dream he may be something, for the fact that he can do nothing, yet is able to imagine everything, if the world esteem this equivalent. He has loved song's results, not song; so, must effect this to obtain those. He succeeds a little, but fails more; tries again, is no better satisfied, and declines from the ideal of song. What is the world's recognition worth? How, poet no longer in unity with man, the whole visible Sordello goes wrong with those too hard for half of him, of whom he is also too contemptuous. He pleases neither himself nor them: which the best judges account for. Their criticisms give small comfort: and his own degradation is complete. Adelaide's death: what happens on it: and a trouble it occasions Sordello. He chances upon his old environment, sees but failure in all done since, and resolves to desist from the like.

His defeat of Eglamor makes Sordello conscious of his own genius.

When his rival dies of grief, Sordello comes to the conclusion that Eglamor had aimed only at popularity, instead of devoting himself to the true end of poetry, the ennoblement of mankind. Sordello wishes to dedicate himself to this, but finds it much more difficult than he expected. He reflects on the difference between traditional poetry and the poetry that he himself aspires to produce:

> Cannot men bear, now, something better?—fly
> A pitch beyond this unreal pageantry
> Of essences? the period sure has ceased
> For such: present us with ourselves, at least,
> Not portions of ourselves, mere loves and hates
> Made flesh. (ll. 563–8)

Yet when he exerts himself to evolve a new style suitable for this new kind of poetry, what is the result?—

> . . . Then came
> The world's revenge: their pleasure, now his aim
> Merely,—what was it? 'Not to play the fool
> 'So much as learn our lesson in your school!'
> (ll. 617–20)

His 'ungrateful audience', epitomized by the hateful Naddo, insists on his writing conventional poetry, leaving him frustrated in his ambition of creating deeply subjective poetry of a new kind, and so

> Remote as ever from the self-display
> He meant to compass, hampered every way
> By what he hoped assistance. (ll. 651–3)

The inspiration of this Book is clearly the debate that was going on in Browning's own mind between himself and his critics, actual and imagined. Naddo is the personification of his unintelligent and therefore sinister critics, and we notice similarities between the advice that he gives Sordello and the advice quoted in a later poem, 'Transcendentalism': Naddo sympathizes with a critic ('Squarcialupe') who complains that Sordello 'can't stoop To sing us out . . . a mere romance', and continues:

> . . . Now, you're a bard, a bard past doubt,
> And no philosopher; why introduce

> Crotchets like these? fine, surely, but no use
> In poetry—which still must be, to strike,
> Based upon common sense; there's nothing like
> Appealing to our nature!   (ll. 788–93)

The portrait of Naddo,

>   . . . busiest of the tribe
> Of genius-haunters,   (ll. 821–2)

who assures Sordello that if he persists in probing the human soul
'Too deeply for poetic purposes' then

>   . . . The knowledge that you are a bard
> Must constitute your prime, nay sole, reward!
>   (ll. 819–20)

—this satirical portrait has an intensity which reveals Browning's
own anxieties at the time. No less revealing is the lack of all clarity
in the accounts that Sordello gives of the poetry that he aspires to
write. All that is really clear is that by the end of Book II he is
disillusioned:

> The Body, the Machine for Acting Will,
> Had been at the commencement proved unfit;
> That for Demonstrating, Reflecting it,
> Mankind—no fitter: was the Will Itself
> In fault?   (ll. 994–8)

Instead of abandoning his quest in despair, however, he suddenly
quits the court of Taurello, leaving Naddo to make the sneering
comment that

> His Highness knew what poets were.   (l. 1008)

In Book II Sordello has 'attained', but only in the deeply ironic
sense in which Paracelsus attains in Part II of the previous poem.
Book III begins, a little like the corresponding part of *Paracelsus*,
with the protagonist aware that he has failed, in the only sense in
which 'success' and 'failure' are meaningful to him. But from the
first Sordello's retreat to Goito seems to hold out the promise of
rebirth, since with it 'the stain O' the world forsakes Sordello'. He
reflects on the great difficulty of the poetic aim which he has set
himself—

> To need become all natures, yet retain
> The law of my own nature. (ll. 39–40)

As elsewhere in the poem, it is clear that what he aspires to is some sort of dramatic poetry. After 'a sweet and solitary year' at Goito, Sordello is summoned back to the world of men and women by Naddo, who calls on him to write a 'marriage-chant' for Palma, who is to marry Boniface for political reasons. Unlike Paracelsus, however, Sordello has not renounced human love. At the end of the first phase of his life he had discovered

> . . . that a soul, whate'er its might,
> Is insufficient to its own delight,
> Both in corporeal organs and in skill
> By means of such to body forth its Will. (ll. 565–8)

In the words of the head-notes, 'nature is one thing, man another—having multifarious sympathies, he may neither renounce nor satisfy; in the process to which is pleasure, while renunciation ensures despair'. Palma, who is the key to a complex political situation, is released from her bond to Boniface, and avows her love for Sordello (although she does not tell him the true story of his birth, which she has heard from the dying Adelaide). She proposes that they should go together to Ferrara and assume the leadership of the Kaiser's party. Sordello obeys Palma,

who thereupon becomes his associate, as her own history will account for,—a reverse to, and completion of, his. How she ever aspired for his sake, circumstances helping or hindering. How success at last seemed possible, by the intervention of Salinguerra: who remedied ill wrought by Ecelin, and had a project for her own glory, which she would change to Sordello's.

In one of the most interesting passages in the Book, Sordello distinguishes between the popular poetry of a minor poet like Eglamor and the poetry that he himself wishes to write:

> . . . Note,
> In just such songs as Eglamor (say) wrote
> With heart and soul and strength, for he believed
> Himself achieving all to be achieved

> By singer—in such songs you find alone
> Completeness, judge the song and singer one,
> And either purpose answered, his in it
> Or its in him: while from true works (to wit
> Sordello's dream-performances that will
> Never be more than dreamed) escapes there still
> Some proof, the singer's proper life was 'neath
> The life his song exhibits, this a sheath
> To that; a passion and a knowledge far
> Transcending these, majestic as they are,
> Smouldered; his lay was but an episode
> In the bard's life.   (ll. 615–30)

Browning's characteristic insistence on the superiority of the Imperfect over the Perfect and his sense that his own poetry so far was merely the prelude to the major poetry that he hoped one day to write both lie behind this passage. We notice his almost Miltonic sense of being a dedicated man, and are reminded of Keats's comment that 'Shakspeare led a life of Allegory; his works are the comments on it'.[11]

At this point Browning himself enters the poem—

> I muse this on a ruined palace-step
> At Venice   (ll. 676–7)

—and the remainder of Book III consists of a long digression, linked to the story of Sordello because that is the story of a poet. The summary reads as follows:

Thus then, having completed a circle, the poet may pause and breathe, being really in the flesh at Venice, and watching his own life sometimes, because it is pleasant to be young, would but suffering humanity allow!—which instigates to tasks like this, and doubtlessly compensates them, as those who desist should remember. Let the poet take his own part, then, should any object that he was dull beside his sprightlier predecessors. One ought not blame but praise this; at all events, his own audience may: what if things brighten, who knows?

Although the most important effects of Browning's Italian visit of 1838 are to be found elsewhere, even within *Sordello* we notice an

11 *Letters of Keats*, ii. 67.

element of fresh vitality as the poet watches the beautiful Italian
girls and wonders which is fittest to be 'queen to me'. At this point,
however, a voice seems to address him—

> . . . 'Let others seek!—thy care
> 'Is found, thy life's provision; if thy race
> 'Should be thy mistress, and into one face
> 'The many faces crowd?'   (ll. 752–5)

There is no doubt that Browning was deeply moved by the poverty
which he saw in Italy, and that this modified his view of the poet's
role in society. It follows that the later part of Book III is of great
importance. It ends with a salute to Landor, 'my patron-friend',
another to Euphrasia Fanny Haworth, 'My English Eyebright', and
a story about 'John the Beloved' which the head-note assures us is
'to the point', but the relevance of which is at first characteristically
obscure.

In Book IV Browning nose-dives into twelfth-century history,
and without the head-notes even the most careful reader would be
likely to lose his way:

Men suffered much, whichever of the parties was victor. How
Guelfs criticize Ghibellin work as unusually energetic in this case.
How, passing through the rare garden, Salinguerra contrived for a
purpose, Sordello ponders all seen and heard, finds in men no machine
for his sake, but a thing with a life of its own, and rights hitherto
ignored by him,—a fault he is now anxious to repair, since he appre-
hends its full extent, and would fain have helped some way. But
Salinguerra is also pre-occupied; resembling Sordello in nothing else.
How he was made in body and spirit, and what had been his career
of old. The original check to his fortunes, which he was in the way to
retrieve, when a fresh calamity destroyed all. He sank into a secondary personage, with the appropriate graces of such. But Ecelin, he set
in front, falling, Salinguerra must again come forward,—why and
how, is let out in soliloquy. Ecelin, he did all for, is a monk now, just
when the prize awaits somebody—himself, if it were only worth
while, as it may be—but also, as it may not be—the supposition he
most inclines to; being contented with mere vengeance. Sordello,
taught what Ghibellins are, and what Guelfs, approves of neither.
Have men a cause distinct from both?

The profusion of historical detail, and the culpable difficulty of the writing, come near to obscuring Browning's main theme, which is the further awakening of Sordello's social conscience. The psychological study of Salinguerra does not quite come off—his long soliloquy has little of the brilliance we might expect in a dramatic monologue by Browning—and the story of 'the famed Roman Crescentius' at the end is merely a further specimen of *obscurum per obscurius*.

In Book V Sordello meditates, and makes a long and rambling speech to Salinguerra. Patient at first, Salinguerra becomes scornful, and so stimulates Sordello to a long defence of his own mode of life. Apparently on a mad impulse, but in fact for subtle political reasons, Salinguerra suddenly decides to abdicate in favour of Sordello, whom he immediately discovers to be his son. Sordello is thus presented—or so it seems—with an opportunity of having a great and beneficial influence on the destiny of mankind. The head-notes provide the following guidance:

Mankind triumph of a sudden? Why, the work should be one of ages, if performed equally and thoroughly; and a man can but do a man's portion. The last of each series of workmen sums up in himself all predecessors. We just see Charlemagne, Hildebrand, in composite work they end and name. If associates trouble you, stand off!— should the new sympathies allow you. Time having been lost, choose quick! He takes his first step as a Guelf; but to will and to do are different: he may sleep on the bed he has made. Scorn flings cold water in his face, arouses him at last, to some purpose, and thus gets the utmost out of him. He asserts the poet's rank and right, basing these on their proper ground, recognizing true dignity in service, whether successively that of epoist, dramatist, or, so to call him, analyst, who turns in due course synthetist. This for one day: now, serve as Guelf! Salinguerra, dislodged from his post, in moving, opens a door to Sordello, who is declared Salinguerra's son, hidden hitherto by Adelaide's policy. How the discovery moves Salinguerra, and Sordello the finally-determined,—the Devil putting forth his potency: since Sordello, who began by rhyming, may, even from the depths of failure, yet spring to the summit of success, if he consent to oppress the world. Just this decided, as it now may be, and we have done.

The most interesting feature of this part of the poem is Sordello's meditation on heroes: men who are ahead of their time, to whom the progress of mankind is wholly due, and yet who are often in a sense failures. As he meditates on these matters, and realizes the narrowness of Salinguerra's devotion to a partisan cause, Sordello comes to understand more deeply the role of the poet in the development of mankind. Thought must precede action, and so (although Shelley is not quoted) 'Poets are the unacknowledged legislators of the world.'[12]

At the end of Part V Sordello mysteriously dies, at the very time when Salinguerra and Palma are excitedly discussing his future, as they wait below:

> Triumph at height, and thus Sordello crowned —
> Above the passage suddenly a sound
> Stops speech, stops walk . . .   (ll. 999–1001)

The fact of his death, however, only becomes apparent to the reader in Part VI, in which we are taken back a few minutes in time to share in the thoughts of Sordello as he meditates on his position. The question posed by Browning is whether Sordello is a success in life or a failure. Having 'aspired', has he 'attained'? Here is the summary:

At the close of a day or a life, past procedure is fitliest reviewed, as more appreciable in its entirety. Strong, he needed external strength: even now, where can he perceive such? Internal strength must suffice then, his sympathy with the people, to wit; of which, try now the inherent force! How much of man's ill may be removed? How much of ill ought to be removed?—if removed, at what cost to Sordello? Men win little thereby; he loses all: for he can infinitely enjoy himself, freed from a problematic obligation, and accepting life on its own terms, which, yet, others have renounced: how? Because there is a life beyond life, and with new conditions of success, nor such as, in this, produce failure. But, even here, is failure inevitable? Or may failure here be success also when induced by love? Sordello knows: but too late: an insect knows sooner. On his disappearance from the stage, the next aspirant can press forward;

---

[12] The last sentence of 'A Defence of Poetry'.

Salinguerra's part lapsing to Ecelin, who, with his brother, played it out, and went home duly to their reward. Good will—ill luck, get second prize: What least one may I award Sordello? This [i.e. the poem]—that must perforce content him, as no prize at all, has contented me.

The paradox about Sordello's success and failure is summed up in lines 822–35:

> The Chroniclers of Mantua tired their pen
> Telling how *Sordello Prince Visconti* saved
> Mantua, and elsewhere notably behaved—
> Who thus, by fortune ordering events,
> Passed with posterity, to all intents,
> For just the god he never could become.
> As Knight, Bard, Gallant, men were never dumb
> In praise of him: while what he should have been,
> Could be, and was not—the one step too mean
> For him to take,—we suffer at this day
> Because of: Ecelin had pushed away
> Its chance ere Dante could arrive and take
> That step Sordello spurned, for the world's sake:
> He did much—but Sordello's chance was gone.

How far Sordello has really 'attained' remains undefined. 'May failure here be success also when induced by love? Sordello knows: but too late.'

Browning's own remark that the 'stress lay on the incidents in the development of a soul' remains the best comment on the principal theme of *Sordello*. As in *Paracelsus*, he is concerned with the part played by a man of exceptional, yet imperfect, powers in creating the fabric of human history. In this case the protagonist is a poet, and there is no doubt that Browning's own hopes and fears lie behind many passages. Sordello's speculations on the task of the poet, and the nature of his role in society and in human destiny, are Browning's own.

The obscurity of *Sordello* is attributable to an uncertainty of focus due primarily to the long period of composition and to Browning's shifting conception both of the subject of the poem and of the role of the poet during these seven years. His main theme is almost buried under a mountain of Italian history, and this gives particular interest to an entry in Harriet Martineau's diary at the end of 1837:

Browning called. 'Sordello' will soon be done now. Denies himself preface and notes. He must choose between being historian or poet. Cannot split the interest. I advised him to let the poem tell its own tale.[13]

Such were Browning's reflections five months after the appearance of Mrs. Busk's 'Sordello'. Unfortunately, however, he did not choose between 'being historian or poet', and his own claim in the preface added in 1863 that 'the historical decoration was purposely of no more importance than a background requires' leads one to speculate with awe on the form the poem might have taken if he had decided to allow more prominence to Italian history.

Browning often thought of revising *Sordello*—an idea loyally encouraged by Elizabeth Barrett, who described the poem as being 'like a noble picture with its face to the wall just now—or at least, in the shadow';[14] but in fact he did no more than tinker with the text, and add the invaluable head-notes which he dropped again in the final edition of his *Poetical Works*. We are more likely to regret his spending so long over the poem than his failure to rewrite it comprehensively. If he had published it sooner 'the exhibition would have been both done and done with: he would have turned his attention to other subjects of thought and feeling, which, whether as congenial to him as the former, were at least new and unexpressed'. The quotation is from Browning's letter about *Death's Jest-Book*, by Thomas Lovell Beddoes, whose literary executor Browning later found himself, and whose poetry he so admired that he intended to take it as his first subject, if he were elected to the Professorship of Poetry at Oxford. The remainder of this passage may be quoted, with reference both to Browning's failure to publish *Sordello* earlier and to his 'attaining' (in an

---

[13] *Harriet Martineau's Autobiography, with memorials by Maria Weston Chapman* (2nd edn., 3 vols., 1877), iii. 207. On 11 April the following year Miss Martineau noted: 'Erasmus Darwin and Browning called who is just departing for Venice to get a view of the localities of Sordello. He is right': p. 219.

[14] Kintner, i. 186.

appropriately ironical sense) by publishing it in 1840, and so escaping from it—as Beddoes never escaped from *Death's Jest-Book*:

had he printed the piece just as it stands, without any delay at all,— he would have at least done justice, in his own mind, to these conceptions . . . whereas, he is prevented somehow from venting these, and so goes round and round them, ends in the exclusive occupation of his soul with them,—does not he? What good was got by suppressing the poem, or what harm could have followed the publication even in the worldly way of looking at things? Suppose it had been laughed at, blackguarded in Blackwood, fallen flat from the press? The worse for the world for the quarter of an hour: Beddoes would not have much cared, but probably made a clean breast and begun on something else.[15]

When Browning wrote these sentences it is hard not to believe that he was remembering the composition of *Sordello* almost thirty years before.[16] *Sordello* did indeed fall 'flat from the press', and every Naddo used it as an opportunity for an epigram. Browning was deeply hurt, but at least he had escaped from the poem, by publishing it, and so was able to turn his attention 'to other subjects of thought and feeling'.[17]

---

[15] *The Browning Box or The Life and Works of . . . Beddoes as reflected in letters by his friends and admirers*, ed. H. W. Donner (1935), p. 104.

[16] *Sordello* was reprinted in the six-volume *Poetical Works* published in the year (1868) in which he wrote this letter.

[17] For a penetrating study of the poem, see 'The Importance of *Sordello*', by Michael Mason, in *The Major Victorian Poets: Reconsiderations*, ed. Isobel Armstrong, 1969.

V

IN AND OUT OF THE THEATRE

*It is all in long speeches—the action, proper, is in them—they are no
descriptions, or amplifications—but here . . in a drama of this kind,
all the events, (and interest), take place in the minds of the actors . .
somewhat like Paracelsus in that respect.*

BROWNING on *Luria*[1]

'*Nearly Ready*. PIPPA PASSES. KING VICTOR AND KING CHARLES.
MANSOOR THE HIEROPHANT.[2] DRAMAS BY R. B.' So runs an
advertisement at the end of *Sordello*, and it serves as a reminder that
the publication of that poem occurred in the middle of a period
during which Browning was also aspiring to celebrity as a writer
of plays.

Since Browning's ambition early took the direction of wishing to
chronicle 'the stages of all life', his thoughts must often have turned
towards the drama. As a boy at Mr. Ready's school he wrote plays
which he persuaded his schoolfellows to act. As we have seen, it was
the experience of watching the acting of Edmund Kean which
inspired the 'childish scheme' by which he was to 'assume &
realize I know not how many different characters' and so write
poems, novels, operas, speeches, '&c &c'. The fact that plays are not
mentioned in the list may be fortuitous, or it may be due to the
unfavourable theatrical conditions of the time: in any case we notice
a connection between Browning's desire to assume various personae
and his later emergence as the supreme master of the dramatic
monologue.

Browning first turned to the theatre as a result of meeting William
Charles Macready, the celebrated actor-manager, late in 1835.
Macready described Browning as looking and speaking 'more like

---

[1] Kintner, i. 381.   [2] *The Return of the Druses.*

a youthful poet than any man I ever saw',[3] and soon conceived a boundless admiration for *Paracelsus*. Years later, on finding that a literary lady had not read the poem,

he lifted his eyebrows; . . . muttered expressions of wonder; . . . [and] once or twice said, 'Oh, good God!' He took a turn or two up and down the room, and then said, 'I really am quite at a loss; I cannot understand it.' I pleaded the claims of the babies. . . . To which he replied: 'Hand over the babies to the nurse, and read *Paracelsus*'.[4]

It is an appropriate prologue to the next phase of Browning's career that he saw in the New Year of 1836 at the Macreadys', and joined in pouring out 'a libation as a farewell to the old year and a welcome to the new'.[5] By the middle of February he told Macready that he was thinking of writing a tragedy about Narses, Justinian's general, so arousing in the actor the hope that he had 'awakened a spirit of poetry whose influence would elevate, ennoble, and adorn our degraded drama'.[6] At the dinner party given by Sergeant Talfourd to celebrate the success of *Ion* Macready openly appealed to Browning to 'write a play . . . and keep [him] from going to America'.[7] For the next few years success in the theatre was to be constantly in Browning's mind. This was the second false path that he was fated to explore before he reached the happiest and most fruitful period of his life.

In the preface to the original edition of *Strafford* Browning acknowledges that he 'had for some time been engaged in a Poem of a very different nature, when induced to make the present attempt', and refers to his 'eagerness to freshen a jaded mind by diverting it to the healthy natures of a grand epoch'. It is easy to believe that he was relieved to put *Sordello* aside for a while. He chose Strafford for his protagonist because he had been doing a good deal of work to help Forster with his prose *Life of Strafford*. Yet he was afraid that he had not given sufficient thought to the nature of the new work on which he had embarked. In the preface to *Paracelsus* he had explained that he had 'endeavoured to write a poem,

[3] Griffin and Minchin, p. 75.

[4] Juliet Lady Pollock, *Macready as I Knew Him* (1884), p. 65, quoted in *The Diaries of William Charles Macready 1833–1851*, ed. William Toynbee (1912), i. 247 n.

[5] Macready, i. 267.   [6] Ibid. 277.   [7] *Life and Letters*, p. 82.

not a drama', but as *Strafford* was designed as a drama, not a poem, it is disconcerting to find him acknowledging that it is a work 'of Action in Character rather than Character in Action'.[8] On 1 November 1836 Macready wrote in his Diary: 'I fear he has such an interest in the individual characters, the biographies of whom he has written, that he is misled as to its dramatic power; character to him having the interest of action.'[9] Three weeks later Macready 'Began *very attentively* to read over the tragedy of *Strafford*, in which I find more grounds for exception that I had anticipated. I had been too much carried away by the truth of character to observe the meanness of plot, and occasional obscurity.' Four months later he was still worried about the play, confessing to 'disappointment at the management of the story' and to being 'by no means sanguine . . . on its success'. Shortly we find him concerned about 'the want of connection in the scenes', and making the experiment of reading the play aloud:

Browning called, whom I accompanied to the theatre. Read over *Strafford* to the persons in the green-room, but did not produce the impression I had hoped—it dragged its slow length along. Read Strafford to Catherine and Letitia [his daughters], and I lament to say they were oppressed by a want of action and lightness; *I fear it will not do*

As the first night drew near, his hopes grew fainter and fainter. 'Browning came to breakfast, very pale, and apparently suffering from over-excitement', he wrote on 22 April:

I think it is unfortunate that without due consideration and time for arranging and digesting his thoughts on a work so difficult as a tragedy, he should have committed himself to the production of one. I should be too glad of any accident that would impede its representation, and give me a *fair* occasion for withdrawing it.

He was depressed not only by 'the want of action, and consequently of interest', but also by 'the unintelligibility of the motives' of the

[8] Preface to original edition.
[9] Macready, i. 355. The quotations which follow are from pp. 362, 380, 385–6, 389, 390.

characters. The last comment of Macready's that demands quotation is both shrewd and unanswerable:

In all the historical plays of Shakspeare, the great poet has only introduced such events as act on the individuals concerned, and of which they are themselves a part; the persons are all in direct relation to each other, and the facts are present to the audience. But in Browning's play we have a long scene of passion—upon what? A plan destroyed, by whom or for what we know not, and a parliament dissolved, which merely seems to inconvenience *Strafford* in his arrangements. There is a sad want of judgment and tact in the whole composition. Would it were over!

In the preface to *Paracelsus* Browning had argued forcefully against the conception of the 'Dramatic Poem', in which 'the canons of the drama' are submitted to in spite of the fact that such 'restrictions' are only advantageous 'so long as the purpose for which they were at first instituted is kept in view'. As *Strafford* was intended for 'stage representation', these restrictions should have been accepted because of the advantages which they bring with them. In fact, however, the 'canons' of the drama are violated in Browning's first play, or observed only in the most half-hearted manner, and the result is a work which is little more 'dramatic' than *Paracelsus* itself. The most interesting passage is the monologue which Strafford addresses to Balfour as he is about to be led away to execution.

In the original advertisement to *Pippa Passes* Browning recalled that 'a Pitfull of goodnatured People' had applauded *Strafford*. Although it had little success on the stage—running for only five nights—the *Morning Herald* 'extolled the play as the "best that had been produced for many years" ',[10] while the *Edinburgh Review* considered it important enough to devote twenty pages to a predominantly unfavourable critique which grudgingly acknowledged some promise in the work of the new dramatist.[11] It is not surprising

[10] Macready, i. 392.

[11] A short extract is given in Litzinger and Smalley. The most interesting passage, however, is the following: 'The worst peculiarity of Mr. Browning's dramatic diction is one which he has in common with many popular writers of the day; and it may be easily discovered how much it is owing to the circumstance of writing for actors, and in that manner which they conceive best calculated to exhibit their powers. It is a fashion of breaking up his language into fragments; conveying a meaning, as it were, by starts and jerks; rarely finishing a sentence at

that Browning should have decided to try again, attempting to avoid the faults of his first attempt: accordingly he modelled *King Victor & King Charles* 'on the simple lines of Alfieri, whose works [he] had been studying very closely'.[12] In turning to the Italian neo-classicist Browning may have been taking a hint from the *Edinburgh Review*:[13] he was certainly doing what Byron had done twenty years before, when he proclaimed that his 'dramatic system' was 'more upon the Alfieri School than the English'.[14] Sismondi tells us that 'every high-minded Italian who lamented over the humiliation of his country was united to [Alfieri] by bonds of mutual sympathy', and it is significant that Browning should have turned to his example at a time when his interest in liberal politics was growing steadily. In fact, however, the fourfold structure of *King Victor* seems to have little in common with that of Alfieri's dramas, and the reader is principally struck by Browning's interest in his characters:

the fiery and audacious temper, unscrupulous selfishness, profound dissimulation, and singular fertility in resources, of Victor—the extreme and painful sensibility, prolonged immaturity of powers, earnest good purpose and vacillating will of Charles—the noble and right woman's manliness of his wife—and the ill-considered rascality and subsequent better-advised rectitude of D'Ormea.[15]

Macready was not impressed: he considered the play 'a *great mistake* . . . and most explicitly told him so, and gave him my reasons for coming to such a conclusion'.[16] So far as can be traced, no performance has ever taken place.

In the months following the completion of *Sordello* Browning seems to have written three further dramatic pieces: *The Return of the Druses*, *Pippa Passes*, and (probably during the autumn of 1840) *A Blot in the 'Scutcheon*. The first- and last-named were intended for

all; and, when he does, cutting it short with disagreeable abruptness. . . . The author of the "Pickwick Papers," with his usual acuteness, has made this fragmentary mode of speech the attribute of a strolling actor; and we really do not know where we could find a parallel to the language of Strafford so easily as in that of his inimitable Mr. Alfred Jingle': *Edinburgh Review*, lxv (July 1837), 143–4.

[12] Griffin and Minchin, p. 126.   [13] *Edinburgh Review*, lxv. 151.
[14] *The Works of Lord Byron: Letters and Journals*, v. 372.
[15] Prefatory note.   [16] Macready, ii. 23

the theatre, and the rejection of the one and the failure of the other led to a long breach between Browning and Macready. On 3 August 1840 Macready read *The Return of the Druses* and wrote in his Diary: 'with the deepest concern I yield to the belief that he will *never write again*—to any purpose. I fear his intellect is not quite clear'. On the 27th there is an equally decisive and amusing entry: 'Browning came before I had finished my bath, and really *wearied* me with his obstinate faith in his poem of *Sordello*, and of his eventual celebrity, and also with his self-opinionated persuasions upon his *Return of the Druses*. I fear he is for ever gone.'

In *A Blot in the 'Scutcheon* Browning further pursued his search for an eligible dramatic form. Offering it to Macready, he described it as 'a sort of compromise between my own notion and yours', and boasted: 'There is *action* in it, drabbing, stabbing, et autres gentil-lesses,—who knows but the Gods may make me good even yet?'[17] There is a remarkable piece of evidence that Browning's abandonment of the political or foreign themes of his earlier plays in favour of a domestic subject (the action takes place in England in the late eighteenth century) made a strong appeal to the man in all England who must be supposed to have understood the taste of the time most surely. Late in 1842 Dickens wrote to give Macready and Forster his opinion:

Browning's play has thrown me into a perfect passion of sorrow. To say that there is anything in its subject save what is lovely, true, deeply affecting, full of the best emotion, the most earnest feeling, and the most true and tender source of interest, is to say that there is no light in the sun, and no heat in blood. It is full of genius, natural and great thoughts, profound and yet simple and beautiful in its vigour. I know nothing that is so affecting, nothing in any book I have ever read, as Mildred's recurrence to that 'I was so young—I had no mother.' I know no love like it, no passion like it, no moulding of a splendid thing after its conception, like it. And I swear it is a tragedy that MUST be played: and must be played, moreover, by Macready. . . . And if you tell Browning that I have seen it, tell him that I believe from my soul there is no man living (and not many dead) who could produce such a work.[18]

17 *Letters*, p. 5.
18 John Forster, *Life of Charles Dickens*, ii. (1873), 25.

This is the sort of praise that writers dream of, and hardly ever receive. Browning did not see the letter, but it was probably decisive in determining that his play should be acted—though not before Macready had cut it to three Acts. We have the evidence of Joseph Arnould that, at the first night, the popular part of the audience were very much moved:

The first night was magnificent . . . and there could be no mistake at all about the honest enthusiasm of the audience. The gallery (and this, of course, was very gratifying, because not to be expected at a play of *Browning*) took all the points quite as quickly as the pit, and entered into the general feeling and interest of the action far more than the boxes—some of whom took it upon themselves to be shocked at being betrayed into so much interest for a young woman who had behaved so improperly as Mildred.[19]

On the second night the gallery was again full, but the rest of the theatre was almost empty, and on the third night it was evident that the play would have to be withdrawn. There can be no doubt that Browning's proud refusal to accept Macready's last-minute offer to act in *A Blot* himself (contrary to his earlier decision) greatly damaged its chances, but it is interesting to notice that even the loyal Arnould doubted whether Macready's participation would have been sufficient to ensure any permanent popularity for the play:

With some of the grandest situations and finest passages you can conceive [he wrote to Domett], it does undoubtedly want a sustained interest to the end of the third act; in fact the whole of that act on the stage is a falling off from the second act; which I need not tell you is for all purposes of performance the most unpardonable fault. Still, it will no doubt—nay, it must—have . . . produced a higher opinion than ever of Browning's genius and the great things he is yet to do, in the minds not only of a clique, but of the general world of readers.[20]

Unfortunately the opinion of 'the general world of readers' seems to have been fairly represented by the reviewer in the *Athenæum*, who wrote as follows:

If to pain and perplex were the end and aim of tragedy, Mr. Browning's

---

[19] *Domett*, p. 65.   [20] Ibid., pp. 66-7.

poetic melodrama, called *A Blot on the 'Scutcheon*, would be worthy of admiration, for it is a very puzzling and unpleasant piece of business. The plot is plain enough, but the acts and feelings of the characters are inscrutable and abhorrent, and their language is as strange as their proceedings.[21]

Perhaps Browning was unlucky, yet it was just as well that he was obliged to renounce the ambition of becoming a popular dramatist. For his own development *A Blot in the 'Scutcheon* was a false direction. It was not in the theatre, nor in scenes of domestic pathos, that Browning was to prove himself master of his own kind of dramatic verse.

It is significant that of all Browning's 'Dramas' it is the one in which he broke away most decidedly from any normal shape of acting play that occupies the most important position in his development. Mrs. Orr tells us how the idea for *Pippa Passes* came to him:

Mr. Browning was walking alone, in a wood near Dulwich, when the image flashed upon him of some one walking thus alone through life; one apparently too obscure to leave a trace of his or her passage, yet exercising a lasting though unconscious influence at every step of it; and the image shaped itself into the little silk-winder of Asolo, Felippa, or Pippa.[22]

So far as the form is concerned, the model is not the drama but the 'Dramatic Scene'. This curious genre flourished in the 1820s and 1830s, Browning's acquaintance B. W. Procter ('Barry Cornwall') being a prolific practitioner. Stimulated (no doubt) by Lamb's *Specimens of English Dramatic Poets, Who Lived About the Time of Shakspeare*, and other anthologies of passages from the older dramatists, poets took to writing detached scenes from plays which they had, as a rule, no intention whatever of completing. The wretched condition of the theatres encouraged a habit which reminds us that the poetry of the Elizabethan dramatists seemed much more important at this time than the acting quality of their plays. Minor poets enjoyed the opportunity of writing an eloquent or pathetic speech for a given moment in an imaginary action, without the

[21] 18 Feb. 1843: reprinted in Litzinger and Smalley, p. 95.
[22] *A Handbook to the Works of Robert Browning* (7th edn., 1896), p. 55.

labour of constructing a dramatic whole. For the most part, the writers of these 'Dramatic Scenes' were not so much poets as (in Eliot's phrase) 'poetical persons'.

Yet Browning's aim, in *Pippa Passes*, is no more that of the writer of 'Dramatic Scenes' than it is that of the dramatist. By presenting a crisis in the life of a number of people he wishes to enforce a religious or moral idea: the truth that human character is always mixed—('Best people are not angels quite', as Pippa remarks)[23]— and that one human being may by innocence and virtue have a beneficial influence on another. It is as characteristic of Browning that the germ of the work should be 'the image . . . of some one walking . . . alone through life' as that this theme should be worked out with Italian characters in an Italian setting. For all her un-conscious influence on others, Pippa is essentially a lonely figure, and so are the protagonists of the four scenes of which (as of four interrelated short stories) the work as a whole consists. It is only in the first scene—that between Ottima and Sebald—that there is any real conflict between the dramatis personae, and at the end of it the two lovers are separated. Jules is isolated from his fellow students. Luigi, who leaves his mother in order to fight for his country, is essentially a 'loner' (like the speaker in 'The Italian in England'). Monsignor, too, is an isolated man. The most memor-able passages are monologues, while (as so often in Browning) passages that are technically dialogue often retain the air of monologue, the speaker being little concerned with the reaction of the person whom he is supposed to be addressing.

In *Pippa Passes*, therefore, we find Browning using an experimental form which is closer to the dramatic monologue than to any normal type of legitimate drama. He takes four men (even in the first scene it is the man who is the protagonist), and shows us each of them at a turning-point in his life. It is Pippa's song which determines the choice made by each of the protagonists: her voice may be taken as a symbol for the inner voice of conscience, an expression of the innocence that is to be found in every human heart. Two of the protagonists are the sort of men who become speakers in the great dramatic monologues. Jules is a young

[23] l. 38 of the last section of Part IV.

sculptor in whose work a powerful churchman is interested, an artist at a turning-point in his career who 'may—probably will—fail egregiously', yet who could conceivably prove to be the 'new painter' who will change the whole course of painting; while Monsignor is a forerunner of Browning's worldly bishops.

The scene between Monsignor and the Intendant is of considerable merit, but Part II, in which Jules is the principal character, is of particular interest because it so clearly points forward to Browning's greatest work, notably to 'Andrea del Sarto'. Jules expresses his love for his books in a way that reminds us of Browning's flair for recapturing the spirit of the Italian Renaissance:

> This minion, a Coluthus, writ in red
> Bistre and azure by Bessarion's scribe—
> Read this line . . . no, shame—Homer's be the Greek
> First breathed me from the lips of my Greek girl!
> This Odyssey in coarse black vivid type
> With faded yellow blossoms 'twixt page and page,
> To mark great places with due gratitude . . . (ll. 39–45)

In his meditations on painting and sculpture Jules is the successor of Aprile in *Paracelsus* and a reminder of certain of the most interesting passages in *Sordello*:

> . . . Why, before I found
> The real flesh Phene, I inured myself
> To see, throughout all nature, varied stuff
> For better nature's birth by means of art:
> With me, each substance tended to one form
> Of beauty—to the human archetype.
> On every side occurred suggestive germs
> Of that—the tree, the flower—or take the fruit,—
> Some rosy shape, continuing the peach,
> Curved beewise o'er its bough; as rosy limbs,
> Depending, nestled in the leaves; and just
> From a cleft rose-peach the whole Dryad sprang.
> But of the stuffs one can be master of,
> How I divined their capabilities!
> From the soft-rinded smoothening facile chalk
> That yields your outline to the air's embrace,

Half-softened by a halo's pearly gloom;
Down to the crisp imperious steel, so sure
To cut its one confided thought clean out
Of all the world. But marble!—'neath my tools
More pliable than jelly—as it were
Some clear primordial creature dug from depths
In the earth's heart, where itself breeds itself,
And whence all baser substance may be worked . . .

(ll. 81–104)

Jules is an idealist, isolated from his fellow students by his un-worldliness, and he addresses Phene very much as Andrea del Sarto addresses Lucrezia:

. . . Sit here—
My work-room's single seat. I over-lean
This length of hair and lustrous front; they turn
Like an entire flower upward: eyes, lips, last
Your chin—no, last your throat turns: 'tis their scent
Pulls down my face upon you . . .   (ll. 3–8)

For a long time, like the silent presence in a dramatic monologue, Phene says nothing, as Jules pours out his ambitions and his soul's dreams. Near the end, when he discovers that she is a prostitute who has been sent to him by his malicious fellow students, he is on the verge of despair. But unlike the speakers in most of the great monologues, Jules is young: his life lies ahead of him, so he is able to abandon sculpture in favour of painting and to escape with Phene to

Some unsuspected isle in far-off seas![24]

The ending of the Scene is optimistic and Shelleyan: Browning's object (here) is not to present a mature man, complete with his destiny, but to show the effect of Pippa's song on an idealistic young man whose 'choice of life' still remains open.

There is no need to pursue Browning into his other three dramatic works: *Colombe's Birthday*, a domestic drama about the triumph of love over the desire for power which was written to be

[24] It is curious that DeVane makes no reference to *Pippa Passes* in 'The Virgin and the Dragon' (*Yale Review*, 37 (1947), reprinted in Drew), since the story of Jules and Phene is a particularly clear example of Browning's deep interest in the myth of Perseus and Andromeda.

acted by Charles Kean and his wife and which contains a certain unity of action and some passages of tolerable verse: *A Soul's Tragedy*, which was not designed for the stage but which contains some witty prose speeches which might remind one of Bernard Shaw:[25] and *Luria*, which was written in 1845–6, 'for a purely imaginary Stage',[26] at the time when Browning was turning away from the theatre. Although he himself was always very touchy about his plays, insisting to the end of his life that the three which were produced 'all succeeded, and . . . owed it to fortuitous circumstances that their tenure on the boards has been comparatively short',[27] no one today—except perhaps the writer of an academic dissertation—is likely to argue that he has been seriously underestimated as a dramatist. What concerns us is the light that his dramas throw on his major poetry.

It has become noticeable that Browning is at his best, in his 'Dramas', when the possibility of stage production is least in his mind. He was not a man of the theatre, and his interest remained an interest in 'Action in Character' rather than in 'Character in Action'. His remark, in the passage quoted at the head of this chapter, that in *Luria* 'all the *events*, (and interest), take place in the *minds* of the actors' is equally applicable to his other dramatic works. In them, as in *Paracelsus* and *Sordello*, his 'stress lay on the incidents in the development of a soul', a fact which we may verify by glancing for a moment at his protagonists. A 'great, misguided man', Strafford is a mixed character who attains nobility when he is

---

[25] For example, the discussion of love between Chiappino and Ogniben. The former says that he 'must have a woman that can sympathize with, and appreciate me . . . a woman that could understand the whole of me, to whom I could reveal alike the strength and the weakness—'. Ogniben replies: 'Ah, my friend, wish for nothing so foolish! Worship your love, give her the best of you to see; be to her like the western lands (they bring us such strange news of) to the Spanish Court; send her only your lumps of gold, fans of feathers, your spirit-like birds, and fruits and gems! So shall you, what is unseen of you, be supposed altogether a paradise by her,—as these western lands by Spain: though I warrant there is filth, red baboons, ugly reptiles and squalor enough, which they bring Spain as few samples of as possible. Do you want your mistress to respect your body generally? Offer her your mouth to kiss: don't strip off your boot and put your foot to her lips! You understand my humour by this time? I help men to carry out their own principles: if they please to say two and two make five, I assent, so they will but go on and say, four and four make ten': *The Poetical Works*, iii. (1889), 290–1.

[26] Kintner, i. 251.

[27] Gosse, p. 44.

put to the test. King Charles rises from weakness to strength when the occasion demands it. In *The Return of the Druses* Djabal rises to dignity, in spite of the 'false life' he has lived for most of the action: killing himself at the end, he remains an inspiration to his people, although he will be regarded as an impostor by the rest of the world. Each of the protagonists in *Pippa Passes* turns from evil when he hears Pippa singing. Colombe triumphantly sacrifices everything for love. *A Soul's Tragedy* was described by Browning himself as 'a wise metaphysical play (about a great mind and soul turning to ill)'.[28] Luria dies as a sort of martyr to Honour and Faith. As the reviewers did not fail to point out, the motivation of these characters is frequently obscure and over-subtle (one is reminded of the disastrous theatrical ventures of Henry James), while Browning shows little interest in the interplay between his characters — the only source of a true dramatic action. He prefers characters (such as thinkers and artists) who react to events, rather than characters who bring events about by their own initiative. As a subject for poetry, Napoleon would only have interested Browning during his final captivity. Although six of the eight works are described as 'Tragedies' there is little evidence that the tragic view of life was meaningful to Browning, abundant evidence that the development of a tragic action was quite beyond his powers. Nothing could be more revealing than his disagreement with Matthew Arnold over *Empedocles on Etna*. In 1853 Arnold refrained from including the work in his *Poems* on the ground that it failed to meet the criterion of tragedy, that 'no poetical enjoyment' can be derived from situations

in which the suffering finds no vent in action; in which a continuous state of mental distress is prolonged, unrelieved by incident, hope, or resistance; in which there is everything to be endured, nothing to be done. In such situations there is inevitably something morbid, in the description of them something monotonous.

Browning was the 'man of genius' at whose request *Empedocles* was reprinted in later editions of Arnold's work. While Arnold was right in believing that the subject was unsuitable for tragedy,

[28] *Domett*, p. 36.

Browning recognized a subject suited to his own strange poetic art. Three decades before, George Darley had diagnosed the weakness of English tragedy in words that apply as unerringly to Browning as to Byron and his contemporaries (to whom they were addressed):

Your tragedies . . . appear to me to be deficient in the first grand leading essential attribute of the drama, viz. action. Your plots are poor, your stories meagre; they have neither boldness of delineation, nor fulness of incident: your scenes are too few, too long, and too seldom themselves subdivided by change of topic, or introduction of new characters; . . . your fables want interest; your matter diversity; in short, your action is nothing, and your poetry every thing.[29]

Only the last clause is inapplicable to Browning. What led him astray as a dramatist was not a striving after 'poetry'—the usual fault of nineteenth-century verse drama—but an exclusive interest in the psychology and motivation of one single character. Elizabeth Barrett showed remarkable understanding when she told Browning, in her second letter to him, that 'A great dramatic power may develop itself otherwise than in the formal drama; & I have been guilty of wishing, before this hour . . . that you w^d give the public a poem unassociated directly or indirectly with the stage.'[30]

While Browning was much occupied with the theatre for ten years, from his meeting with Macready at the end of 1835 to the completion of *Luria* in 1846, his main dramatic activity was probably concentrated in the period immediately before and after his work on the final version of *Sordello*.[31] Although by the end of this time he was on the threshold of his great creative years, outwardly there was little to encourage him. Having been regarded as a promising young poet a few years before, he now found himself nearing thirty without having written anything that had received any measure of general approbation. He was still living with his parents, and Mrs. Procter was not the only candid friend who thought it a pity that he

---

[29] 'A Second Letter to the Dramatists of the Day', by 'John Lacy', in the *London Magazine*, viii (July–December 1823), 140–1.

[30] Kintner, i. 10.

[31] *Strafford* and (probably) *King Victor and King Charles* were written in 1836–7, *The Return of the Druses*, *Pippa Passes*, and *A Blot in the 'Scutcheon* probably in 1839–40. The writing of the three remaining plays may be regarded as a sort of postscript.

'had not seven or eight hours a day of occupation'.[32] It is regrettable that we do not know more about Browning's life at this point. We do know, however, that he had met Carlyle by early 1839, and that he 'soon became a familiar figure at Cheyne Row'; and it is clear that he found kindness and inspiration in Carlyle's conversation, in spite of its astringency and the sage's standard advice 'to give up poetry'.[33] The fact that his mother was half German and had been brought up in Scotland must have helped him to understand Carlyle, who obviously discerned the earnestness underlying the flippancy with which the young poet sometimes concealed his serious purposes. Carlyle must have noticed how often Browning employed the scriptural phraseology, with reference to his own vocation as a writer, which is ubiquitous throughout his own writings.

It is fortunate that one correspondence survives which throws a good deal of light on what was clearly a time of inward stirring and growth. In the second letter in the collection edited by Sir Frederic Kenyon as *Browning and Alfred Domett* we find Browning defending *Sordello* against the charge of unnecessary obscurity and hoping that he will be vindicated by his plays. 'I wish I had thought of this before', Browning writes after the passage already quoted on p. 40; 'meantime I am busy on some plays . . . that shall be plain enough if my pains are not thrown away'.[34] The whole passage makes it clear how difficult Browning found it to anticipate the reaction of theatre-goers or of readers.

What men require, I don't know [he wrote two years later]. . . . I shall . . . print the Eastern play you may remember hearing about— finish a wise metaphysical play . . ., and print a few songs and small poems which Moxon advised me to do for popularity's sake! These things done (and my play out), I shall have tried an experiment to the end, and be pretty well contented either way.[35]

Elsewhere in the same letter Browning made a remarkably penetrating comment on his own position. He was writing to Domett in New Zealand:

---

[35] Griffin and Minchin, p. 138. [33] Ibid., p. 136. [34] *Domett*, p. 29.
[35] Ibid., pp. 35–6.

Live properly you cannot without writing, and to write a book now will take one at least the ten or dozen years you portion out for your stay abroad. I don't expect to do any real thing till then: the little I, or anybody, can do as it is, comes of them *going to New Zealand*—partial retirement and stopping the ears against the noise outside; but all is next to useless—for there is a creeping, magnetic, assimilating influence nothing can block out. When I block it out, I shall do something.[36]

'The true best of me is to come', Browning wrote a few sentences later, and within two or three months he seems to have written 'My Last Duchess' and a number of shorter poems in which he confirms the impression that he has found his proper territory. He was clearly stimulated by a close reading of Tennyson's *Poems* of 1842,[37] while Moxon's fortunate advice must have encouraged him to add to the slender collection of 'small poems' which he had already written. 'I seem only beginning to see what one . . . might do, writing',[38] as he wrote to Domett in May 1843, and his own description of himself as one of 'God's Elect' who is obliged to tolerate disingenuous and unintelligent criticism is a reminder of the seriousness with which he regarded his own poetic career. About this point in his life the caterpillar turned into a butterfly. This lends particular interest to a passage in a letter by one of the most intelligent of his friends, Joseph Arnould, whose brilliant career at Oxford (where he won the Newdigate Prize for an English Poem) was to lead him to a knighthood and the position of Judge of the Supreme Court at Bombay. In 1843 he wrote as follows:

Browning's conversation is as remarkably good as his books, though so different: in conversation anecdotal, vigorous, showing great thought and reading, but in his language most simple, energetic, and accurate. From the habit of good and extensive society he has improved in this respect wonderfully. We remember him as hardly doing justice to himself in society; now it is quite the reverse—no one could converse with him without being struck by his great conversational power—he relates admirably; in fact, altogether I look upon him as *to be* our foremost literary man.

---

[36] *Domett*, p. 35.　　　　　　　　　　　　[37] Cf. pp. 92–3, below.
[38] *Domett*, pp. 55–6, followed by quotations from pp. 86, 46, 49, and 54.

'He relates admirably' is a statement of great importance, when we recall the evident affinity of many of Browning's finest poems to the art of the short story. Since Domett had left for New Zealand only the previous year, the wonderful improvement observed by Arnould in Browning's conversational powers presumably occurred relatively quickly.

Browning's increasing confidence at this time may be shown by the 'outrageous laughters' with which he greeted the prosing talk of a solemn American visitor of Carlyle's: an earnest man who wished to 'convert [England] to something or other'. Visits to Carlyle continued. In December 1842 Browning told Domett that he had recently spent an evening with him, and that 'he talked nobly— seemed to love Goethe more than ever'. 'What shall I tell you?', he asked when he wrote to New Zealand again the following May:

—that we are dead asleep in literary things, and in great want of a 'rousing word' (as the old Puritans phrase it) from New Zealand or any place *out* of this snoring dormitory. Carlyle has just given us a book, however; not the study on 'English History' (Cromwell, &c.) that he was engaged on when you were with us—but there, what, in short, I shall send you by next ship [*Past and Present*]. Carlyle came here a few weeks ago—walked about the place, and talked very wisely and beautifully. He cannot get on for the row and noise.

It is noticeable that Browning was by no means overawed by 'the sage of Chelsea'. Early in 1845 he tells Domett of the progress of *Oliver Cromwell*, and comments: 'Himself seems to entertain a boundless admiration for the man. I spent this day fortnight's evening with Carlyle, and never remember him more delightful; the intensity of his Radicalism, too, is exquisite.'[39]

The sense of creative discontent and expectancy which seems to have dominated Browning at this time is illustrated by a letter which he sent to New Zealand in October 1843:

I make no new friends, which sometimes seems a pity—but I strengthen myself with the old—find better and better reasons for

[39] *Domett*, p. 111. In an early letter to Browning, Elizabeth Barrett wrote of 'the great teacher of the age, Carlyle, who is also yours & mine', adding: 'He fills the office of a poet—does he not?—by analyzing humanity back into its elements . . .': Kintner, i. 29.

the faith that was in me. . . . We are all here, in the same quiet way. People read my works a little more, they say, and I have some real works here, in hand . . . nothing more can be done at present with plays.[40]

Nothing could testify more clearly to Browning's sense of vocation than the matter-of-fact way in which he uses the phrase 'the faith that was in me'. In November his growing confidence appears again, in another letter to New Zealand:

Thank you heartily for your criticism, which is sound as old wine. The fact is, in my youth (*i.e.* childhood) I wrote *only* musically—and after stopped all that so effectually that I even now catch myself grudging my men and women their half-lines. . . . But you will find a difference, I think, in what has reached you already, even, and *more* in what *shall* reach you, D.V.[41]

As is emphasized elsewhere, Moxon's suggestion that Browning should put together some of his shorter poems for one of the *Bells and Pomegranates* pamphlets proved of the greatest importance, since it offered him a means of escape from the frustrations of a poet who had written long poems which hardly anyone had read and plays which no producer (now) was prepared to put on the stage. In July 1844 Joseph Arnould commented approvingly on the second group of the shorter poems:

Do you remember F. A. Ward? He is now sub-editor of *Hood's Magazine*, and in this capacity has acted well in wrenching from our Robert several little morceaux, sketches by a master, which have appeared in said Magazine, and being more exoteric than even his *sketches* generally are, may do him some further service with the public.[42]

The previous month 'The Laboratory' had appeared in *Hood's*. About the same time Browning was the subject of a half-chapter in R. H. Horne's 'menagerie of modern lions and lionesses',[43] *A New Spirit of the Age*. Arnould reported this fact to Domett, commenting that 'Browning is ever active; from one height scaling another.'[44] Three days later, Browning wrote a letter which makes it clear that he felt a new access of confidence and excitement:

[40] *Domett*, pp. 92, 94.   [41] Ibid., p. 96.   [42] Ibid., p. 103.
[43] Ibid., p. 102.   [44] Ibid., p. 101.

I feel myself so much stronger, if flattery not deceive, that I shall stop some things that were meant to follow [*Colombe's Birthday*], and begin again. I really seem to have something fresh to say. In all probability, however, I shall go to Italy first (Naples and Rome), for my head is dizzy and wants change. I never took so earnestly to the craft as I think I shall—or may, for these things are with God.[45]

He left on this second, more leisurely, Italian journey in the early autumn of this same year, and one of its results was clearly 'The Bishop Orders his Tomb at Saint Praxed's Church', published in *Hood's Magazine* in March 1845. Already, by then, he had written the first of the extraordinary love-letters to Elizabeth Barrett in which he came as near to revealing the intricacies of his own mind and heart as he was ever to do in writing. Our concern (meanwhile) is with the 'sketches by a master' which he published in *Bells and Pomegranates*, nos. iii and vii, in 1842 and 1845. Let us look first at those of the poems in these two collections which Browning later classified as 'Dramatic Romances'.

[45] Ibid., p. 106.

VI

THE EARLY DRAMATIC ROMANCES

Je crois que son séjour dans le drame a été comme le professorat à Bâle de Paracelse. . . . Pour tenter sa première tentative, il avait fallu, que pour un moment au moins il perdît de vue et l'état intellectuel du public, et l'indocilité des langues humaines, et tous les autres obstacles qui empêchent un homme comme lui de transmettre à d'autres le fond de son âme. Le drame et été le lendemain: j'ai bon espoir de voir arriver un troisième et plus beau jour.   MILSAND[1]

'For I'—so I spoke— 'am a poet:
'Human nature,—behoves that I know it!'
    'The Glove'

WHEN Browning was young his ambitions were grand, not to say grandiose. He wished to trace the development of a soul, and to do so on the ample scale of a sort of *Bildungsroman* in verse, as in *Paracelsus* and *Sordello*. The purely lyrical impulse (as it is usually understood) was not strong in him, and although he occasionally published a short poem in some periodical he seems to have attributed little importance even to such an accomplished achievement as 'Porphyria's Lover'. After the failure of *Sordello* the problem of finding a publisher became acute, and in this situation Edward Moxon came to the rescue, remarking 'that at that time he was bringing out some editions of the old Elizabethan dramatists in a comparatively cheap form, and that if Mr. Browning would consent to print his poems as pamphlets, using this cheap type, the expense would be very inconsiderable'.[2] In an Advertisement to the first pamphlet, which contained *Pippa Passes*, Browning described it as 'the first of a series of Dramatical Pieces, to come out at intervals', and added: 'I amuse myself by fancying that the cheap mode in

---

[1] 'La Poésie anglaise depuis Byron: II: Robert Browning', *Revue des deux mondes*, 11 (1851), 687–8.
[2] Gosse, p. 52.

which they appear will for once help me to a sort of Pit-audience again.' Soon Moxon made a further suggestion which may have proved of the greatest importance in helping to determine the course taken by Browning's poetic career. He suggested that Browning should include 'a few songs and small poems . . . for popularity's sake',[3] and the result was the third of the pamphlets, which bore the title *Dramatic Lyrics* and had a brief Advertisement of its own:

Such Poems as the following come properly enough, I suppose, under the head of 'Dramatic Pieces;' being, though for the most part Lyric in expression, always Dramatic in principle, and so many utterances of so many imaginary persons, not mine.

It is clear that the word 'Dramatic' is used in the title partly to emphasize that Browning was not departing from his original plan of including only dramatic works in the *Bells and Pomegranates* series, and that the word 'Lyric' is being used in a very general sense.[4] When Browning attempted to *classify* his shorter poems as 'Dramatic Lyrics', 'Dramatic Romances', and 'Men and Women' poems, as he first did in *The Poetical Works* in 1863, we notice that (apart from the three 'Cavalier Tunes' with which the pamphlet opens) only three of the poems in the original *Dramatic Lyrics* are classified as 'Dramatic Lyrics', whereas eight are classified as 'Dramatic Romances'—and this last group includes both the longest and the best poems in the collection.[5]

This later distinction between a Dramatic Romance and a Dramatic Lyric is by no means clear cut: 'Time's Revenges', for example, which Browning classified as a Dramatic Romance, might seem more at home among the Dramatic Lyrics, while the opposite is clearly arguable in the case of 'The Confessional', which he classified as a Dramatic Lyric. Yet the attempted classification is

---

[3] *Domett*, p. 36.

[4] In 1863 Browning qualified his observation, merely stating that 'Such Poems as *the majority* in this volume' are '*often* Lyric in expression' (my italics). From the first he must have been aware that the word 'Lyric' is inapplicable to 'My Last Duchess' and 'The Pied Piper' (for example), and so in 1863 he made his attempt to classify his shorter poems.

[5] The longest are 'The Pied Piper', 'Waring', and 'In A Gondola': the best (in my opinion) are 'My Last Duchess', 'Porphyria's Lover', 'The Pied Piper', and perhaps 'Count Gismond'.

a useful guide to Browning's thought on his own poetry, and in the present chapter we shall be concerned with those of the shorter poems published in 1842 and 1845[6] which he later classified as 'Dramatic Romances'.

Unexpected insight into the nature of a Dramatic Romance is provided by Edmund Gosse, in an interesting reminiscence of Browning in old age:

In recounting a story of some Tuscan nobleman who had shown him two exquisite miniature-paintings, the work of a young artist who should have received for them the prize in some local contest, and who, being unjustly defrauded, broke his ivories, burned his brushes, and indignantly forswore the thankless art for ever, Mr. Browning suddenly reflected that there was, as he said, 'stuff for a poem' in that story, and immediately with extreme vivacity began to sketch the form it should take, the suppression of what features and the substitution of what others were needful; and finally suggested the non-obvious or inverted moral of the whole, in which the act of spirited defiance was shown to be, really, an act of tame renunciation, the poverty of the artist's spirit being proved in his eagerness to snatch, even though it was by honest merit, a benefit simply material. The poet said, distinctly, that he had never before reflected on this incident as one proper to be versified; the speed, therefore, with which the creative architect laid the foundations, built the main fabric, and even put on the domes and pinnacles of his poem was, no doubt, of uncommon interest. He left it, in five minutes, needing nothing but the mere outward crust of the versification. It will be a matter of some curiosity to see whether the poem so started and sketched was actually brought to completion.[7]

As Browning was an old man when he spoke to Gosse, it is not surprising that the poem seems never to have been written. Yet any reader of the anecdote must be struck by the fact that Browning's approach to the writing of the projected poem was so close to that of a novelist or short-story writer. The anecdote provides us with a valuable clue to the sort of thing we are to expect in the Dramatic Romances.

[6] In *Dramatic Romances and Lyrics*, the seventh of the *Bells and Pomegranates* pamphlets.

[7] Gosse, pp. 85–7.

In this unwritten poem, as in most short stories, it is possible to distinguish two constituent elements: the story or plot, and the moral or the view of life which the story suggests. A third element which is important in many short stories, as in many of Browning's Dramatic Romances, is the character of the narrator. If the projected poem had been written in the first person, as a narration by the disappointed artist, it would have been very different from what it would have been if it had been written in the third person—and probably much subtler: 'Pictor Ignotus' may serve as an analogue.[8] When Gosse met Browning the poet's dramatic powers had greatly diminished, and it is possible that what he envisaged was a poem in the third person. In the Dramatic Romances published in the 1840s, on the other hand, there are only two or three where the narrator appears to be indistinguishable from the poet himself: 'The Pied Piper', which is sub-titled 'A Child's Story', 'The Boy and the Angel', and possibly 'Waring'.[9] In the great collection of 1855 there are only three Dramatic Romances of this type, although two of them 'The Statue and the Bust' and 'Childe Roland'—are of major importance.

When we consider the Dramatic Romances chronologically we find that Browning did not progress from the technically simple to the technically complex. On the contrary, the first Dramatic Romance that he published, 'Porphyria's Lover', is a highly sophisticated poem in which he presents a study of insane jealousy in the form of a dramatized short story. 'My Last Duchess', which

---

[8] See pp. 208–13 below.

[9] 'The Boy and the Angel', a 'little parable poem' as Arthur Symons well described it (*An Introduction to . . . Browning*, p. 78), enforces the same moral as *Pippa Passes*, '*All service ranks the same with God*'. The most remarkable feature of this poem is the economy of the clipped couplets, which are at times reminiscent of Blake. Seventy-eight lines suffice to tell the story, and at times tetrameters give way to trimeters—or even to a spondaic dimeter, as in l. 19:

> Night passed, day shone,
> And Theocrite was gone. (19–20)

'Waring', a less impressive poem, is interesting because of the cavalier manner in which Browning treats the fact which undoubtedly inspired it, Alfred Domett's departure for New Zealand in 1842. This 'fancy portrait' is written in the sort of informal verse that suggests swift composition, yet it is far from a transcript of what actually happened. Domett did not leave England in winter, and Browning was so far from being ignorant of his destination that he corresponded with him for the next few years.

is also among the earliest of the Dramatic Romances, is another of
the most sophisticated of these poems—and the most brilliant of
the whole remarkable collection. In the present attempt to analyse
Browning's art it will be best to abandon chronology and to start
with those of the Dramatic Romances in which there is little or no
element of the 'dramatic', progressing towards those in which the
character of the speaker becomes more important.

'The Pied Piper' makes an excellent introduction to Browning's
art as a writer of short stories, not only because it is the first of his
poems that most of us encounter, but also because it is a reminder
of the importance of the poet's father. In one of his latest poems,
'Development', Browning gives us a delightful picture of his father
rearranging the furniture in the sitting-room to explain to his son
the strategy of the Siege of Troy,[10] and it is clear that Robert
Browning Senior was an inspired entertainer of children. Word
and picture often went together in his stories, as we know from
the numerous manuscripts which survive. An undated story called
'The Old Schoolfellow',[11] for example, consists of twenty-one
leaves, each headed by a careful and vivid wash drawing, with
seven or eight lines of writing below. The pictures illustrate the
heads of the men in the story, which is simply a description of
a confidence trick. The narrator receives a letter from a man who
claims to be a former schoolfellow of his who has now grown rich:
hopeful of great things from his old acquaintance, the narrator
borrows a carriage and sets out to visit him—only to find, on his
return from a fruitless excursion, that his house has been burgled in
his absence. Take away the arrest of the thief at the end, and the
result might be a sketch for a story by de Maupassant. Technically,
one notices that the story is told in a series of extremely brief
dramatic monologues: it is in fact a sort of strip cartoon. Another
story in the same notebook describes how a farmer who sets out to

[10] The passionate interest of his father in warfare and in the science of fortification
is illustrated by manuscripts at the Armstrong Browning Library at Waco. There
are numerous and careful geometrical drawings illustrating military dispositions and
fortifications: 'Vauban's 1st. Method, Freitach or Dutch Method, De Nille's or
French Method, Muller's Method', and so on. One is inscribed 'New Method RB'.
There was a good deal of My Uncle Toby about Robert Browning Senior, but he had
a whole stable of hobby-horses.

[11] At Waco.

find his brother is rooked by a card-sharper: this too is carefully illustrated. When Browning describes himself telling a child a story, therefore, in 'The Englishman in Italy', it is clear that he is writing of an experience that had been familiar to him as a boy, as well as in adult life when he himself became the story-teller:

> Fortù, Fortù, my beloved one,
>   Sit here by my side,
> On my knees put up both little feet!
>   I was sure, if I tried,
> I could make you laugh spite of Scirocco.
>   Now, open your eyes,
> Let me keep you amused till he vanish
>   In black from the skies.

In that poem the narrator describes Italian scenes, rather than telling a story; but 'The Pied Piper' remains as evidence that Browning learned the nature of a good children's story in the nursery, and never forgot it.[12]

'The Pied Piper' was written for young Willie Macready, the eldest son of the actor-manager, when he was ill in bed:

He had a talent for drawing, and asked me to give him some little thing to illustrate; so, I made a bit of a poem out of an old account of the death of the Pope's legate at the Council of Trent—which he made such clever drawings for, that I tried at a more picturesque subject, the Piper.[13]

It was a story 'well known to the family', and came from an encyclopedic work by a seventeenth-century writer, Nathaniel Wanley, *The Wonders of the Little World*.[14]

---

[12] It is remarkable that the poet's father began a poem of his own about the Pied Piper, in 1842, 'not knowing that Robert had written on this subject; having heard him mention it [the account goes on] I stopped short'. This version was printed in the *Bookman* for May 1912. It has the raciness, and the comical rhymes, that are to be found in the poem by the son. A specimen of it is printed in Griffin and Minchin, p. 21.

[13] *Letters*, p. 197.

[14] 'At Hammel, a town in the Dutchy of Brunswick, in the year of Christ 1284, upon the twenty-sixth day of June, the town being grievously troubled with rats and mice, there came to them a piper, who promised, upon a certain rate, to free them from them all: it was agreed; he went from street to street, and playing upon his pipe, drew after him out of the town all that kind of vermin, and then demanding his

The opening of 'The Pied Piper', and the mixture of verse forms in which it is written, are slightly reminiscent of Scott, and the poem has the improvised air that he had made popular thirty years before. The rushing movement of the verse makes the story vivid and exciting. As we read these hurrying and tumbling stanzas we are reminded of Gosse's description of Browning as a talker, when he was at his ease in the company of someone whom he liked: 'His talk assumed the volume and the tumult of a cascade. His voice rose to a shout, sank to a whisper, ran up and down the gamut of conversational melody.'[15] It is easy, and agreeable, to imagine stanza ii read in such a voice:

> Rats!
> They fought the dogs and killed the cats,
>   And bit the babies in the cradles,
> And ate the cheeses out of the vats,
>   And licked the soup from the cooks' own ladles,
> Split open the kegs of salted sprats,
> Made nests inside men's Sunday hats,
> And even spoiled the women's chats
>   By drowning their speaking
>   With shrieking and squeaking
> In fifty different sharps and flats.

The fact that 'The Pied Piper' contains all the elements required to please children has been proved conclusively by its triumphant history as a nursery classic. Children love an animal story, and they

wages was denied it. Whereupon he began another tune, and there followed him one hundred and thirty boys to a hill called Koppen, situate on the north by the road, where they perished, and were never seen after. This piper was called the Pied Piper, because his clothes were of several colours. This story is writ, and religiously kept by them in their annals at Hammel, read in their books, and painted in their windows and churches, of which I am a witness by my own sight. Their elder Magistrates, for the confirmation of the truth of this are wont to write in conjunction, in their publick books, such a year of Christ, and such a year of the transmigration of the children, &c. It is also observed in the memory of it, that in the street he passed out of, no piper is admitted to this day. The street is called Burgelosestrasse; if a bride be in that street, till she is gone out of it there is no dancing to be suffered': Book VI, ch. xxvi, para. 23. DeVane and others have pointed out that at least two details in Browning's poem—the opening of the mountain to swallow up the children, and the lame child who gets left behind—are not to be found in Wanley, but do occur in *Restitution of Decayed Intelligence*, by Richard Verstegan. DeVane quotes the passage *in extenso*.

[15] Gosse, p. 81.

love even more an incident which escapes from the humdrum reality of everyday life. They also love a story which makes grown-ups seem foolish, and that is exactly what happens to the adult inhabitants of Hamelin (as epitomized by the Mayor, who is treacherous, dull, and 'wondrous fat'). When these ordinary grown-ups are at a complete loss there enters the Piper,

> . . . a wandering fellow
> With a gipsy coat of red and yellow!

He is just the sort of person to fascinate children, an adult who yet comes from beyond the usual world of grown-ups, an 'outsider' with supernatural powers. When the story turns its corner, at stanza xi—the point at which the Mayor breaks his promise to the Piper—the grown-ups are once again made to look foolish, and the children themselves become prominent as the Piper leads them away for ever. Children always sympathize with the poor lame boy, who is left behind when the mountain closes, and take a healthy satisfaction in the unambiguous moral which is presented at the end:

> So, Willy, let me and you be wipers
> Of scores out with all men—especially pipers!
> And, whether they pipe us free from rats or from mice,
> If we've promised them aught, let us keep our promise!

Unlike 'Porphyria's Lover', 'The Pied Piper' is hardly a *Dramatic Romance* at all—only the most self-conscious of critics will find it necessary to try to distinguish between the narrator and Browning himself—yet it resembles that earlier poem in being a most skilful composition which has an obvious affinity to the short story. First of all, it is interesting: like Willie Macready, we all want to know what is going to happen next. Secondly, it has a definite and satisfying structure: first we hear of the plague of rats that is afflicting Hamelin, then there is the dramatic arrival of the strange Piper, and his removal of the rats, followed by the turning-point of the story and the extraordinary and fascinating revenge taken by the Piper when he dances off followed by every child in the village. Thirdly, it has a moral—as is fitting in a children's story, and as happens (also) in many of Browning's poems for adult readers.

Fourthly, the verse form is skilfully handled so as to provide a perfect medium for the speaking voice—and Browning is one of the greatest masters of the speaking voice in the whole history of English poetry.

It is a natural transition to 'Incident of the French Camp', a poem which Browning placed at the beginning of the Dramatic Romances and which exemplifies the genre at its simplest. Perhaps it is because of our modern distrust of the heroic that one is tempted to say that this would be a perfect story for Willie Macready when he had grown up a little. Browning told an inquirer that the poem was based on a true incident, but that he had changed the hero from a man to a boy. It is not known for certain when the poem was written, but if DeVane is right in his conjecture that it was in 1842 then it may conceivably have been inspired in some degree by a highly successful volume of verse that appeared in that year, Macaulay's *Lays of Ancient Rome*:

> Then off there flung in smiling joy,
>   And held himself erect
> By just his horse's mane, a boy:
>   You hardly could suspect—
> (So tight he kept his lips compressed,
>   Scarce any blood came through)
> You looked twice ere you saw his breast
>   Was all but shot in two.
>
> But fiercely ran the current,
>   Swollen high by months of rain:
> And fast his blood was flowing;
>   And he was sore in pain,
> And heavy with his armour,
>   And spent with changing blows:
> And oft they thought him sinking,
>   But still again he rose.[16]

---

[16] The first stanza is Browning's, the second Macaulay's ('Horatius', st. lxi). On 13 December 1842 Browning wrote to Domett that 'The only novelty we have had in books as yet has been Macaulay's "Lays of Rome" ', adding that so far he has only seen extracts (*Domett*, pp. 48–9). Browning makes it clear that he does not like what he has seen of the book, but that does not preclude his deriving some hint or stimulus from it.

The juxtaposition may at least serve to emphasize that when Browning is at his best he tends to be remarkably concise (when he is at his worst he is one of the long-winded bores of English literature). Whereas 'Horatius' consists of some 700 lines, 'Incident of the French Camp' is told in forty lines, with all the economy of a skilful short-story writer who keeps a surprise ending up his sleeve. If the question is asked how far the poem is 'Dramatic', the answer must be that while the portrayal of the character of the narrator is not an important part of the poet's purpose, the use of a narrator gives the story immediacy. We are in the presence of an old soldier to whom the sight of Napoleon was familiar, and this makes the tale of martial heroism the more impressive.

In 'The Flight of the Duchess' the narrator plays a distinctly more important part. The opening is striking:

> You're my friend:
>   I was the man the Duke spoke to;
>   I helped the Duchess to cast off his yoke, too;
> So here's the tale from beginning to end,
>   My friend!

It is so skilfully done that we take it for granted that the telling of the story has a context: something has happened, some remarks have been exchanged by the speaker and his auditor, before we have come within earshot. Although the division of the poem into two parts was due to interruptions, Browning had the address to turn it to use precisely in the manner of a serial-writer:

> . . . The old one, many a year,
> Is in hell, and the Duke's self . . . you shall hear.
>
> Well, early in autumn . . .

DeVane observes that 'The Flight of the Duchess' is 'peculiarly characteristic of Browning, and is hence a favorite'. The latter part of the statement is certainly no longer true. The poem is too long, and it is easy to give some credence (at least) to Browning's own remark that as a result of the interruptions he 'lost altogether the thing as it was in my head at the beginning'.[17] That the whole

---

[17] *Letters*, p. 217.

tendency of the poem was changed is unlikely, on the other hand, as its ultimate inspiration seems to have been the Scots ballad, 'The Gypsy Laddie'. But it suffered from the fact that its composition extended over a period of three years,[18] and in this case the criticisms of Elizabeth Barrett—no other poem is referred to so often in their letters—may not have been wholly beneficial. 'The Flight of the Duchess' has obvious and interesting affinities with other poems by Browning about love, and it is clear that his growing passion for Elizabeth Barrett helped to shape the course of the narrative, and perhaps led to something of its vagueness. We miss the sureness of handling which is characteristic of Browning at his best. Yet the use of the narrator is quite skilful. Although he has no admiration for the Duke as a man, he is a loyal servant of the family. Having been devoted to Jacynth, a beautiful servant girl, he knew a great deal of what was going on. The young Duchess liked him, and he helped her to escape. Later he married Jacynth, who bore him ten children, and he is now speaking as an elderly man. He is a simple person, though far from a fool, and he tells us that he still dreams of going off to join the gipsies himself one day, and ends by expressing his wonder at the odd way in which things turn out, 'The world's . . . see-saw'. We conclude that in this poem the narrator is used to make an improbable story more credible, and to enforce a romantic moral. He is essentially an observer, but he also plays an ancillary part in the main action.

A shorter poem, 'The Glove', offers interesting points of comparison with 'The Flight of the Duchess'. It is literary in inspiration, being based on Leigh Hunt's 'The Glove and the Lions'—a poem so close (in its turn) to Schiller's 'Der Handschuh' as to be little more than a translation. The first hundred lines of Browning's poem are essentially an elaboration of the Schiller–Hunt version of the story, and conclude with the verdict of the King that the lady who required her admirer to risk his life to recover her glove deserves the scorn with which De Lorge subsequently treats her. At this point the narrator becomes particularly important in Browning's poem, however. At line 105 he tells us that he did not agree with the King:

[18] The known facts about the composition of the poem are summarized by DeVane.

Not so, I; for I caught an expression
In her brow's undisturbed self-possession
Amid the Court's scoffing and merriment,—
As if from no pleasing experiment
She rose . . .

The narrator vindicates the lady's action, and Elizabeth Barrett told Browning that 'all women should be grateful' for the poem, 'though the chivalry of the interpretation, as well as much beside, is so plainly yours, . . could only be yours perhaps'.[19] The way in which Browning sends the lady off with a young lover who has been watching her actions with admiration from the wings is highly romantic, and the choice of Ronsard as the narrator was therefore appropriate. Whether or not DeVane is right in believing that Browning's own experience, and his reading of the *Mémoires* of the Marquis de Lassay, influenced Browning's attitude to the story, there is more than 'chivalry'—characteristic as that is—in his handling of the tale. In this relatively slight poem, as in his master-pieces, Browning is probing at the truth of human nature and human motivation. According to his interpretation it is not vanity that makes the lady act as she does, but her imperative need to discover the true character of her admirer. Brave as De Lorge is, he lacks other important qualities, as Browning shows by making him a *mari complaisant* at the end of the poem. That the lady has acted quite rightly is the 'non-obvious or inverted moral of the whole',[20] and Ronsard is the speaker of the lines that stand as an epigraph to the present chapter. In this poem the narrator is used primarily as a mouthpiece for the unusual interpretation of the lady's motive—though we also notice the relative sophistication introduced into what would otherwise be a slight poem by this dramatic element.

In 'Count Gismond' the narrator is more important, being no longer a mere spectator, nor even an ancillary personage. Browning's characteristic 'chivalry' is again prominent in this tale of a woman whose character was defamed, many years ago, only to be vindicated by the man who has since become her husband and the father of her two sons. She is telling the story to a friend, as her children play in

[19] Kintner, i. 252.
[20] Gosse, quoted on p. 78, above.

the distance. Mother-like, she swiftly changes the subject when the
younger of her children comes running up:

> Our elder boy has got the clear
>   Great brow; tho' when his brother's black
> Full eye shows scorn, it . . . Gismond here?
>   And have you brought my tercel back?
> I was just telling Adela
> How many birds it struck since May.

One or two recent critics have suggested that the speaker may not
in fact be innocent,[21] but the whole tone of the poem is against
them. The only lie the Countess tells occurs when she fibs about
the subject of her conversation, in the stanza quoted. No one but a
literary critic could remark without embarrassment (as one has
done in a letter to me) that he 'find[s] the poem much more interesting if the speaker's guilt is assumed'. The Pre-Raphaelites, who
loved this poem, were closer to the truth about it than such
aberrations of psychological criticism.

In 'The Italian in England' Browning is as much concerned with
the character of the speaker as with the story that is told. This
accomplished poem has suffered from Browning's yoking of it with
'The Englishman in Italy', which is a poem of a completely different sort. Unlike the latter, 'The Italian in England' is narrative in
form, and it begins with the abruptness of a skilful short story:

> That second time they hunted me
> From hill to plain, from shore to sea . . .

It is the story of one of the many adventures in the life of a passionate political partisan, a patriot working for the liberation of his
country from the yoke of Metternich, and deals with a group of
people with whom Browning is known to have felt a strong sympathy. Harry W. Rudman conjectured that it 'was suggested by the
life and personality of Mazzini, who was "the Italian in England"
par excellence',[22] and it is highly probable that Browning had read

---

[21] John V. Hagopian, 'The Mask of Browning's Countess Gismond', *PQ* 40 (1961),
153–5; J. W. Tilton and R. D. Tuttle, 'A New Reading of "Count Gismond" ', *SP* 59
(1962), 83–95; Sister M. M. Holloway, 'A Further Reading of "Count Gismond" ',
SP 60 (1963), 549–53.

[22] *Italian Nationalism and English Letters* (1940), p. 71. Mrs. Sutherland Orr tells us

Carlyle's letter to *The Times* on the scandal arising from the opening of Mazzini's correspondence. Carlyle described Mazzini as

a man of genius and virtue, a man of sterling veracity, humanity, and nobleness of mind, one of those rare men numerable, unfortunately, but as units in this world, who are worthy to be called martyr souls, who in silence piously in their daily life, understand and practise what is meant by that.[23]

The story holds our attention admirably, but as it progresses it is the character of the speaker that fascinates us, as we come to appreciate his single-minded and almost fanatical devotion to his political cause:

> How very long since I have thought
> Concerning   much less wished for   aught
> Beside the good of Italy,
> For which I live and mean to die!
> I never was in love.

In fact love is the subject of the poem: above all the speaker's love for Italy, but also his love (which even now he will not fully acknowledge) for the beautiful Italian girl who saved his life so many years ago. If he were to be granted three wishes—he tells his auditor—the first would be to throttle Metternich: the second would be that his friend Charles, who betrayed the cause, should die of a broken heart: and the third concerns the girl who saved him:

> . . . I should wish to stand
> This evening in that dear, lost land,
> Over the sea the thousand miles,
> And know if yet that woman smiles
> With the calm smile.

The theme of love renounced is common in Victorian poetry, but we

that 'Mr. Browning is proud to remember that Mazzini informed him he had read this poem to certain of his fellow-exiles in England to show how an Englishman could sympathize with them' (*Handbook*, p. 306 n.). Rudman (p. 71 n.) tells us that 'During 1846, Mazzini sent his mother bit by bit a translation, which is said still to exist in Florence in his autograph.' It should also be remembered that Browning's Italian master in England, Angelo Cerutti, was an Italian refugee.

[23] *The Times*, Wednesday, 19 June 1844: quoted by Rudman, p. 62.

notice that Browning handles it with a welcome absence of sentimentality. The conclusion of the poem is admirably managed:

> . . . I'd talk this out,
> And sit there, for an hour about,
> Then kiss her hand once more, and lay
> Mine on her head, and go my way.
>
> So much for idle wishing—how
> It steals the time! To business now.

It is clear that 'idle wishing' has stolen no time at all from the
speaker, who is a completely dedicated patriot: only in this exceptional moment of retrospection, as he tells someone of his
adventures, is the love that he has refused to acknowledge even to
himself allowed a brief and guarded expression. This is a poem that
'grows on you the more you know of it',[24] as Elizabeth Barrett
remarked, and it is one of the finest of Browning's studies of a
mind obsessed.

Obsession is also the theme of the greatest of all the early
Dramatic Romances, 'My Last Duchess', as it had been of the first
Dramatic Romance to be written, 'Porphyria's Lover'. 'Porphyria's
Lover' and 'Johannes Agricola' were first published together, in the
Monthly Repository, as two separate poems: later they were grouped
together, as 'Madhouse Cells': in 1863 they were separated, but
both classed as (Dramatic) Romances: and then in 1868 and in
Browning's final collected edition 'Johannes Agricola' became one
of the 'Men and Women' poems, 'Porphyria's Lover' remaining one
of the Dramatic Romances. Unlike 'Johannes Agricola', which contains no plot, 'Porphyria's Lover' is a brilliantly disquieting short
story, in which the speaker describes how the girl whom he loved
came to him one evening from a 'gay feast' to which he had not been
invited,

> And made her smooth white shoulder bare,
> And all her yellow hair displaced,
> And, stooping, made my cheek lie there,
> And spread, o'er all, her yellow hair.

[24] Kintner, i. 268.

He wonders how to prolong his happiness. The poem turns on the words 'I found / A thing to do', and ends by describing how he strangled the girl with her own long hair:

> . . . all her hair
> In one long yellow string I wound
> Three times her little throat around,
> And strangled her. No pain felt she;
> I am quite sure she felt no pain.

He tells us that Porphyria

> . . . guessed not how
> Her darling one wish would be heard.
> And thus we sit together now,
> And all night long we have not stirred,
> And yet God has not said a word!

Although most modern readers probably think of 'My Last Duchess' simply as a 'dramatic monologue', Browning himself can have had little hesitation in placing it among his Dramatic Romances, as soon as he hit on that category. Like 'Porphyria's Lover', this poem tells a story—the story of how a man killed a woman,[25] told in his own words. The original inspiration probably came from Browning's first visit to Italy, in search of material for *Sordello*, but other influences also came into play. In 1842, as Donald Smalley has pointed out, Browning was reviewing a book about Tasso,[26] and in looking up the facts about Tasso's life he is certain to have come on a brief account of Alfonso II, fifth Duke of Ferrara, the patron of Tasso who imprisoned him. This Duke, who married a young girl of fourteen and then left her for two years, only to return a year or so before she died (very probably as the result of poison), may well have suggested Browning's speaker. Another hint for the poem probably came from a tale in Tennyson's *Poems*, published in two volumes in 1842.

Having failed with *Sordello*, and finding himself less and less

---

[25] As DeVane notes, when Browning was asked what happened to the Duchess in his poem he replied: 'the commands were that she should be put to death, . . . or he might have had her shut up in a convent.' A reader of the poem is likely to suppose that she was put to death.

[26] *Chatterton*, Introduction.

successful in his attempts to convince Macready and the English public that he was a great dramatic poet in the usual sense of the term, Browning was at a low ebb when he found himself confronted by the spectacle of a poet of his own generation publishing a collection of short poems which was to prove the foundation-stone of a great reputation. An important letter to Alfred Domett shows that Browning studied Tennyson's poems with close attention, and it is particularly interesting to notice that he had access to a copy belonging to someone who had 'luckily transcribed from the proof-sheet' certain words and lines which Tennyson apparently deleted at the last moment.[27] One remark in the letter has an obvious bearing on Browning's own work: his comment that ' "St. Simeon Stylites" . . . I think perfect'. This poem is a study of a religious fanatic, in the form of a monologue spoken a few hours before his death, which has something in common with 'Johannes Agricola'. It is another poem in the same collection that seems to have influenced Browning, however. We know that 'The Gardener's Daughter; or, The Pictures' greatly impressed Browning's friend Joseph Arnould, and we know that it was mentioned when Browning and Tennyson met at some later time, Tennyson observing that 'he felt his life to be in flower' when he wrote the poem.[28] It is a monologue in which an old man describes how he first met his wife, when they were both young. The conclusion is as follows:

> But this whole hour your eyes have been intent
> On that veil'd picture—veil'd, for what it holds
> May not be dwelt on by the common day.
> This prelude has prepared thee. Raise thy soul;
> Make thine heart ready with thine eyes: the time
> Is come to raise the veil.
>   Behold her there,
> As I beheld her ere she knew my heart,
> My first, last love; the idol of my youth,
> The darling of my manhood, and, alas!
> Now the most blessed memory of mine age.

Is it too fanciful to remember another portrait of a dead wife, with a curtain in front of it, too, in another country and another age?

---

[27] *Domett*, p. 40, followed by a quotation from p. 41.   [28] *Wedgwood*, p. 75.

It seems probable that Tennyson's blameless old man helped to inspire the cold Renaissance aristocrat who is the speaker in 'My Last Duchess', a man so much less admirable, and so much more interesting. One of the principal impulses to creation, in the case of Browning, was an impulse with which we are more familiar when we study the lives of novelists: the impulse to reject romance in favour of reality. As he read Tennyson and other poets of the time Browning must often have been moved to protest, as Fielding was when he read *Pamela*, as George Eliot was when she read 'Silly Novels by Lady Novelists', as Tolstoy was when he read romantic descriptions of modern warfare.

In his letter about Tennyson's poems Browning emphasizes that most of them are '*dramatic* utterances coloured by an imaginary speaker's moods'.[29] Yet one has only to compare Tennyson's poems with Browning's own to see the much fuller meaning of the word 'dramatic' when it is applied to the work of the latter. The genuinely dramatic 'St. Simeon Stylites' is much less characteristic of Tennyson than 'The Gardener's Daughter'. Tennyson tells us that the old man who narrates the story is an artist, but we have to be told—whereas in Browning we would know from the smell of the paint. With Tennyson the mood or the story comes first, and remains predominant, the element of characterization usually being subordinate. With Browning it is quite different. It is impossible to think of 'My Last Duchess' without remembering the character of the speaker whose arrogant pride and jealousy are so brilliantly evoked. In this poem, as in 'Porphyria's Lover', Browning is as interested in the teller as in the tale.

'My Last Duchess' remains a Dramatic Romance, however, a brilliant short story in verse. Like the born story-teller that he is, Browning keeps a surprise for the end: a surprise that is not a mere structural device, since it throws a retrospective light on the monologue as a whole. The silent visitor whom the Duke has been addressing—to whom he has been discoursing on the charm of his first young wife, a charm that was too undiscriminating for his own exclusive taste, so that he has been obliged to permit or encourage her to die—turns out to be an emissary from a Count whose

[29] *Domett*, p. 97.

beautiful daughter the Duke is thinking of making his second wife
—provided that she brings with her a sufficient dowry.

Is the Duke mad? If he is—and there are sentimental dogmatists
who maintain that every murderer is mad—then it might even be
suggested that he is less directly responsible for his wife's death
than he supposes. If he is mad, of course, there is always the possibility that the whole story of his marriage is a fantasy—the
possibility (even) that there is no emissary for him to talk to. Such
a reading of the poem is obviously absurd, but the possibility of
such an interpretation serves to emphasize the need for extreme
tact in interpreting and criticizing any 'dramatic' poem. A critic
desirous of the praise of originality has only to introduce the hypothesis that the speaker is not telling the truth and he can claim
a liberty of interpretation which is entirely without limitation. An
example has already been given—that of critics who believe that
the speaker in 'Count Gismond' is a liar who is not in fact innocent
of the unchaste behaviour of which she was once accused.

Browning was particularly interested in insanity and every sort
of mental imbalance, but when one of his dramatis personae is lying
the poet usually or always makes it quite clear. Sometimes he
explicitly draws our attention to the unbalanced condition of his
speaker: if 'Porphyria's Lover' had not at one point been labelled
as one of two 'Madhouse Cells' critics might claim greater liberty
of interpretation than is now reasonable. More often, however,
Browning tells us what we need to know about the psychological
condition of his speaker by subtler means, and in particular by the
movement of the verse which he makes him speak. The speaker in
'Porphyria's Lover' is obviously (to put it mildly) over-excited.
The speaker in 'Count Gismond' is naturally excited as she begins
the story of how she was wronged, many years before; but by the
end of the poem she has completely regained her composure, as is
shown by the quieter tone of the last stanza, and the presence of
mind with which she changes the subject for the sake of her young
son. The speaker in 'A Light Woman' is obviously an experienced
and intelligent man of the world, as will be argued later: otherwise
a very different interpretation of that poem from the interpretation
which is obviously correct might become a temptation. The speaker

in 'Mesmerism' (another later poem) raises doubts, by the rhythm of his speech, about his complete sanity.

This test gives us a clear answer to the question whether the Duke is mad. On the contrary, everything about the movement of the verse, from the casual assurance of the opening—

> That's my last Duchess painted on the wall,
> Looking as if she were alive. I call
> That piece a wonder, now . . .

—to the arrogant affability of the conclusion—

> . . . Nay, we'll go
> Together down, sir. Notice Neptune, though,
> Taming a sea-horse, thought a rarity,
> Which Claus of Innsbruck cast in bronze for me!

—makes it clear that he is almost frighteningly in charge of the situation. Most readers, asked to name the metrical form of the poem without referring to the text, remember it as blank verse. In fact 'My Last Duchess' is written in boldly enjambed pentameter couplets, with the rhyme so muted that it affects us at a subconscious rather than a conscious level. This helps to make the poem the brilliant artefact that it is, and to enhance our feeling that the Duke is as sane a man as Iago.[30]

[30] 'As for Browning! Mon cher—if our Henry, if Turguénef, if Bourget had written their masterpieces in verse they would have been like that. The subtility, the tact of omission, the Morbidezza! "My Last Duchess", par exemple, is pure Henry James . . .' Dowson to Arthur Moore, ?31 March, 1890: *The Letters of Ernest Dowson*, ed. Desmond Flower and Henry Maas (1967), p. 146.

VII

THE EARLY DRAMATIC LYRICS

I do my best at all times—and really hope to be doing better already.
BROWNING to Alfred Domett, February 1845[1]

MOST poets write a great deal of lyric poetry when they are young, but as we have seen Browning's career was unusual in this respect, as in others. The only poems published in the *Dramatic Lyrics* of 1842 which he later classified as 'Dramatic Lyrics'[2] were the three 'Cavalier Tunes' (possibly inspired by the bicentenary of the beginning of the Civil War), 'Soliloquy of the Spanish Cloister' (which DeVane conjectures to have been written after the completion of *Sordello* in May 1839), 'Cristina' (which was probably written soon after the Queen of Spain resigned her regency in 1840), and 'Through the Metidja to Abd-el-Kadr' (which was dated '1842' when it first appeared, to make it clear that it related to the fighting between the Algerian chieftain and the French). We notice that all except the 'Soliloquy of the Spanish Cloister' were probably occasional in origin, and that the only lyric of the period which deals with love—'Cristina'—portrays it, as does the earlier 'Porphyria's Lover', as a destructive force. In those of the poems published in 1845 (in *Dramatic Romances and Lyrics*) which Browning later classified as 'Dramatic Lyrics' love is much more prominent;

---

[1] *Domett*, p. 111.

[2] To recapitulate: Browning described most of his shorter poems as 'dramatic' because they are 'so many utterances of so many imaginary persons, not mine' (cf. p. 77, above). In 1842, in the title *Dramatic Lyrics*, 'Lyric' is clearly used to cover any short poem. In 1845, however, Browning used the title *Dramatic Romances and Lyrics* (for the seventh of the *Bells and Pomegranates* pamphlets) because he considered the word 'Lyric' inapplicable to a narrative poem like 'The Pied Piper'. The difference which he tried to bear in mind, in distinguishing between 'Dramatic Lyrics' and 'Dramatic Romances', was simply that a poem in which the narrative element is prominent should be placed in the latter category.

but again it is mainly the destructive force of love that is portrayed
—as notably in 'The Laboratory' and 'The Confessional'—while
we find a continuing tendency for the most interesting of the poems
to be those which are least clearly distinguishable from 'Dramatic
Romances', in that each of them implies a whole situation or story.
It is also noticeable that hardly any of these poems can be related
to what we know of Browning's own life, while even these which
might appear to bear a relatively direct relation to some known
historical fact often turn out to be less straightforward than one
might expect.

An excellent example is 'How They Brought the Good News
from Ghent to Aix'. If ever there was a simple and straightforward poem—one might imagine—it is this. We learn it at school,
and the masterly handling of the anapaestic measure ensures
that we never forget it. Yet no poem better illustrates Browning's
characteristic elusiveness and obliquity. He was often asked
about the factual basis of the ride, and in 1884 he wrote to an
unidentified correspondent who was obviously a schoolmaster
anxious to provide his pupils with the relevant background
material:

The incident of the 'Ride' is altogether imaginary. I wrote the poem
at sea, off the African coast, after many weeks' parting with a certain
good horse 'York', on whose back I would fain have found myself—
hence the suggestion of a gallop in relief of an invested town whereto
access, by a certain road hitherto impracticable, was discovered to be
open for once. As I had no map, and wrote swiftly on the inside-cover
of a book I was reading, the places mentioned were remembered or
guessed at loosely enough.

Commending this account to the indulgence of your young
gentlemen. . . .[3]

In another letter he had given a briefer but similar account, saying
that the poem was the result of his 'sitting down under the bulwark
of a ship off the coast of Tangiers'—and adding that the book was
Bartoli's *Simboli*. In a third letter Browning states that what he had
in mind was 'a merely general impression of the characteristic

---

[3] *New Letters*, p. 300. The next letter quoted occurs on p. 203 of the same book,
while the other may be found on pp. 215–16 of *Letters*.

warfare and besieging which abound in the Annals of Flanders. This accounts for some difficulties in the time and space occupied by the ride in one night'. It would be impossible to find a clearer example of the fact that with Browning it was much less often a matter of experiencing and writing than of imagining and writing. We could no more have guessed that 'How They Brought the Good News' was composed at sea, off the coast of Africa, than that 'Love among the Ruins' may have been composed in the centre of Paris. The former poem is in fact an inspired variation on a traditional boyhood dream in which a brave young soldier rides heroically through the enemy lines bearing a vital message—a dream which may also have contributed something to 'Incident of the French Camp'. It is an odd coincidence that the name of the horse in the poem is Roland, for 'How They Brought the Good News' is a dream that may be contrasted with the nightmare that is 'Childe Roland to the Dark Tower Came': a poem that is equally without any definite historical reference, so that the precise significance of the 'Dark Tower' remains in dispute to the present day.

It is noteworthy that the speaker in the good dream is riding his favourite horse, whereas the speaker in the nightmare makes his painful way on foot. Riding was clearly a powerful imaginative stimulus to Browning, as it had been both to Scott and to Byron. 'Boot, saddle, to horse, and away!' is the refrain of one of the lively 'Cavalier Tunes', while DeVane plausibly conjectures that Browning may have composed 'Through the Metidja to Abd-el-Kadr' as he rode 'on his good horse York, whose gallop seems to me as much the real inspiration of this poem as it was of "How They Brought the Good News" '—a conjecture supported by the known fact that Browning was ordered to ride every day, for his health, in the summer of 1842, the year in which the poem was written. Whether or not we regard 'Through the Metidja' as 'one of Browning's metrical triumphs' (with DeVane), it is certainly something of a metrical curiosity.[4] The line 'As I ride, as I ride' occurs fifteen times in forty lines, three times in each stanza, while there is only the one rhyme sound throughout the poem, which even includes

---

[4] For George Saintsbury's appreciative comments on it see *A History of English Prosody*, iii (1910), 223.

further medial rhymes on the same sound. The penultimate stanza
may serve as an example:

> As I ride, as I ride,
> Ne'er has spur my swift horse plied,
> Yet his hide, streaked and pied,
> As I ride, as I ride,
> Shows where sweat has sprung and dried,
> —Zebra-footed, ostrich-thighed—
> How has vied stride with stride
> As I ride, as I ride!

In certain other of Browning's poems riding again takes on some-
thing of a symbolical significance, much as dancing does in Yeats.[5]
   The most straightforward love poem among the early Dramatic
Lyrics is 'Garden Fancies: I: The Flower's Name':

> Here's the garden she walked across,
>   Arm in my arm, such a short while since:
> Hark, now I push its wicket, the moss
>   Hinders the hinges and makes them wince!

This is simply Album verse of the better sort. There is no evidence
of the reality of passion, and if (as is possible) the inspiration of the
poem was purely literary it remains true that the imagined situation did not fire Browning's imagination, as it did (for example) in
'Soliloquy of the Spanish Cloister'. The song,

> Nay but you, who do not love her,
> Is she not pure gold, my mistress?

begins well, but continues unremarkably. 'The Lost Mistress' has
more reality about it:

> All's over, then: does truth sound bitter
>   As one at first believes?
> Hark, 't is the sparrows' good-night twitter
>   About your cottage eaves!

DeVane conjectures that this poem was written 'from apprehended
experience', the fear that his premature declaration of love had
ruined his chances with Elizabeth Barrett. It is possible, yet such

---

[5] See, e.g. 'The Last Ride Together'.

a hypothesis would be more tempting in the case of a poet more given than Browning was to making direct use of his own experience. There is no reason at all to suppose that the remarkable pair of lyrics 'Meeting at Night' and 'Parting at Morning' were inspired by any experience of Browning's own, yet they are extremely vivid, and they illustrate as well as anything could the nature of a 'Dramatic Lyric'. In the twelve lines of the first poem the man describes his arrival near the trysting place in a little boat:

> Then a mile of warm sea-scented beach;
> Three fields to cross till a farm appears;
> A tap at the pane, the quick sharp scratch
> And blue spurt of a lighted match,
> And a voice less loud, thro' its joys and fears,
> Than the two hearts beating each to each!

In the second lyric, which consists of only four lines, the speaker (who has often been supposed to be the woman, but who is in fact the man again, as Browning himself pointed out)[6] reflects as follows:

> Round the cape of a sudden came the sea,
> And the sun looked over the mountain's rim:
> And straight was a path of gold for him,
> And the need of a world of men for me.

These poems are as remarkable for what is left out as for what is included: there is no description of the lady, and virtually none of the lovers' meeting: instead we are given only the briefest natural description and a line or two of reflection by the speaker. It is impossible to imagine a love story told more concisely than in this poem, which the Imagists must surely have admired.

'Cristina' raises an interesting problem of interpretation of the sort that occurs frequently with Browning's poetry. The title suggests that it relates to Maria Cristina, who was Queen of Spain from 1829 to 1840, in which year she was forced to resign the

---

6 When he was asked whether the last line was 'an expression by her of her sense of loss of him, or the despairing cry of a ruined woman?' he replied: 'Neither: it is *his* confession of how fleeting is the belief (implied in the first part) that such raptures are self-sufficient and enduring—as for the time they appear': *New Poems*, p. 176. This is by no means the only instance in Browning's poetry where the reader is left uncertain of the identity of the speaker.

regency. Cristina was a celebrated coquette, and must be one of the few queens ever to have been the subject of a sexual assault by her Prime Minister. The speaker is in love with the Queen:

> She should never have looked at me
>   If she meant I should not love her!
> There are plenty . . . men, you call such,
>   I suppose . . . she may discover
> All her soul to, if she pleases,
>   And yet leave much as she found them:
> But I'm not so, and she knew it
>   When she fixed me, glancing round them.

It is a poem about love at first sight in which the speaker maintains that the lady's failure to acknowledge her love is a failure in courage by which she has been the loser. He himself (on the other hand) has succeeded:

> She has lost me, I have gained her;
> Her soul's mine; and thus, grown perfect,
> I shall pass my life's remainder.

W. L. Phelps rightly pointed out that 'four of Browning's fundamental articles of faith are expressed' in this poem:

the doctrine of the elective affinities; the doctrine of success through failure; the doctrine that time is measured not by the clock and the calendar, but by the intensity of spiritual experiences; [and] the doctrine that life on earth is a trial and a test, the result of which will be seen in the higher and happier development when the soul is freed from the limitations of time and space.[7]

While all this is true, and while Browning originally yoked the poem with 'Rudel to the Lady of Tripoli' under the joint title 'Queen-Worship', grave doubts surely arise about the complete sanity of the speaker. It is possible to take the uncertain rhythm of the opening as an indication of the speaker's lack of mental equilibrium, and it seems almost certain that this is one of Browning's characteristic studies of abnormal psychological conditions.[8] The speaker may be compared with the speakers in 'Porphyria's Lover' and 'Mesmerism'.

---

[7] *Robert Browning: How to Know Him*, by W. L. Phelps (1919), p. 116.
[8] The view that Browning wishes to stress the mental oddity of the speaker was

The suffering caused by love is the theme of two of the finest of these poems—poems which might well have been classified as Dramatic Romances rather than Dramatic Lyrics. In 'The Laboratory' we notice the skill with which Browning expresses the passion of a jealous woman who is planning to murder her rival:

> He is with her, and they know that I know
> Where they are, what they do: they believe my tears flow
> While they laugh, laugh at me, at me fled to the drear
> Empty church, to pray God in, for them!—Í am hére.

Here Browning is using his metrical form with the boldness of the Jacobeans in their handling of blank verse, and with the same motive—to catch the accents of the passionate speaking voice. The opening of the poem is abrupt and cacophonous, and it is interesting to read Elizabeth Barrett's comment on it:

> The Laboratory is hideous as you meant to make it:—only I object a little to your tendency . . which is almost a habit . . & is very observable in this poem I think, . . of making lines difficult for the reader to read . . see the opening lines of this poem. Not that music is required everywhere, nor in *them* certainly, but that the uncertainty of rhythm throws the reader's mind off the *rail* . . & interrupts his progress with you and your influence with him. Where we have not direct pleasure from rhythm, & where no peculiar impression is to be produced by the changes in it, we sh^d be encouraged by the poet to *forget it altogether*; should we not?[9]

The first line of 'The Laboratory' is certainly 'difficult for the reader to read':

> Now that I, tying thy glass mask tightly

—and while that represents a revision of the line as it was when Elizabeth Barrett objected to it—

> Now I have tied thy glass mask on tightly

—we notice that the revision can hardly have been made in the interests of easy reading or 'music'. While it would be foolish to

expressed by Clyde S. Kilby in *The Explicator*, ii, item 16 (November 1943). When the poem is printed in long lines, as in *Selections from the Poetical Works of Robert Browning* (1872), the effect is to emphasize the oddity of the speaker.

9 Kintner, i. 131.

deny the charge that harshness sometimes becomes a bad habit
with Browning (as it does at times with Donne) there is no doubt
that it is entirely justified in this poem, where it is used to emphasize both the macabre setting and the rancorous hatred of the
woman who is the speaker. Attention has already been drawn to
the skilful rhythm of the second stanza, with the sinister heavy
emphasis on the last three words: 'I am here'. A similar skill may be
seen in the first stanza, from the clogged and hindered utterance of
the opening line to the sudden dramatic directness of the last, with
its dactyls which are almost gay:

> Now that I, tying thy glass mask tightly,
> May gaze thro' these faint smokes curling whitely,
> As thou pliest thy trade in this devil's-smithy—
> Which is the poison to poison her, prithee?

It is astonishing to reflect that the subject of this poem is in a sense
the subject of 'Œnone'. What one remembers about Tennyson's
poem is the slow music and the mournful vowels—so much so that
the conclusion is disconcerting:

> O mother, hear me yet before I die.
> Hear me, O earth. I will not die alone,
> Lest their shrill happy laughter come to me
> Walking the cold and starless road of Death
> Uncomforted, leaving my ancient love
> With the Greek woman . . .

Violent effective action is the last thing we would expect from the
woman who has been making so musical a complaint. The speaker
in 'The Laboratory', on the other hand, is intent on action: on
murder: and we have no doubt that she will be successful. In this
sombre psychological study Browning shows a different aspect of
the same dramatic insight into a woman's mind that he was later
to show in 'Any Wife to Any Husband':

> Not that I bid you spare her the pain;
> Let death be felt and the proof remain:
> Brand, burn up, bite into its grace—
> He is sure to remember her dying face!

Since its first publication in *Dramatic Romances and Lyrics* in 1845

'The Confessional' has always been printed immediately after 'The Laboratory', as a sort of companion poem. Like its predecessor it begins dramatically, though in a very different rhythm:

> It is a lie—their Priests, their Pope,
> Their Saints, their . . . all they fear or hope
> Are lies, and lies—there! through my door
> And ceiling, there! and walls and floor,
> There, lies, they lie—shall still be hurled
> Till spite of them I reach the world!

In the second stanza we find that the speaker is—or rather was—a beautiful young girl who is now confined in a dungeon, having seen her lover executed as the result of the treachery of her confessor. The story unfolds with something of the tragic simplicity and starkness of a ballad:

> That horrible black scaffold dressed,
> That stapled block . . . God sink the rest!
> That head strapped back, that blinding vest,
> Those knotted hands and naked breast,
> Till near one busy hangman pressed,
> And, on the neck these arms caressed . . .
>
> No part in aught they hope or fear!
> No heaven with them, no hell!—and here,
> No earth, not so much space as pens
> My body in their worst of dens
> But shall bear God and man my cry,
> Lies—lies, again—and still, they lie!

Whether or not the poem is to be read as a study of the cruelty of the Inquisition, it has certainly a great deal in common with short stories on that subject which are to be found in Victorian periodicals. It seems to be more of a Dramatic Romance than a Dramatic Lyric, but whichever it is the final scene is unforgettable. The image of a man being hanged, or otherwise executed, was clearly a potent one in Browning's imagination.[10]

Hatred plays its part in each of the three remaining Dramatic Lyrics that call for our attention, and it is interesting to notice that

[10] See, for example, 'The Patriot: An Old Story', and 'Childe Roland', l. 100.

'The Lost Leader' is one of the most personal of all Browning's
early poems. If there seems something odd about such a vehement
attack on a man in his seventies who had been 'proud to drink
[Browning's] health' a few years before, we must remember the
strength of Browning's liberal political feelings at this time, and his
lifelong hatred of traitors and turncoats. If the speaker of 'The
Italian in England' were granted three wishes—he tells his interlocutor—the second would be that

> Charles, perjured traitor, for his part,
> Should die slow of a broken heart
> Under his new employers.

The speaker in 'Childe Roland' steels himself to go through with
his terrifying ordeal by remembering the disgrace that had come
on Cuthbert and the manner in which Giles, 'the soul of honour',
had died, a 'Poor traitor, spit upon and curst!' Browning was clearly
nauseated by the eulogies that were now heaped on the old man of
the Lakes—such as that contained in a letter from Harriet Martineau
to Elizabeth Barrett, on which he commented at length:

Was ever such a '*great*' poet before? Put one trait with the other—
the theory of rural innocence—alternation of 'vulgar trifles' with
dissertating with style of 'the utmost grandeur that *even you* can
conceive' (speak for yourself, Miss M . . . !)—and that amiable
transition from two o'clock's grief at the death of one's brother to
three o'clock's happiness in the 'extraordinary mesmeric discourse'
of one's friend. All this, and the rest of the serene & happy inspired
daily life which a piece of 'unpunctuality' can ruin, and to which the
guardian 'angel' brings as crowning qualification the knack of poking
the fire adroitly—of this—what can one say but that—no—best hold
one's tongue and read the Lyrical Ballads with finger in ear: did not
Shelley say long ago 'He had no more *imagination* than a pint-pot' tho'
in those days he used to walk about France and Flanders like a man—
Now, he is 'most comfortable in his worldly affairs' and just this comes
of it! He lives the best twenty years of his life after the way of his own
heart—and when one presses in to see the result of the rare experiment . . what the *one* alchemist whom fortune has allowed to get all
his coveted materials and set to work at last in earnest with fire and
melting-pot what *he* produces after all the talk of him and the like of

him why—you get *pulvis et cinis*—a man at the mercy of the tongs and shovel![11]

It is instructive to compare the obscurity of parts of this letter with the splendidly direct rhetoric of the poem:

> Just for a handful of silver he left us,
> Just for a riband to stick in his coat—
> Found the one gift of which fortune bereft us,
> Lost all the others she lets us devote.

It is not surprising that Browning became embarrassed by the poem, later in his life. He was constantly asked whether Wordsworth was really the subject of his attack, and he frequently felt obliged to reply. One of two answers to this question written in 1875 runs as follows:

I have been asked the question you put to me . . . I suppose a score of times: and I can only answer, with something of shame and contrition, that I undoubtedly had Wordsworth in my mind—but simply as 'a model;' you know, an artist takes one or two striking traits in the features of his 'model,' and uses them to start his fancy on a flight which may end far enough from the good man or woman who happens to be 'sitting' for nose and eye.

I thought of the great Poet's abandonment of liberalism, at an unlucky juncture, and no repaying consequence that I could ever see. But—once call my fancy-portrait *Wordsworth*—and how much more ought one to say,—how much more would not I have attempted to say![12]

It would have been curious to have had a poem of the sort found in the 'Men and Women' group based on a probing attempt to understand Wordsworth's point of view; but the only successful poem of this type which Browning wrote on a contemporary was 'Bishop Blougram's Apology', where his emotions are less deeply involved. 'Mr. Sludge, the "Medium"', also deals with a contemporary, but in it, in spite of its length, Browning's feelings were so strong that the result is more of a satire than of a dramatic monologue in the usual sense.

[11] Kintner, i. 464.
[12] *Life and Letters*, p. 123. DeVane quotes the other letter of 1875 on the subject, from *Letters*, pp. 166–7.

If 'The Lost Leader' is regarded as a satire, we notice that it lacks the lethal quality of Pope's 'Atticus'. In a pure satire, any good qualities conceded to the subject are used to strengthen the attack, as happens with Atticus and with Achitophel.[13] In some degree this is what happens in the later part of the first stanza of Browning's poem:

> We that had loved him so, followed him, honoured him,
> Lived in his mild and magnificent eye,
> Learned his great language, caught his clear accents,
> Made him our pattern to live and to die!
> Shakespeare was of us, Milton was for us,
> Burns, Shelley, were with us,—they watch from their graves!
> He alone breaks from the van and the freemen,
> —He alone sinks to the rear and the slaves!

Yet there is an element of 'candour' in Browning's attack which is not to be found in Augustan satire—an element which is emphasized by the conclusion of his magnificent invective, when he suddenly turns round and hopes to see Wordsworth in the end,

> Pardoned in heaven, the first by the throne!

The charge against Wordsworth is the most serious charge that Browning can make against anyone: the charge that this greatly endowed man has become a 'lost soul' (l. 21). This makes the final relenting all the more striking; and we notice that Wordsworth is not to be admitted to heaven contemptuously (as happens to Southey in Byron's *The Vision of Judgment*), but in forgiveness, because he will have received 'the new knowledge'.

'Sibrandus Schafnaburgensis' is an imprecation written in a very different spirit. 'I like your burial of the pedant so much!', wrote Elizabeth Barrett, in a phrase that may conceivably have proved the germ of 'A Grammarian's Funeral' a few years later: '—you have quite the damp smell of funguses and the sense of creeping things through and through it'.[14] Elsewhere she repeats that the poem is 'a great favourite with me—it is so new, and full of a creeping,

---

[13] *An Epistle to Arbuthnot*, ll. 193 ff.; *Absalom and Achitophel*, ll. 180–91 (lines added in the second edition): cf. the present writer's *Augustan Satire* (1952), p. 68, n. 2.
[14] Kintner, i, 130–1.

crawling grotesque life'.[15] In so far as it is a narrative, it might well be described as a comic Dramatic Romance. Exasperated by the dullness of an old book which he has been reading, the narrator—who may well be supposed to be Browning himself—has taken his revenge by dropping it into the damp hollow of a tree:

> Splash, went he, as under he ducked,
>   —At the bottom, I knew, rain-drippings stagnate:
> Next, a handful of blossoms I plucked
>   To bury him with, my bookshelf's magnate;
> Then I went in-doors, brought out a loaf,
>   Half a cheese, and a bottle of Chablis;
> Lay on the grass and forgot the oaf
>   Over a jolly chapter of Rabelais.

Nothing could be more characteristic of the 'Gothic', off-beat, un-expected side of Browning's imagination than stanzas vii and viii, in which he imagines the torments suffered by the book when it is discovered by the insects:

> How did he like it when the live creatures
>   Tickled and toused and browsed him all over,
> And worm, slug, eft, with serious features,
>   Came in, each one, for his right of trover? . . .
> All that life and fun and romping,
>   All that frisking and twisting and coupling,
> While slowly our poor friend's leaves were swamping
>   And clasps were cracking and covers suppling!

In the end he repents, in lines that bear a slight resemblance to part of 'The Lost Leader'. Restoring Sibrandus to his shelves, the speaker addresses him as follows:

> A.'s book shall prop you up, B.'s shall cover you,
>   Here's C. to be grave with, or D. to be gay,
> And with E. on each side, and F. right over you,
>   Dry-rot at ease till the Judgment-day!

More serious is the hatred in 'Soliloquy of the Spanish Cloister', though it is likely that Browning wrote the poem in the same light-hearted spirit as 'Sibrandus Schafnaburgensis'. The 'Soliloquy' is so

[15] *New Poems*, pp. 141–2.

well known that quotation is hardly necessary, but it is interesting to juxtapose stanza ii and a comment by the *Edinburgh Review* on the idiom of Byron's *Beppo*:

> At the meal we sit together:
> *Salve tibi!* I must hear
> Wise talk of the kind of weather,
> Sort of season, time of year:
> *Not a plenteous cork-crop: scarcely*
> *Dare we hope oak-galls, I doubt:*
> *What's the Latin name for 'parsley'?*
> What's the Greek name for Swine's Snout?

This is 'good verse', as the critic commented on Byron's poem, 'entirely composed of common words, in their common places; never . . . one sprig of what is called poetical diction . . . running on in an inexhaustible series of good easy colloquial phrases, and . . . fall[ing] into verse by some unaccountable and happy fatality'.[16]

---

[16] xxix (February 1818), 303.

VIII

RETROSPECT AND PROSPECT:
THE LOVE LETTERS

I really did understand of you before I was told, exactly what you told me. Yes—I did indeed. I felt sure that as a poet you fronted the future—& that your chief works, in your own apprehension, were to come.   ELIZABETH BARRETT[1]

His love for Elizabeth Barrett was the crowning happiness of Browning's life. Its influence on his poetry is much harder to assess, but it seems likely that courtship and marriage, by delaying and then virtually halting his writing for a period of years, had ultimately a beneficial effect. Certain as he was that he was a dramatic poet, Browning was not easily convinced that his future did not lie in the theatre. Although he had already written a handful of his finest short poems, he did not regard these as being of central importance. What he needed was an appreciative and understanding reader with whom he could discuss what he had done already, and what he hoped to do in the future. In Elizabeth Barrett he found an extremely intellectual practitioner of verse who admired what he had written and understood his situation and his ambitions with the intuition of a highly feminine woman.

Five months before their correspondence began, in a passage from a letter to Domett already quoted in part, we find Browning in an optimistic mood:

I feel myself so much stronger, if flattery not deceive, that I shall stop some things that were meant to follow [*Colombe's Birthday*], and begin again. I really seem to have something fresh to say. In all probability, however, I shall go to Italy first (Naples and Rome), for

---

[1] Kintner, i. 22.

my head is dizzy and wants change. I never took so earnestly to the craft as I think I shall—or may, for these things are with God.[2]

His first visit to Italy, hurried as it had been, had clearly been of importance in Browning's development. It helped him to finish, and so to escape from, *Sordello*, and almost certainly inspired 'My Last Duchess', written four years later. He wrote the great majority of the poems collected as *Dramatic Romances and Lyrics* before and during his second visit to Italy, which lasted from the late summer until the middle of December 1844. His first letter to Elizabeth Barrett was written three weeks after his return.

During the early months of their courtship Browning worked on *Luria* and made numerous revisions in the text of his shorter poems, often at the suggestion of Elizabeth Barrett. While several of these shorter poems may have been written during this period, the only one which can certainly be assigned to it is 'The Flight of the Duchess', the original idea for which had come to him some three years earlier. It is not hard to see why Elizabeth Barrett was embarrassed by Browning's profuse expressions of gratitude for her help with his poems: 'The actual *good* you get out of me, may be stated at about *two commas & a semi-colon*—do I overstate it, I wonder? . . . The worst is, that it sets me wishing impotently, to do some really good helpful thing for you—and I cannot, cannot.'[3] Browning's reply is of the greatest interest:

I have told you, and tell you and will tell you . . . because it is simple truth,—that you have been 'helping' me to cover a defeat, not gain a triumph. If I had not known you *so far* THESE works might have been the *better*,—as assuredly, the greater works, I trust will follow, —they would have suffered in proportion! If you take a man from prison and set him free . . do you not probably cause a signal interruption to his previously all-ingrossing occupation, and sole labour of love, of carving bone-boxes, making chains of cherry-stones, and other such time beguiling occupations—does he ever take up that business with the old alacrity?—No! But he begins ploughing, building—(castles he makes, no bone-boxes now). I may plough & build. . .[3a]

What Browning wanted was to be understood, and Elizabeth Barrett understood him as no one else was ever to understand him.

    [2] *Domett*, p. 106.   [3] Kintner, ii. 577.   [3a] Ibid. 580.

This made it possible for him to write a series of letters in which he revealed more of himself than he had ever done before, or would ever choose to do again. As we read these letters were are reminded of Browning's description of '*real* letters' (as distinct from 'clever writing' of the sort that is to be found in the letters of Harriet Martineau):

they move & live—the thoughts, feelings, & expressions even,—in a self-imposed circle limiting the experience of two persons only—*there* is the standard, and to *that* the appeal—how should a third person know? His presence breaks the line, so to speak . . . so that the significance is lost at once, and whole value of such letters—the cypher changed, the vowel-points removed.[4]

There are certainly many passages which read as if they were written in Hebrew, or cipher, and Elizabeth had already acknowledged that 'People say of you & of me . . . that we love the darkness & use a sphinxine idiom in our talk'. The subtlety and allusiveness of these letters may explain why so little use has been made of them by many recent critics of Browning; but it cannot excuse it, for they throw more light on Browning's life and work than any others that he was ever to write. Of the topics to which he returns time and time again, five are of particular importance: his conscious dedication of his life to poetry: his awareness that his major work still lay in the future: his speculation about the form that major work would take: his search for an audience for his poetry: and his growing discontent with life in Victorian England.

In one of his earliest letters Browning admits that he is 'vain and ambitious some nights', and that he means 'to be a Poet, if not *the* Poet'.[5] As we have seen, he regarded poetry as a vocation, in the full sense of the word: 'I desire in this life (with very little fluctuation for a man & too weak a one) to live and just write out certain things which are in me, and so save my soul.' He had need of his determination, for he was thirty-three, and had earned nothing. Like Tennyson at a similar age, but with even less to encourage him,[6] he was in the awkward situation of being obliged to watch his contemporaries

---

[4] Kintner, i. 463–4, 51.   [5] Ibid. 75, followed by 206.
[6] Tennyson's fame was established by the publication of his *Poems* in 1842, three months before his thirty-third birthday.

making progress in their careers, while he himself apparently made none. 'My friend the Countess began proceedings', he wrote in one letter, '. . . by asking "if I had got as much money as I expected by any works published of late?"—to which I answered, of course, "exactly as much".'[7] In the same letter in which he wrote the Miltonic sentence already quoted elsewhere,[8] he emphasized that his 'whole scheme of life, (with its wants, material wants at least, closely cut down,) was long ago calculated—and it supposed *you*, the finding such an one as you, utterly impossible'. Fortunately Elizabeth Barrett had a small income of her own, so that (as she wrote) they had 'sufficient or more than sufficient means of living, without modifying by a line that "good free life" of yours which you reasonably praise—which, if it had been necessary to modify, *we must have parted . . .*'. Replying to Mrs. Procter's reported wish that Browning had a regular occupation, like her own husband, Elizabeth Barrett insisted that 'to put race horses into dray carts, was not usually done nor advised'.

In one of her first letters she had assured Browning that she knew enough of him, from a careful reading of his poetry, to be certain that his

greatest works are to come . . . when the author of 'Paracelsus' and the 'Bells and Pomegranates' says that he is only 'going to begin' we may well . . . rejoice & clap our hands. Yet I believe that, whatever you may have done, you *will* do what is greater. It is my faith for you.[9]

The fact that she shared his own belief in his future potential must have been immensely heartening:

What I have printed gives *no* knowledge of me [he wrote in reply]—it evidences abilities of various kinds, if you will—and a dramatic sympathy with certain modifications of passion . . *that* I think: . . [but] these scenes and song-scraps *are* such mere and very escapes of my inner power . . . don't think I want to say I have not worked hard . . . but the work has been *inside* . . .

[7] Kintner, i. 165.
[8] p. 2, above, followed by quotations from Kintner, i. 193, 426–7, and ii. 615–16.
[9] Kintner, i. 14–15, followed by quotations from 17–18, 26, 345, and 493.

The short poems which he had already printed, like those which he was now collecting for *Dramatic Romances and Lyrics*, seemed to Browning mere preliminaries to be cleared out of the way (like his last two plays) before he could approach the next stage of his poetic career: 'first I have some Romances and Lyrics, all dramatic, to dispatch, and *then*, I shall stoop of a sudden under and out of this dancing ring of men & women hand in hand; and stand still awhile.' '*Let* me get done with these', he wrote in another letter, either of the *Dramatic Romances and Lyrics* or of the *Bells and Pomegranates* series as a whole, 'and better things will follow'. A little later he wrote that 'There are some things in the "Tragedy" [*A Soul's Tragedy*] I should like to preserve and print now, leaving the future to spring as it likes, in any direction,—and these half-dead, half-alive works fetter it, if left behind'. Soon we find him describing *Luria* as 'infinitely worse than I thought . . . a pure exercise of *cleverness*, even where [it is] most successful', and explaining:

If I go on, even hurry the more to get on, with the printing,—it is to throw out and away from me the irritating obstruction once & for-ever. I have corrected it, cut it down, and it may stand and pledge me to doing better hereafter.[10]

A few weeks later he repeated that he did not wish to be judged by what he had written so far:

My poetry is far from the 'completest expression of my being' [a phrase from the preface to Elizabeth Barrett's *Poems* of 1844]—I hate to refer to it, or I could tell you why, wherefore. . . . Still, I should not so much object, if, such as it is, it were the best, the flower of my life . . but that is all to come, and thro' you, mainly, or more certainly.

On 13 July 1846 he wrote a letter to Domett which may stand as a full and final statement of his own view of his position, at this point in his career:

As to the obscurity and imperfect expression, the last number of my 'Bells,' which you get with this [No. VIII, comprising *Luria* and *A Soul's Tragedy*], must stand for the best I could do, *four or five* months ago, to rid myself of those defects—and if you judge I have succeeded

---

10 Kintner, i. 551, followed by ii. 725.

in any degree, you will not fancy I am likely to relax in my endeavour now. As for the necessity of such endeavour I agree with you alto-gether: from the beginning, I have been used to take a high ground, and say, all endeavour elsewhere is thrown away. Endeavour *to think* (the real *thought*), to *imagine*, to *create*, or whatever they call it—as well endeavour to add the cubit to your stature! *Nascitur poeta*—and that conceded to happen, the one object of labour is naturally what you recommend to me, and I to myself—nobody knows better, with what indifferent success. But here is, without affectation, the reason why I have gone on so far although succeeding so indifferently: I felt so instinctively from the beginning that unless I tumbled out the dozen more or less of conceptions, I should bear them about forever. . . . If the real work should present itself to be done, I shall begin at once and in earnest.[11]

While Browning and Elizabeth Barrett agreed that his great work lay in the future, neither of them knew what form it would take. Long before they first met, Elizabeth had been reflecting on the dilemma confronting the Victorian poet, and in one of her first letters to Browning she set out one of her speculations:

I am inclined to think that we want new *forms* . . as well as thoughts. The old gods are dethroned. Why should we go back to the antique moulds . . classical moulds, as they are so improperly called? If it is a necessity of Art to do so, why then those critics are right who hold that Art is exhausted and the world too worn out for poetry. I do not, for my part, believe this: & I believe the so-called necessity of Art to be the mere feebleness of the artist. Let us all aspire rather to *Life*—& let the dead bury their dead. If we have but courage to face these conventions, to touch this low ground, we shall take strength from it instead of losing it; & of that, I am intimately persuaded. For there is poetry *everywhere* . . the 'treasure' (see the old fable) lies all over the field.[12]

Browning had already distinguished between her poetry and his, and expressed a hope for the future:

you *do* what I always wanted, hoped to do, and only seem now likely to do for the first time. You speak out, *you*,—I only make men & women speak—give you truth broken into prismatic hues, and fear the pure white light, even if it is in me: but I am going to try.

[11] *Domett*, pp. 127–8.   [12] Kintner i. 43, followed by 7.

It is clear that Browning was no more content with short dramatic poems than he was with plays: he had set his heart on writing some sort of long poem—with perhaps an earlier poem of some unspecified kind as the conclusion of one part of his career, and the beginning of another.[13] As early as 11 February 1845 he wrote: 'I never have begun, even, what I hope I was born to begin and end,— "R. B. a poem".'[14] A few days later he added: 'as I think I told you, I always shiver involuntarily when I look .. no, glance .. at this First Poem of mine to be. '*Now*', I call it, what, upon my soul,—for a solemn matter it is,—what is to be done *now*, believed *now*, so far as it has been revealed to me—solemn words, truly.'[15] It is fortunate that Browning never wrote what sounds a very Carlylean sort of poem: *Christmas-Eve and Easter-Day* is as near as he ever came, at least until his major period was over, to writing a poem of this sort.[16] What matters, in any event, is to notice Browning's ambition of writing a long poem, and his sense that he would be supported in this endeavour by the criticism of Elizabeth Barrett: 'when I try and build a great building I shall want you to come with me and judge it and counsel me before the scaffolding is taken down.'[17]

Whether or not it was consistent with such an ambition, there is one point on which Browning almost always insisted: that he was (in some sense) essentially a dramatic poet. I have already quoted the passage in which Elizabeth Barrett pointed out that 'A great

[13] In May 1846 he wrote: 'will it not be better to let me write one last poem this summer,—quite easily, stringing every day's thoughts instead of letting them fall, —and laying them at the dear feet at the summer's end for a memorial? I have been almost determining to do this, or try to do it, as I walked in the garden just now. A poem to publish or not to publish; but a proper introduction to the afterwork': Kintner, ii. 725. Elizabeth Barrett was worried about the headaches from which he was suffering at this time, and would only encourage the idea if he would 'promise to keep from all excesses, & to write very very gently' (ibid. 731). DeVane suggests, not very convincingly, that 'By the Fireside' may be the eventual outcome of this project.

[14] Ibid. i. 17.   [15] Ibid. 26.

[16] A passage in the letter written on 13 Jan. 1845 states that Browning had already begun a poem in which he would try to give 'the pure white light': 'it seems bleak melancholy work, this talking to the wind (for I have begun)—yet I don't think I shall let *you* hear, after all, the savage things about Popes and imaginative religions that I must say' (ibid. 7). Dowden (cited in Kintner's note) may be right to associate this with *Christmas-Eve and Easter-Day*, but it is most uncertain.

[17] Kintner, i. 123, followed by 22 and 29–30.

dramatic power may develop itself otherwise than in the formal drama.' A week or two later she returned to the topic:

I have wondered at you sometimes, not for daring, but for bearing to trust your noble works into the great mill of the 'rank, popular' playhouse, to be ground to pieces between the teeth of vulgar actors and actresses. . . . I love the drama too. I look to our old dramatists as to our Kings & princes in poetry. I love them through all the deeps of their abominations. But the theatre in those days was a better medium between the people and the poet; and the press in those days was a less sufficient medium than now.

Her next letter continues the same theme:

You are not to think that I blaspheme the Drama. . . . It is the theatre which vulgarizes these things; the modern theatre in which we see no altar! . . . And also, I have a fancy that your great dramatic power would work more clearly & audibly in the less definite mould . . . the dramatic faculty is strong in you.

By early 1846 Browning had moved a great way towards her view: expressing dissatisfaction with *A Soul's Tragedy*, he comments:

I have lost, of late, interest in dramatic writing, as you know—and, perhaps, occasion. . . . I mean to take your advice and be quiet awhile and let my mind get used to its new medium of sight—, seeing all things, as it does, thro' you: and then, let all I have done be the prelude and the real work begin—I felt it would be so before, and told you at the very beginning—do you remember?[18]

Condemned to make a brief speech at a meeting of the Literary Fund in May, Browning told her that he would 'try and speak for about five minutes on the advantages of the Press over the Stage as a medium of communication of the Drama'. 'I refer to this silly business', he wrote of troubles about *A Blot in the 'Scutcheon* later that same month, 'only to show you what success or non-success on the stage means and is worth. It is all behind me now—so far behind!' Elizabeth Barrett was afraid that he misunderstood her reservations about the drama and dramatic poetry:

You have the superabundant mental life & individuality which admits of shifting a personality & speaking the truth still. *That is*

[18] Ibid. 455, followed by ii. 701 and 730.

the highest faculty, the strongest & rarest, which exercises itself in Art,—we are all agreed there is none so great faculty as the dramatic. Several times you have hinted to me that I made you careless for the drama, & it has puzzled me to fancy how it could be, when I understand myself so clearly both the difficulty & the glory of dramatic art.

What she wants, she maintains, is that he should 'take the other crown besides'

—& after having made your own creatures speak in clear human voices, to speak yourself out of that personality which God made, & with the voice which He tuned into such power & sweetness of speech. I do not think that, with all that music in you, only your own personality should be dumb, nor that having thought so much & deeply on life & its ends, you should not teach what you have learnt, in the directest & most impressive way, the mask thrown off. . . . And it is not, I believe, by the dramatic medium, that poets teach most impressively.[19]

The fact that Browning's best poetry is not that in which he sets out to 'teach . . . impressively' reminds us that what Elizabeth Barrett gave him was not infallible criticism or an unerring prophecy of the course his poetic career would take, but simply intelligent guidance which greatly increased his confidence in himself and his understanding of his own powers. In one of her letters she misquotes his line—

When is man strong until he feels alone?

—with the comment: 'What man . . what woman? For have I not felt twenty times the desolate advantage of being insulated here & of not minding anybody when I made my poems?'[20] Yet she has no doubt that she is 'better & stronger for being within [his] influences & sympathies'. Until he met her, Browning had been conspicuously unsuccessful in finding an audience. In spite of the perceptiveness of W. J. Fox, John Forster, and one or two others, writing had for him too been a lonely affair. 'I am rather exacting, myself, with my own gentle audience', he acknowledged at the beginning of their correspondence, 'and get to say spiteful things

[19] Kintner, ii. 731–2.   [20] Ibid. i. 263.

about them when they are backward in their duties of appreciation.'[21] She hastened to reassure him, saying that he had 'not one but many enthusiastic admirers, the "fit & few" in the intense meaning, yet not the *diffused* fame which will come to you presently'. In her, Browning realized that he had found his perfect reader and critic, and in a letter written in January 1846 we find him apostrophizing her as 'my Audience', a single phrase that tells a great deal. Earlier he had been equally explicit:

You do not understand what a new feeling it is for me to have someone who is to like my verses or I shall not ever like them after! So far differently was I circumstanced of old, that I used rather to go about for a subject of offence to people; writing ugly things in order to warn the ungenial & timorous off my grounds at once. I shall never do so again at least![22]

It is interesting to speculate how far the curiously unattractive titles of Browning's later volumes—*Prince Hohenstiel-Schwangau*, *Red Cotton Night Cap Country*, and the rest—might have been modified if his wife had still been alive to counsel him. She herself was often accused of unnecessary obscurity: in April 1846 she described a letter she had received from a friend, 'giving indeed a very encouraging opinion of my poems generally, but desiring me to consider, that poets write both for the learned & the unlearned, & that in fact I am in the habit of using a great many hard words . . .'[23] Readers of Browning had more than 'hard words' to contend with, however, and not the least of Elizabeth Barrett's merits was the fact that she had some understanding of the situation of an ordinary intelligent reader, confronted for the first time with one of Browning's strange obliquities:

And now when you come to print these fragments, would it not be well if you were to stoop to the vulgarism of prefixing some word of introduction, as other people do, you know, . . a title . . a name? You perplex your readers often by casting yourself on their intelligence in these things—and although it is true that readers in general are stupid & cant understand, it is still more true that they are lazy & wont understand . . & they dont catch your point of sight at first

[21] Ibid. 11, followed by quotations from 15 and 382.
[22] Ibid. 95.   [23] Ibid. ii. 625.

unless you think it worth while to push them by the shoulders &
force them into the right place. Now these fragments . . you mean to
print them with a line between . . & not one word at the top of it . .
now don't you!—And then people will read

'Oh, to be in England'

and say to themselves . . 'Why who is this? . . who's out of England?'
Which is an extreme case of course; but you will see what I mean . . &
often I have observed how some of the very most beautiful of your
lyrics have suffered just from your disdain of the usual tactics of
writers in this one respect.[24]

A little later she asked him to explain what he meant by the title
Bells and Pomegranates, something that he himself considered so self-
evident that she was driven to repeat her suggestion five months
later:

I persist in thinking that you ought not to be too disdainful to explain
your meaning in the Pomegranates. . . Consider that Mr. Kenyon &
I may fairly represent the average intelligence of your readers,—&
that *he* was altogether in the clouds as to your meaning . . had not the
most distant notion of it,—while I, taking hold of the priest's
garment, missed the Rabbins & the distinctive significance, as
completely as he did.[25]

In April 1846, after stating her conviction that 'The mission of Art,
like that of Religion, is to the unlearned . . to the poor & to the
blind . . . at least it seems so to me', she goes on to comment on
'the manifest advance in clearness & directness of expression' in
A Soul's Tragedy, while disclaiming any share of the credit:

The fact is, that your obscurities, . . as far as they concern the *medium*,
. . you have been throwing off gradually & surely this long while—
you have a calmer mastery over imagery & language, & it was to be
expected that you should. For me, I am the fly on the chariot.[26]

A final important theme running through these letters is Browning's deep interest in Italy, and his growing discontent with life in
Victorian England. Near the beginning of the correspondence he
made a curious reference to Italy which drew an immediate challenge from Elizabeth Barrett: in connection with a translation of
The Improvisatore, by Hans Christian Andersen, Browning wrote:

[24] Kintner, i. 222.   [25] Ibid. 553.   [26] Ibid. ii. 643.

That a Dane should write so, confirms me in an old belief—that Italy is stuff for the use of the North, and no more: pure Poetry there is none, nearly as possible none, in Dante even—materials for Poetry in the pitifullest romancist of their thousands, on the contrary—strange that those great wide black eyes should stare nothing out of the earth that lies before them![27]

When Elizabeth Barrett demurred, Browning immediately retracted, describing what he had written as 'nonsense', referring to Italy as the country 'where my heart lives', and saying that 'all Northern writers' visit Italy 'and discover the sights and sounds' to the great enrichment of their imaginations.[28] Six months later he tells her that his best work is still to come and that they 'shall see Italy together'. A few days later, worried about his complaints of headaches, Elizabeth Barrett wrote to him: 'Is it England that disagrees with you? & is it change away from England that you want? . . require, I mean. If so—why what follows & ought to follow?'[29] He was determined not to go to Italy alone, and he had no difficulty in persuading her that together there they could spend 'a year or two and be as happy as day & night are long'. She replied:

For Italy . . you are right—We should be nearer the sun, as you say, & further from the world, as I think—out of hearing of the great storm of gossiping. . . Even if you liked to live altogether abroad, coming to England at intervals, it would be no sacrifice for me.[30]

In a discussion of modern aristocracy she was soon writing as follows:

People in general would rather be Marquises than Roman artists, consulting their own wishes & inclination. I, for my part, ever since I could speak my mind & knew it, always openly & inwardly preferred the glory of those who live by their heads, to the opposite glory of those who carry other people's arms. . . Happiness goes the same way to my fancy. There is something fascinating to me, in that Bohemian way of living . . all the conventions of society cut so close & thin, that the soul can see through . . beyond . . above. It is 'real life' as you say . . whether at Rome or elsewhere. . . People are apt to suffocate their faculties by their manners . . English people especially.[31]

---

[27] Kintner, i. 50.   [28] Ibid. 54.   [29] Ibid. 281.   [30] Ibid. 425–6.
[31] Ibid. ii. 585, 596, 605, 616, 822.

'This corrupt social life' is a phrase she uses, a day or two later, in opposing Browning's defence of duelling. 'I want to leave society for the Siren's isle', he writes in one of his next letters. On 12 April she tells him, with satisfaction: 'The peculiarity of our circumstances will enable us to be free of the world . . of our friends even . . of all observation & examination, in certain respects.' In their love for Italy they found themselves, not for the first time, united in their disagreement with the revered Carlyle:

Carlyle is wanting to visit only one foreign country [Browning wrote on 28 June 1846]—*Iceland*. The true cradle of the Northmen and the virtues . . all that is worth a northman's caring to see is there, he thinks, and nowise in Italy—Perhaps! Indeed, so I *reason* and say— Did I not once turn on myself and speak against the Southern spirit, and even Dante, just because of that conviction?—(or *imperfect* conviction, whence the uneasy exaggeration).

If there was any real conflict between Browning's reason and his instinct in this matter, it is fortunate that he followed his instinct. Unlike Tennyson and Arnold, he escaped—for the central period of his creative life—from the restrictions of Victorian England. It was not the intellectual life of contemporary Italy that appealed to him —deeply as he sympathized with the struggle for political independence. As he was to write many years later, after his wife's death and his return to England: 'I never read a line in a modern Italian book that was of use to me,—never saw a flash of poetry come out of an Italian *word*: in art, in action, *yes*,—not in the region of ideas: I always said, they *are* poetry, don't and can't *make* poetry.'[32] In Italy Browning found a country where he could be alone with his own soul,[33] a country where the sectarianism of his early surroundings melted away in the sunshine and the history, where men and women and masterpieces of painting and sculpture wooed the eye as they had seldom done in the smoke and grime of early Victorian London, a country where Shelleyan dreams of man as he should be yielded to a fascinated observation of man as he is— where contemplation of the present led naturally to speculation on the past, and in particular on that period of the past which Michelet had described as 'the discovery of man', the Italian Renaissance.

[32] *Dearest Isa*, p. 238.   [33] Ibid., p. 239.

The last of the *Bells and Pomegranates* pamphlets was dedicated
to Landor, whose early praise of *Paracelsus* Browning treasured
throughout his life. In November 1845 Landor had published lines
'To Robert Browning' which are one of the noblest compliments
Browning was ever paid, and which serve as the perfect transition
between the first part of his poetic career and the happy years of
married life which he was now to spend in Italy:

> There is delight in singing, tho none hear
> Beside the singer: and there is delight
> In praising, tho the praiser sit alone
> And see the prais'd far off him, far above.
> Shakspeare is not *our* poet, but the World's,
> Therefor on him no speech; and brief for thee,
> Browning! Since Chaucer was alive and hale
> No man hath walked along our roads with step
> So active, so inquiring eye, or tongue
> So varied in discourse. But warmer climes
> Give brighter plumage, stronger wing: the breeze
> Of Alpine highths thou playest with borne on
> Beyond Sorrento and Amalfi, where
> The Siren waits thee, singing song for song.[34]

[34] It is amusing to contrast Landor's prophecy with a characteristically xeno-
phobic passage by Charles Kingsley, a few years later: 'How can Mr. Browning help
England? By leaving henceforth "the dead to bury their dead", in effete and ener-
vating Italy, and casting all his rugged genial force into the questions and the
struggles of that mother-country to whom, and not to Italy at all, he owes all his
most valuable characteristics': *Fraser's Magazine* (February 1851), reprinted in
Litzinger and Smalley, pp. 147–8.

IX

A FALSE DIRECTION:
CHRISTMAS-EVE AND EASTER-DAY

The book before us is the work of a poet; though if this fact should
gain but a limited recognition, the writer will have only himself to
blame.[1]

THERE is nothing tidy about Browning's career. It would be
satisfying to say that when he married and left for Italy he abandoned the 'false lights'[2] which he had pursued in his early long
poems and his plays and concentrated on writing the brief dramatic
poems for which he is principally remembered. It would be satisfying—but it would not be true.

As we have seen, Browning wrote the first two of these poems
in his early twenties and more than thirty others before he met
Elizabeth Barrett. During the twenty months of his courtship
he was concerned with tidying up and publishing what he had
already written, and with excited speculations about the future,
rather than with much new creative work. When he arrived in
Italy there was a great deal to take his mind off poetry for a while.
He was happy, he had innumerable arrangements to make, he had
a wife to look after, he had buildings and pictures and masterpieces
of sculpture to inspect, he had bookstalls to explore.[3] When his

---

[1] *Athenæum*, 6 Apr. 1850, p. 370 (Litzinger and Smalley, p. 138).

[2] The title of the chapter on the early work in *The Poetry of John Dryden*, by Mark
Van Doren. The phrase is, of course, Dryden's own.

[3] In July 1847 Joseph Arnould told Domett that 'Browning is spending a luxurious
year in Italy—is, at this present writing, with his poetess bride dwelling in some
hermit hut in "Vallombrosa, where the Etruscan shades high overarched embower".'
Two months later he wrote again: 'Browning and his wife are still in Florence: both
ravished with Italy and Italian life; so much so, that I think for some years they will
make it the Paradise of their poetical exile' (*Domett*, pp. 140–1). Paradise is not the
place for work, and this Paradise was no exception.

thoughts turned to poetry, as we may be sure that they often did, he was by no means certain which path to follow. His wife wanted him to speak for himself 'out of that personality which God made, & with the voice which He tuned into such power & sweetness of speech',[4] while his own ambitions also pointed in the direction of a long poem that should be more personal and 'subjective' than anything he had yet written.

The first poem that we know Browning to have written, after his arrival in Italy, is 'The Guardian-Angel', a lyrical description of a painting by Guercino which he saw at Fano one day in the summer of 1848. There is nothing dramatic about the poem, and the tone is religious, verging on sentimentality. Browning's thoughts are stretching back to his childhood, while in the final lines he apostrophizes Alfred Domett. When we turn to the long poem that Browning now wrote, *Christmas-Eve and Easter-Day*, we find some of the same characteristics in a composition that is otherwise extremely different. The stimulus which led him to write this work was probably the emotional crisis produced caused by the birth of his child and the death of his mother in 1849. When he heard that his mother was dead he was plunged into profound grief:

My husband has been in the deepest anguish [his wife wrote to Mary Russell Mitford], and indeed, except for the courageous consideration of his sister, who wrote two letters of preparation . . . when in fact all was over, I am frightened to think what the result would have been to him. He has loved his mother as such passionate natures only can love, and I never saw a man so bowed down in an extremity of sorrow—never.[5]

In such circumstances a man is led to question his own beliefs about life and death, and Browning found himself in this situation at a critical moment in the history of English religious thought. Newman had moved over to Rome, Strauss's book, *The Life of Jesus Critically Examined*, was exerting a widespread and disquieting influence, while Clough (whom the Brownings may well have met in Florence in 1849) had resigned his Fellowship at Oriel. The storm

---

[4] p. 118, above.   [5] *Life and Letters*, p. 155.

which drives the narrator into the 'little chapel' at the beginning of *Christmas-Eve* may be taken as a symbol for the emotional weather in the poet's heart, and we notice that near the end of the poem it is the storm that makes 'a mild indifferentism'[6] in religious matters impossible for the speaker, attractive as he might otherwise find it. The birth of his son and the death of his mother naturally drew Browning's mind back to his own early days in Camberwell, 'the headquarters of Non-Conformity'.[7] It is worth noticing that his wife's religious background was very similar:

I used to go with my father always, when I was able, to the nearest dissenting chapel of the Congregationalists [she had written to him in an early letter]—from liking the simplicity of that praying and speaking without books—& a little too from disliking the theory of state churches. There is a narrowness among the dissenters which is wonderful,—an arid, grey Puritanism in the clefts of their souls: but it seems to me clear that they know what the 'liberty of Christ' *means*, far better than those do who call themselves 'churchmen'; & stand altogether, as a body, on higher ground.[8]

The structure of *Christmas-Eve*, the first part of this curious bipartite composition, is extremely simple. One evening the narrator enters a little dissenting chapel, looks round him at the poor and often squalid congregation, listens to the sermon, and (as he and we later discover) falls asleep. In his dream he emerges from the chapel, speculates about religion, and has a vision of Christ:

> All at once I looked up with terror.
> He was there.   (430–1)

He next dreams of St. Peter's in Rome, but leaves it quickly and reflects further about religion. In the final part of his dream he finds himself in a church in Göttingen, listening to a sermon or lecture delivered by an arid German professor: here again a brief and grotesque descriptive passage is followed by a long argument about his own beliefs. Awakening, he finds himself still in the little chapel, listening to the interminable sermon. If he had not been dreaming—he reflects—he would never have

---

6 l. 1148.   7 DeVane, p. 198.
8 Kintner, i. 141.

> Seen the raree-show of Peter's successor,
> Or the laboratory of the Professor!
> For the Vision, that was true, I wist,
> True as that heaven and earth exist.   (1242–5)

He decides to cleave to the simple religion in which he was brought
up, and in token of this

> I put up pencil and join chorus
> To Hepzibah Tune, without further apology,
>   The last five verses of the third section
>   Of the seventeenth hymn of Whitfield's Collection,
> To conclude with the doxology.   (1355–9)

The best way to derive any enjoyment from *Christmas-Eve* is to
read it quickly—a tempo which the nature of the versification in
fact imposes on a responsive reader. Read in this way, the narrative
carries one along, in many parts, and the Hogarthian description of
the chapel congregation at the beginning illustrates Browning's
skill in a rough-and-tumble type of satire:

> My old fat woman purred with pleasure,
> And thumb round thumb went twirling faster,
> While she, to his periods keeping measure,
> Maternally devoured the pastor.   (173–6)

Something of the same power appears in the description of the
German Professor, 'Three parts sublime to one grotesque', later in
the poem.[9] As the greater part of *Christmas-Eve* consists of reflections
on the subject of religion, however—'So sat I talking with my
mind'[10]—it is impossible to avoid the conclusion that the free
metrical form which Browning has chosen is completely unsuited
to his subject-matter. One of the invariable characteristics of a
successful poem—whether it is Marvell's lines 'To his Coy Mistress',
Pope's *Rape of the Lock*, Gray's *Elegy*, or Byron's *Don Juan*—
is the sense that it gives the reader that it could never have
been written in any other idiom or metrical form. In *Religio Laici*
(a modestly successful poem) Dryden chose—as he informs the
reader—'unpolish'd, rugged Verse',

> As fittest for Discourse, and nearest Prose.

[9] l. 811.   [10] l. 1132.

The trouble about the style of *Christmas-Eve* is that while it often comes near to prose, it is not obviously fit for 'Discourse'. The double and comic rhymes sometimes remind us of *Hudibras*, as at lines 677–82:

> As more-enduring sculpture must,
> Till filthy saints rebuked the gust
> With which they chanced to get a sight
> Of some dear naked Aphrodite
> They glanced a thought above the toes of,
> By breaking zealously her nose off.

Such a manner of writing is quite unsuited to theological discussion.

'Whether you will like Robert's new book I don't know', Elizabeth Barrett wrote rather anxiously to Mrs. Jameson,

but I am sure you will admit the originality and power in it. . . .
There is nothing *Italian* in the book; poets are apt to be most present with the distant. A remark of Wilson's used to strike me as eminently true—that the perfectest descriptive poem (descriptive of rural scenery) would be naturally produced in a London cellar.[11]

Wilson's observation is curiously applicable to Browning, since we know that 'How They brought the Good News' was written at sea off the African coast and 'Love Among the Ruins' may have been written in the busy centre of Paris. It is true that the scene shifts to St. Peter's at one point in *Christmas-Eve*, but in fact Browning had not yet visited Rome, and in any case, in spite of two fine lines—

> And wondered how these fountains play,
> Growing up eternally   (548–9)

—he does not allow his narrator to describe the scene in the cathedral in anything like the detail that we find in the description of the little chapel. The narrator is at least as anti-Catholic as his creator: he hopes that the Pope—

> Turned sick at last of to-day's buffoonery,
> Of posturings and petticoatings,
> Beside his Bourbon bully's gloatings
> In the bloody orgies of drunk poltroonery!   (1324–7)

---

11 *E.B.B.* i. 441–2.

—will at last see the light, and be saved through the grace of Christ. Although there is emphasis throughout the poem on the importance of love and charity, the portrayal of Catholicism is no more sympathetic than Butler's portrayal of the sects in *Hudibras*— partly (one notices) because Browning associates Catholicism with reactionary political views.

If there is 'nothing *Italian*' in the poem, neither is there anything German. In spite of the apostrophe to the German professor—

> Unlearned love was safe from spurning—
> Can't we respect your loveless learning?
> Let us at least give learning honour!   (1096–8)

—the pedant of Göttingen is in fact treated with scant respect. The failure to reach any imaginative sympathy with Catholic and New Critic is striking, in a poem written by the poet who was to create Bishop Blougram and Cleon and a host of other characters whose views of life are completely different from those of their creator. The truth is that this poem is the work of Browning's conscience and his will, and that between them they refused to allow his imagination sufficient freedom to make from the confrontation of contrasting religious views a convincing imaginative work.

Whereas *Christmas-Eve* opens with the lively description of the 'little chapel' and its worshippers, *Easter-Day* plunges at once into religious discussion and rumination:

> How very hard it is to be
> A Christian! Hard for you and me,
> —Not the mere task of making real
> That duty up to its ideal,
> Effecting thus, complete and whole,
> A purpose of the human soul—
> For that is always hard to do;
> But hard, I mean, for me and you . . .

Initially we are given no clue about the identity of the speaker, whom we might naturally suppose to be the poet himself. To complicate the issue, the narrator is very soon quoting arguments put forward by an interlocutor who finds it even more difficult to adhere to the Christian faith. At times it is only the inverted commas which remind us who is speaking—as the narrator himself seems to acknowledge in Section viii:

> Do you say this, or I?—Oh, you!
> Then, what, my friend?—(thus I pursue
> Our parley)—you indeed opine
> That the Eternal and Divine
> Did, eighteen centuries ago,
> In very truth . . . Enough! you know
> The all-stupendous tale,—that Birth,
> That Life, that Death! . . .

Later, before he describes his own vision, the speaker mentions that they are both acquainted with the speaker in *Christmas-Eve*:

> On such a night three years ago,
> It chanced that I had cause to cross
> The common, where the chapel was,
> Our friend spoke of, the other day—
> You've not forgotten, I dare say.   (372–6)

The two critical points that must be made are the inferiority of much of the verse, and the failure to 'dramatize' effectively.

To illustrate the first point the whole of the brief Section xi may be quoted, to refute any suggestion of unfairly selective quotation:

> 'Proved, or not,
> 'Howe'er you wis, small thanks, I wot,
> 'You get of mine, for taking pains
> 'To make it hard to me. Who gains
> 'By that, I wonder? Here I live
> 'In trusting ease; and here you drive
> 'At causing me to lose what most
> 'Yourself would mourn for had you lost!'

It is astonishing to find the author of 'My Last Duchess' handling verse so ineptly. As in *Christmas-Eve*, it is clear that Browning has chosen the wrong metre. In Section ix, for example, he puts the following words into the mouth of a man who has been martyred:

> . . . Twice
> I fought with beasts, and three times saw
> My children suffer by his law;
> At last my own release was earned:
> I was some time in being burned.

The last line balances uneasily for a moment on the line between
the impressive and the absurd, only to fall, with a dull thud, into
the latter category. It would be instructive to compare lines 435–
58 with a passage from Matthew Green's little masterpiece, *The
Spleen*, which may well have helped to inspire them.[12] This is one
of the better passages in Browning's poem, yet he lacks the sureness of touch and tone that Green owed in part to the Augustan tradition of civilized wit. Browning sets himself a much
more severe test when he has to describe the vision that has come
to the speaker, and there is no doubt that he fails to rise to the
occasion:

> I felt begin
> The Judgment-Day: to retrocede
> Was too late now. 'In very deed,'
> (I uttered to myself) 'that Day!'   (546–9)

It is like something from Pope's *The Art of Sinking in Poetry*, and
contrasts most unfavourably with Clare's sombre vision of the Last
Day in his remarkable poem, 'The Dream'. When Christ Himself
speaks—as he does at some length—we can only be struck by the
unintentional impiety of putting such inferior verse into the
mouth of the Son of God. Pope had claimed that in the weaker
passages of *Paradise Lost* 'God the Father turns a School-Divine':[13]
here, in *Easter-Day*, Browning makes Him argue and threaten like
a Dissenting preacher.

In the last section of the poem the speaker looks back three years,
to the time when he had his astonishing vision:

> Since then, three varied years are spent,
> And commonly my mind is bent
> To think it was a dream—be sure
> A mere dream and distemperature . . .   (1011–14)

---

[12]   Thus, thus I steer my bark, and sail
            On even keel with gentle gale.
            At helm I make my reason sit,
            My crew of passions all submit . . .
[13] *The First Epistle of the Second Book of Horace, Imitated*, l. 102.

Easter-Day ends on a note of uncertainty sustained by hope:

> But Easter-Day breaks! But
> Christ rises! Mercy every way
> Is infinite,—and who can say?

In this last section we catch a glimpse of the possibility that Browning might have rendered the poem truly dramatic by making the speaker a distinct person in whom the reader could have taken an interest. This he was to do later, in different ways, in 'Karshish', 'Bishop Blougram's Apology', and 'Caliban upon Setebos'. Nothing of the sort happens, however, as Mrs. Sutherland Orr points out in her sensible description of *Christmas-Eve and Easter-Day* as

two distinct poems, printed under this one head: and each describing a spiritual experience appropriate to the day, and lived through in a vision of Christ. This vision presents itself to the reader as a probable or obvious hallucination, or even a simple dream; but its utterances are more or less dogmatic; they contain much which is in harmony with Mr. Browning's known views; and it is difficult at first sight to regard them in either case as proceeding from an imaginary person who is only feeling his way to the truth. This, however, they prove themselves to be.[14]

In another sense, however, the two poems do not '*prove* themselves to be' the utterances of two imaginary persons: the poet states that they are, but we are in some doubt whether to believe him.

Mrs. Browning told a correspondent that she had 'complained of the *asceticism* in the second part, but he said it was "one side of the question". Don't think that he has taken to the cilix [hair-shirt]'—she added—'indeed he has not—but it is his way to *see* things as passionately as other people *feel* them.'[15] That is well said, yet it is hard not to conclude that Browning is here simply using the dramatic formula as an excuse for not committing himself explicitly. He was to put 'one side of the question' when he wrote 'Bishop Blougram's Apology', after all. The difference is that in that case he seems to have started by contemplating the problem of how a man like Wiseman could subscribe to a theology that was entirely unacceptable to himself and to most intelligent Englishmen of the day—but then to have been drawn on by his dramatic imagination

---

[14] *Handbook*, p. 179.   [15] *E.B.B.* i. 449.

not only into presenting a brilliant apologia for a man with whom he disagreed fundamentally, but also into putting into Blougram's mouth certain of his own deepest convictions about human life (and doing so in memorable verse). In *Christmas-Eve and Easter-Day* Browning was in a sense too much in earnest, and his imagination was working virtually without the intermediary that was almost always essential, not only to enable him to write a memorable poem, but even to make it possible for him to give effective expression to his own views about human life. The poem is more characteristically 'Victorian' than most of Browning's poetry. It was one of the three poems to be reviewed in *The Germ*, the short-lived periodical published by the Pre-Raphaelite Brotherhood, and it is interesting to notice that the others were *The Strayed Reveller, and Other Poems* by Matthew Arnold, and Clough's *The Bothie of Tober-Na-Vuolich*. Browning and his wife were reading these volumes at the end of 1849, as we know from a letter of Mrs. Browning's:

> I am disappointed in the book on the whole [she wrote of *Ambarvalia*]. What I like infinitely better is Clough's ... 'long vacation pastoral' ... Try to get it, if you have not read it already. I feel certain you will like it and think all the higher of the poet ... Arnold's volume has two good poems in it: 'The Sick King of Bokhara' and 'The Deserted Merman'. I like them both. But none of these writers are *artists*, whatever they may be in future days.[16]

Precisely the same observation may be made of the author of *Christmas-Eve and Easter-Day*. As he wrote it, Browning seems to have been too much in earnest, too 'sincere', to allow his dramatic imagination to spread its wings—and 'Worry is a feeble Muse'. No one has ever been interested in the dramatis personae of the poem: Browning himself was not interested enough to give names to the speakers. The result is that their apologetics are not more but less cogent than those of the speakers of dramatic monologues with whom Browning himself had less in common. Browning was like a man with a stutter whose impediment disappears when he is acting in a play. Yet the writing of this poem may well have eased his conscience, which had been stirred to its depths by the

---

[16] Ibid. 429.

death of his mother, and so have left him free, after a further fallow period, to give life to the Men and Women whose voices were to create the poetry of his great two-volume collection five years later.

X

THE DRAMATIC LYRICS OF 1855

What a magnificent series is *Men and Women*. Of course you have it half by heart ere this.[1]

ON 5 June 1854 Browning told Forster that he had written a number of poems of all sorts and sizes and styles and subjects—not written before last year, but the beginning of an expressing the spirit of all the fruits of the years since I last turned the winch of the wine press. The manner [he added] will be newer than the matter. I hope to be listened to, this time, and I am glad I have been made to wait this not very long while.[2]

But for *Christmas-Eve and Easter-Day*, he had written little poetry since his marriage and departure from England. We know that he was reflecting on the nature of poetry, and of his own poetic powers, in the autumn of 1851, for at that time he wrote a preface to a collection of letters attributed to Shelley (but later proved to be forgeries) in which he attempted to distinguish between 'the subjective poet' and 'the objective poet'. His statement that none of the poems in his new collection had been written 'before last year' (i.e. 1853) is not strictly correct, since we know that 'The Guardian-Angel' had been written in 1848. It is possible that three other poems were written at the beginning of 1852,[3] but what is certain is

---

[1] *Letters of Rossetti*, i. 278 (To William Allingham).
[2] *New Letters*, p. 77.
[3] Griffin and Minchin (p. 189) state that ' "Love among the Ruins", "Women and Roses", and "Childe Roland" are said to have been composed in Paris on three successive days, the 1st, 2nd, and 3rd January, 1852.' One of their authorities for this statement seems to have been Mrs. Sutherland Orr, who wrote that Browning 'repeatedly determined to write a poem every day, and once succeeded for a fortnight in doing so. He was then in Paris, preparing *Men and Women*. *Childe Roland* and *Women and Roses* were among those produced on this plan' (*Life and Letters*, p. 362). Lilian Whiting, on the other hand reports Browning as giving the following account

that after a long fallow period, about which he sometimes felt guilty, Browning resolved to settle down to writing poetry, and that the most fruitful year was 1853. On 24 February he told Milsand that he was writing'—a first step towards popularity for me —lyrics with more music and painting than before, so as to get people to hear and see'.[4] In March he wrote to Kenyon:

I am trying if I can't take people's ears at last by the lyrical tip,—if they have one,—and make songs & such like at a great rate ... I ... think I may have found out and set right some old cranks & hitches which used to stop my success so cruelly.[5]

On 10 August William Wetmore Story told a friend that both Browning and his wife were 'busily engaged in writing', and on the same day Elizabeth Barrett wrote that Browning was 'working at a volume of lyrics', adding that she had seen only a few of them, and that these seemed to her 'as fine as anything he has done'.[6] The poems in *Men and Women* were the result of an extraordinary and relatively brief burst of creative activity. Thirty of the fifty-one poems in the two volumes were later classified as Dramatic Lyrics, twelve as Dramatic Romances, and eight as 'Men and Women' poems.[6a]

At no other time did Browning write so much lyrical poetry, and at no other time did he write so much on the subject of love. It does not follow that most of these poems deal with his own love for Elizabeth Barrett. If (indeed) we compare his poems with her *Sonnets from the Portuguese*—and the opportunity of studying both sides of a love encounter through the evidence of poems written by the two lovers is a most unusual one—we are bound to be struck

---

of the matter, in 1887: 'one year in Florence I had been rather lazy; I resolved that I would write something every day. Well, the first day I wrote about some roses. . . . The next day "Childe Roland" came to me as a kind of dream' (*The Brownings*, Boston 1911, p. 261). This would point to 1853. Cf. Johnstone Parr: 'The Date of Composition of Browning's *Love Among the Ruins*', *PQ* 32 (1953), 443–6.

[4] Griffin and Minchin, p. 189.

[5] Letter dated 'Florence, March 17, '53', now at Wellesley College. I am grateful to the authorities there for permission to quote from this letter here and on p. 225, below.

[6] *Story*, i. 267; *Life and Letters*, p. 187.

[6a] 'In A Balcony' was separated from the other poems.

by the profound differences between the work of the two poets.
Whereas the *Sonnets* form an avowedly autobiographical sequence,
tracing the development of the writer's love, Browning avoids the
sonnet as rigorously as Donne himself did in his love poetry, while
his lyrics are 'dramatic' and form no kind of sequence. For a long
time, indeed, his wife did not show him her sonnets—'all this delay,
because I happened early to say something against putting one's
loves into verse'.[7] Tempting as it is to speculate about the relation
of this poem or that to his own life, it is seldom a helpful approach.
What seems to have happened is that the experience of fortunate
love stimulated Browning to explore the feelings of men and
women in a variety of imaginary situations. He is often at his most
brilliant in expressing the feelings of a lover when the situation
which he is describing is one of which he had no personal experience
and when the voice with which he speaks is the voice of a human
being very different from himself.

He had already written several poems in which the speaker is a
woman—notably 'The Laboratory' and 'The Confessional'—and it
is remarkable that three of the finest of the Dramatic Lyrics of 1855
which deal with love are spoken by women. The happiest of them is
'A Woman's Last Word', in which we find the lovers in bed after a
quarrel. The woman submits her will to the man, weeps a little, and
prepares to fall asleep. The opening is well managed:

> Let's contend no more, Love,
>   Strive nor weep:
> All be as before, Love,
>   —Only sleep!

Throughout the ten brief stanzas the words seem to fall naturally
into the metrical scheme, without distortion or effort. In stanzas ii
to vi there is an interesting sequence of imagery. First of all the
woman thinks of the two of them as being

> In debate, as birds are,
>   Hawk on bough!

This image of the hawk lurking near the defenceless birds suggests

---

[7] *Wedgwood*, p. 114: 'then again, I said something else on the other side'—so she
showed him her poems.

'the tree' and 'the serpent's tooth', and in the fifth stanza the idea that knowledge may be dangerous leads directly to the Garden of Eden:

> Where the apple reddens
> Never pry—
> Lest we lose our Edens,
> Eve and I.

In the sixth stanza the woman appeals to her lover to be a god and a man at the same time:

> Be a god and hold me
> With a charm!
> Be a man and fold me
> With thine arm!

'In a Year' (misleadingly yoked, in Browning's odd way, with 'In Three Days') is a very different poem. The verse movement, as in 'A Woman's Last Word', expresses weariness:

> Never any more,
> While I live,
> Need I hope to see his face
> As before.

The triumphant simplicity of the technique compels our admiration:

> Was it something said,
> Something done,
> Vexed him? was it touch of hand,
> Turn of head?
> Strange! that very way
> Love begun:
> I as little understand
> Love's decay.

This is ordinary speech, but in a condensed form—the shorthand of feeling and of passion.

'Any Wife to Any Husband', the masterpiece of these three lyrics, is a more complicated poem. The choice of subject vividly illustrates the depth of Browning's imaginative interest in a woman's experience of love: he is (perhaps) the only English poet to have taken as a subject a dying wife's prospective jealousy of her possible successor. The poem gains from being read in association with certain of the *Sonnets from the Portuguese*, notably xliii—'How do I love thee? Let me count the ways'—which ends with the lines:

> . . . I love thee with the breath,
> Smiles, tears, of all my life!—and, if God choose,
> I shall but love thee better after death.

The stanza form is very different from that of the preceding poems:

> My love, this is the bitterest, that thou—
> Who art all truth, and who dost love me now
>   As thine eyes say, as thy voice breaks to say—
> Shouldst love so truly, and couldst love me still
> A whole long life through, had but love its will,
>   Would death that leads me from thee brook delay.

The slow-moving pentameters, and the relatively complex rhyme scheme (aabccb) are the fitting expression of a more troubled utterance. The verse movement has something of the freedom and complexity of dramatic blank verse: the accents shift about freely, as in Shakespeare, and sensitive reading is called for. Everywhere one is struck by the true understanding of a woman's feelings:

> Oh, I should fade—'t is willed so! Might I save,
> Gladly I would, whatever beauty gave
>   Joy to thy sense, for that was precious too.
> It is not to be granted. But the soul
> Whence the love comes, all ravage leaves that whole;
>   Vainly the flesh fades; soul makes all things new.

Part of the inspiration of the poem no doubt derives from Browning's own fear that he himself would act as the wife dreads that her husband will act (Elizabeth Barrett was, after all, six years older than himself, and much less robust). Stanzas x and xi, must often have come into Browning's mind after his wife's death. The poem ends brilliantly, with the dying woman's confidence in her husband's future fidelity restored (as it seems), only to be broken in upon again by her prospective jealousy as she foresees the way that things will almost certainly go:

> What did I fear? Thy love shall hold me fast
> Until the little minute's sleep is past
> And I wake saved.—And yet it will not be!

Of the Dramatic Lyrics about love which are spoken by men, two of the best are notably more optimistic in their attitude than those spoken by women. If 'Love among the Ruins', with its Italian setting, was one of the poems written in an apartment in the Avenue des Champs Elysées, then the subject no more reflects Browning's immediate circumstances than the setting. Although the poem is a celebration of love, and was clearly set at the beginning of the whole collection as a declaration of faith, it is by no means directly autobiographical. Whether or not the speaker is to be regarded as an Italian (l. 9), Elizabeth Barrett was no 'girl with eager eyes and yellow hair', nor is there any particular reason for searching for such a girl in Browning's earlier life.

Our attention is at once caught by the curious rhythm of the verse:

> Where the quiet-coloured end of evening smiles,
>> Miles and miles
> On the solitary pastures where our sheep
>> Half-asleep
> Tinkle homeward thro' the twilight, stray or stop
>> As they crop—
> Was the site once of a city great and gay,
>> (So they say)
> Of our country's very capital, its prince
>> Ages since
> Held his court in, gathered councils, wielding far
>> Peace or war.

Initially the trochees seem reflective, if not hesitant. The effect of the long lines, each followed by a short line consisting of a single Cretic, is curiously hypnotic, and the whole poem leads irresistibly to the unanswerable affirmation in the final line,

> Love is best!

Throughout the poem the present is juxtaposed with the past, as the thoughts of the narrator move from the quiet, lonely beauty of the present scene to the barbaric splendours of the past. In each of the first four stanzas (we notice), the first six lines are devoted to the present, the other six to the past. In the fifth stanza, only two and a half lines can be spared for the past, as the poet tells us

> That a girl with eager eyes and yellow hair
>> Waits me there
> In the turret whence the charioteers caught soul
>> For the goal,
> When the king looked, where she looks now, breathless, dumb
>> Till I come.

In the sixth stanza it is the first half that is devoted to the past, while the second describes the present. In the final stanza the past is described, and dismissed as folly, before the triumphant affirm-ation of the conclusion.

Poets are more apt to contrast the glories of the past with the commonplace quality of the present, or the innocence of the past with the corruption of the present, than to dismiss the past in favour of the present, as Browning does in his 'Sicilian Pastoral'.[8] The unusual tone of the lyric may be brought out by comparison with *Palmyra*, a poem by Peacock also inspired by ancient ruins. The motto is the lines from Pindar which proclaim that Time is the conqueror of all happiness, and the poem is accompanied by prose quotations from Wood's *Ruins of Palmyra*, Volney's *Travels in Syria*, Gibbon, and Ossian.[9] The eleventh stanza is characteristic:

> Yes, all are flown!
> I stand alone
> At ev'ning's calm and pensive hour,
>> Mid wasted domes,
>> And mould'ring tombs,
> The wrecks of vanity and pow'r.

Like Browning, Peacock stresses the folly of the grandeur of the

---

[8] The title in a manuscript draft of the poem in the Lowell Collection at Harvard.

[9] 'I have seen the walls of Balclutha, but they were desolate. The fire had re-sounded in the halls: the voice of the people was heard no more. The stream of Clutha was removed from its place, by the fall of the walls. The thistle shook, there, its lonely head: the moss whistled to the wind. The fox looked out from the windows, the rank grass of the wall waved round his head . . . .' Browning may have retained a subconscious memory of these lines. We know that he wrote an imitation of Ossian at the age of five.

past; yet for him the revels of 'happiness and love' also belong to the past, while the conclusion of his poem is Christian. Browning's concern is to celebrate love, whose transcendental power makes the past seem meaningless. It is a subject that one can imagine handled, though with differences, by a poet of the seventeenth century—by Marvell, even, or by Browning's favourite, Donne.

Two lines in 'Two in the Campagna' might also be by one of the masters of the seventeenth century:

> How is it under our control
> To love or not to love?

The opening of the poem, however, has a quality that differentiates it from the work of a seventeenth-century poet:

> I wonder do you feel to-day
>   As I have felt since, hand in hand,
> We sat down on the grass, to stray
>   In spirit better through the land,
>   This morn of Rome and May?

The movement of the verse is matter-of-fact: it is clear that the speaker is an intelligent man who wants to think his thought out to the end, and above all to be honest with his lover. As he surveys the scenery of the Campagna—

> Such life here, through such lengths of hours,
>   Such miracles performed in play,
> Such primal naked forms of flowers,
>   Such letting nature have her way
> While heaven looks from its towers!

—he sees everything growing and changing, and appeals to the lady for openness:

> I would that you were all to me,
>   You that are just so much, no more.
> Nor yours nor mine, nor slave nor free!
>   Where does the fault lie?

Instead of using the subject as an opportunity for an audacious display of wit, in the manner of a poet of the seventeenth century, the speaker is serious and troubled:

> . . . Must I go
> Still like the thistle-ball, no bar,
>   Onward, whenever light winds blow,
> Fixed by no friendly star?

The secret of constancy in love, which the speaker seems to regard
as an intellectual thing that he is always on the point of grasping,
but can never quite run down, eludes him in the end:

> Just when I seemed about to learn!
>   Where is the thread now? Off again!
> The old trick! Only I discern—
>   Infinite passion, and the pain
> Of finite hearts that yearn.

From his matter-of-fact opening he has moved to a conclusion that
belongs essentially to the nineteenth century, and which recalls
the idol of his youth. Irving Babbitt described Shelley's lines—

> The desire of the moth for the star,
>   Of the night for the morrow,
> The devotion to something afar
>   From the sphere of our sorrow

—as 'perhaps the most perfect expression of romantic longing'[10]:
in 'Two in the Campagna' Browning humanizes the same theme
by dramatizing it as well as localizing it, and so implying a whole
psychological situation.

A very different poem is 'By the Fire-Side', a domestic meditation
of which DeVane remarks: 'here and in *One Word More* the poet
speaks more intimately than anywhere else of himself and his
wife.' Yet even here (we notice) Browning is not presenting us with
a direct transcription of his own experience, as (in DeVane's words)
'the event which Browning describes . . . had taken place at 50
Wimpole Street in London in 1845', while the subject of the poem
is a series of reflections that the poet imagines as coming to him
when he is an old man. In the opening lines the speaker visualizes
himself sitting by the fire, ostensibly 'deep in Greek', yet with his
thoughts wandering:

> And we slope to Italy at last
> And youth, by green degrees.

---

[10] *Rousseau and Romanticism* (Cambridge, Mass., impression of 1947), p. 226.

In stanza vi it is not altogether clear at first whether the hand that
leads him is that of his wife, or of Italy—

> I follow wherever I am led,
>   Knowing so well the leader's hand:
> Oh woman-country, wooed not wed,
>   Loved all the more by earth's male lands,
>   Laid to their hearts instead!

We conclude that it is the hand of Italy, and realize that as well as
being a love poem to his wife this is also a love poem to Italy,
reminiscent at times of 'De Gustibus' and 'An Englishman in Italy':

> Look at the ruined chapel again
>   Half-way up in the Alpine gorge!
> Is that a tower, I point you plain,
>   Or is it a mill, or an iron-forge
> Breaks solitude in vain?
>
> A turn, and we stand in the heart of things;
>   The woods are round us, heaped and dim;
> From slab to slab how it slips and springs,
>   The thread of water single and slim,
> Through the ravage some torrent brings!

He then addresses his 'perfect wife' and rejoices in

> . . . an age so blest that, by its side,
> Youth seems the waste instead.

As he looks back on the early course of their love, he remembers
how they managed to overcome 'the trouble' that might have made
it an ordinary thing, thanks to the magnanimity of the lady and to
the blessing of fortune:

> The forests had done it; there they stood;
>   We caught for a moment the powers at play:
> They had mingled us so, for once and good,
>   Their work was done—we might go or stay,
> They relapsed to their ancient mood.

They have been fortunate in their generation:

> So, earth has gained by one man the more,
>   And the gain of earth must be heaven's gain too;

> And the whole is well worth thinking o'er
>> When autumn comes: which I mean to do
> One day, as I said before.

A number of other Dramatic Lyrics also deal with the subject of love. 'A Pretty Woman' is a refusal to love a Society butterfly. 'Respectability' contrasts the stifling conventionality of married life with the freedom which the speaker and his mistress enjoy: if they had married (he asks),

> How much of priceless life were spent
>> With men that every virtue decks,
>> And women models of their sex,
> Society's true ornament,—
> Ere we dared wander, nights like this,
>> Thro' wind and rain, and watch the Seine,
>> And feel the Boulevart break again
> To warmth and light and bliss?

'Evelyn Hope' is inspired by a middle-aged man's dream of loving and being loved by a young girl. We notice that there is nothing 'Platonic' about the speaker's fantasy of loving her in some after-life:

> Why your hair was amber, I shall divine,
>> And your mouth of your own geranium's red—
> And what you would do with me, in fine,
>> In the new life come in the old one's stead.

'Women and Roses' contains lines of which Blake would not have been ashamed—

> Dear rose without a thorn,
> Thy bud's the babe unborn:
> First streak of a new morn

—and lines that remind one of the seventeenth century:

> What is far conquers what is near.
> Roses will bloom nor want beholders,
> Sprung from the dust where our flesh moulders.

This strange and haunting little poem, suggested by a vivid dream inspired by a bunch of roses which a friend sent his wife, is another of the poems perhaps written as a result of a New Year's resolution.

'In Three Days' is a simple and successful poem in which Browning expresses a lover's delighted anticipation of a reunion. 'A Lovers' Quarrel' contains one or two good stanzas describing the time spent by two lovers snowed up together in an isolated house, but 'A Serenade at the Villa' is a more successful whole:

> What they could my words expressed,
>   O my love, my all, my one!
> Singing helped the verses best,
>   And when singing's best was done,
> To my lute I left the rest.

This poem was probably inspired by the idea of running a race with Sir Thomas Wyatt rather than by immediate personal experience.[11]

If only a handful of Browning's love lyrics deserve the compliment of comparison with those of Donne, Dame Helen Gardner's estimate of the nature of Donne's sources of inspiration is interestingly relevant:

Donne, I believe, was stimulated by situations, some literary, some imagined, some reflecting the circumstances of his own life, by things seen on the stage or read in the study, or said by friends in casual conversation, to make poems. Whatever experiences literary or actual lie behind his poems have been transmuted in his imagination, which has worked on them to produce poems that are single and complete, as a play is single and complete. While other poets were producing sequences which, whether truly or not, at least purported to be based on their own fortunes in love, Donne produced a corpus of discrete poems. No links are suggested between them.[12]

Whether or not the quarrel that lies behind the twin lyrics, 'Before' and 'After', originated in a love affair is not revealed. As in 'Meeting at Night' and 'Parting at Morning' we are here presented with two Dramatic Lyrics inspired by a situation which could equally have resulted in a Dramatic Romance. The speaker of the first lyric is in favour of the duel (which he is supervising) because he believes that it is the only means of discovering which of the men is the guilty party, 'the wronger': the speaker of the second is

---

[11] Cf. 'One Way of Love', stanza ii.
[12] *John Donne: The Elegies and The Songs and Sonnets*, ed. Helen Gardner (1965), p. xviii.

the survivor, who is innocent, but who feels that he has disgraced himself by participating in a duel—an interesting fact, as Browning had supported the practice of duelling in a letter to Elizabeth Barrett in 1846.[13] The economy of 'After' makes it one of Browning's most striking achievements:

> Take the cloak from his face, and at first
> Let the corpse do its worst!
>
> How he lies in his rights of a man!
> Death has done all death can.
> And, absorbed in the new life he leads,
> He recks not, he heeds
> Nor his wrong nor my vengeance; both strike
> On his senses alike,
> And are lost in the solemn and strange
> Surprise of the change.

Browning's remark to Milsand that he was writing 'lyrics with more music and painting than before' has sometimes been taken as a reference to the poems in *Men and Women* which deal with these two arts, but it seems more likely that Browning meant that he was trying to write more musically than before, and to include more descriptive passages. In any event the two lyrics about painting— 'The Guardian-Angel' and 'Old Pictures in Florence'—are of no great importance, but three of the finest of the remaining lyrics are concerned with music, although they are by no means simple poems. They are 'A Toccata of Galuppi's', 'Master Hugues of Saxe-Gotha', and 'Saul'.

Browning was a great poet who frequently wrote verse that does not look like the work of a great poet. Often that was because he was writing badly, but sometimes an understanding of his poetic purpose leads the reader to revise his initial judgement. The opening of 'A Toccata of Galuppi's' is a case in point:

> Oh Galuppi, Baldassaro, this is very sad to find!
> I can hardly misconceive you; it would prove me deaf and blind;
> But although I take your meaning, 'tis with such a heavy mind!

---

[13] Kintner, ii. 601 ff.

This reads like the work of a versifier attempting trochees for the first time, with a notably awkward and prosaic result. If we jump to the seventh stanza, however, we find something very different:

> What? Those lesser thirds so plaintive, sixths diminished, sigh on sigh,
>
> Told them something? Those suspensions, those solutions—'Must we die?'
>
> Those commiserating sevenths—'Life might last! we can but try!'

For these lines there is no need to apologize. What has happened? Is it merely that Browning has chosen a metrical form that is ideal for the description of music, but unsuited to ordinary speech? It would appear that the truth is not so simple, and that it is less easy than it might appear to state the precise subject of the poem that we are considering.

The speaker is a man very different from Browning himself: so much is clear. 'I was never out of England—it's as if I saw it all.' Stanza xi suggests that he is rather an arrogant man:

> But when I sit down to reason, think to take my stand nor swerve,
> While I triumph o'er a secret wrung from nature's close reserve,
> In you come with your cold music till I creep thro' every nerve.

He imagines the music speaking to him as follows:

> 'Yours [i.e. your soul] for instance: you know physics, something of geology,
> 'Mathematics are your pastime; souls shall rise in their degree;
> 'Butterflies may dread extinction,—you'll not die, it cannot be!'

The toccata conjures up in the mind of the Englishman an idea of Venice in the eighteenth century:

> What, they lived once thus at Venice where the merchants were the kings,
> Where Saint Mark's is, where the Doges used to wed the sea with rings?

The description is brilliantly done:

> Did young people take their pleasure when the sea was warm in May?
> Balls and masks begun at midnight, burning ever to mid-day,

When they made up fresh adventures for the morrow, do you say?

Was a lady such a lady, cheeks so round and lips so red,—
On her neck the small face buoyant, like a bell-flower on its bed,
O'er the breast's superb abundance where a man might base his
　　head?

Musingly, he imagines the conversations of the participants in this
fête galante:

Then they left you for their pleasure: till in due time, one by one,
Some with lives that came to nothing, some with deeds as well
　　undone,
Death stepped tacitly and took them where they never see the sun.

Only a great poet could have written that last line, and it may be
doubted whether any other poet has succeeded so brilliantly in
describing the reveries that pass through the mind as one listens to
a piece of music. Here are the concluding stanzas:

'As for Venice and her people, merely born to bloom and drop,
'Here on earth they bore their fruitage, mirth and folly were
　　the crop:
'What of soul was left, I wonder, when the kissing had to stop?

'Dust and ashes!' So you creak it, and I want the heart to scold.
Dear dead women, with such hair, too—what's become of all
　　the gold
Used to hang and brush their bosoms? I feel chilly and grown old.

'A Toccata of Galuppi's' is a brilliant description of music, or
rather of the effect of music on one particular man. But he is an
imaginary man, and we are left with the question of what exactly
Browning means by the poem. DeVane's comment shows his
awareness of the problem:

Does [Browning] mean to condemn Galuppi's music? Or is Galuppi
ironical or mocking in what his music says to the untravelled and
unsophisticated speaker of the poem? It seems clear to me that
Browning intends the speaker to be the kind of person who expects
Venice to be the very symbol of romance, made up of canals, doges,
gaiety, and love—in short, just such a place as Browning had pictured
in *In A Gondola*. Instead, Galuppi's music is disconcerting to the
speaker. It is cold, intellectual, and even taunting, and almost

persuades him that he with all his learning will die just as surely as the light people of the Venetian past have died. Browning is not the speaker any more than he is Galuppi's music, but his sympathies incline toward the unsophisticated Englishman.

It is clear, I think, that Browning does not mean 'to condemn Galuppi's music', yet to say that his 'sympathies incline toward the unsophisticated Englishman' gives a misleading account of a complicated poem. Just because it removes us from the here and now—the present spatial and temporal framework of our lives, which we can to some extent control—music *is* disconcerting, as religion is disconcerting:

> Hark, the dominant's persistence till it must be answered to!

To the possible counter-suggestion that the poem is primarily a satire on the speaker one might respond by recalling Eliot's description of 'wit', in his essay on 'Andrew Marvell'. Observing that wit 'is confused with cynicism because it implies a constant inspection and criticism of experience', he goes on to suggest that it 'involves, probably, a recognition, implicit in the expression of every experience, of other kinds of experience which are possible', and to claim that this is a quality 'which we find as clearly in the greatest as in poets like Marvell'.[14] It is certainly a quality that we find in many of Browning's finest poems, and notably in 'A Toccata of Galuppi's', where the poet is less concerned to satirize the speaker than to convey the effect of music on a human soul.

In 'Master Hugues of Saxe-Gotha' there is an element of comedy that is not to be found in the previous poem. The tone is admirably set in the opening stanza:

> Hist, but a word, fair and soft!
>   Forth and be judged, Master Hugues!
> Answer the question I've put you so oft:—
>   What do you mean by your mountainous fugues?
> See, we're alone in the loft.

The scene is vividly described: the poor organist in his loft as the church 'empties apace' and the sacristan goes about extinguishing the lights. The organist is a fanciful man, who amuses himself with

---

[14] *Selected Essays* (1934), p. 303.

the idea that 'the church-saints [go] on their rounds' in the evening, tidying up and setting everything to rights. Brilliant executant as he is—

> Played I not off-hand and runningly,
> Just now, your masterpiece, hard number twelve?

—his fancy plays round the figure of the composer himself, whom he visualizes 'with brow ruled like a score' and eyes 'Like two great breves, as they wrote them of yore, Each side that bar, your straight beak!' He further imagines the composer praising his playing—'Good, the mere notes!'—yet wishing that he could understand his 'intent', the quality that singled him out from the herd of common composers of his day. So he describes the fugue that he has been playing:

> First you deliver your phrase
>   —Nothing propound, that I see,
> Fit in itself for much blame or much praise—
>   Answered no less, where no answer needs be:
> Off start the Two on their ways.
>
> Straight must a Third interpose,
>   Volunteer needlessly help;
> In strikes a Fourth, a Fifth thrusts in his nose,
>   So the cry's open, the kennel's a-yelp,
> Argument's hot to the close.

Whereas the man who plays or listens to 'A Toccata of Galuppi's' is set dreaming about past days in Venice, the organist of this poem is concerned (and perplexed) by the problem of extracting any significance from the complicated mathematics of Master Hugues:

> Is it your moral of Life?
>   Such a web, simple and subtle,
> Weave we on earth here in impotent strife,
>   Backward and forward each throwing his shuttle,
> Death ending all with a knife?

Although the organist believes in Master Hugues, and loves his music, he becomes exasperated by his inability to understand its meaning, and as the conclusion of the poem approaches the element of comedy increases, until he threatens to be disloyal to that composer, and to go over to the side of Palestrina, 'who emancipated his art from a pedantry which was tending to reduce it to mere arithmetical problems':[15]

> Hugues! I advise *meâ pœnâ*
>   (Counterpoint glares like a Gorgon)
> Bid One, Two, Three, Four, Five, clear the arena!
>   Say the word, straight I unstop the full-organ,
> Blare out the *mode Palestrina*.

At this point his candle goes out and we leave him indignantly asking the sacristan if he wants him to be found dead in the morning, having broken his neck trying to get down the stairs of the loft in the dark.

'Saul' also deals with the effect of music, but in a religious context. Curiously enough, the ultimate suggestion for this poem came from a remark made to Christopher Smart by an eighteenth-century don. In the last paragraph of the preface to Smart's 'Ode for Musick on Saint Cecilia's Day', as DeVane points out, Browning found the following words:

It would not be right to conclude, without taking notice of a fine subject for an Ode on S. Cecilia's Day, which was suggested to the Author by his friend the learned and ingenious Mr. Comber, late of Jesus College in this University [Cambridge]; that is David's playing to King Saul when he was troubled with the evil Spirit. He was much pleased with the hint at first, but at length was deterred from improving it by the greatness of the subject, and he thinks not without reason. The chusing too high subjects has been the ruin of many a tolerable Genius.

Comber's allusion was of course to the story of David and Saul as told in 1 Samuel 16: 14–23, and particularly in the last verse:

And it came to pass, when the *evil* spirit from God was upon Saul, that David took an harp, and played with his hand: so Saul was refreshed, and was well, and the evil spirit departed from him.

The poem that Browning wrote is as different from an ordinary 'Ode

---

[15] 'Biographical and Historical Notes to the Poems', in *The Poetical Works*, xvii. (1894), 240.

on Saint Cecilia's Day' of the seventeenth or eighteenth century as is Smart's own remarkable work, 'A Song to David', which was no doubt in his mind.[16]

The greater part of 'Saul', as it was first published, seems to have been written by 3 May 1845, soon after Browning's first meeting with Elizabeth Barrett. In August he showed it to her, and her reply makes it clear that he was conscious of difficulties in the subject:

> But your 'Saul' is unobjectionable as far as I can see, my dear friend. He was tormented by an evil spirit—but how, we are not told . . & the consolation is not obliged to be definite . . is it? A singer was sent for as a singer—& all that you are called upon to be true to, are the general characteristics of David the chosen, standing between his sheep & his dawning hereafter, between innocence & holiness, & with what you speak of as the 'gracious gold locks' besides the chrism of the prophet, on his own head . . . I cannot tell you how the poem holds me . . . I do beseech you . . . to go on with the rest.[17]

It appears that Browning had thrown away 'sixty lines', though whether these correspond to the tenth section of the poem, as published in its longer version in 1855, we have no means of telling. About 29 October Elizabeth Barrett wrote again about the poem, in a way that suggests that Browning was thinking of printing the shorter version of 'Saul' without any indication that it might later be lengthened:

> 'Saul' is noble & must have his full royalty some day. Would it not be well, by the way, to print it in the meanwhile as a fragment confessed . . sowing asterisks at the end. Because as a poem of yours it stands there & wants unity, & people can't be expected to understand the difference between incompleteness & defect, unless you make a sign.[18]

In 1845, accordingly, the words '(*End of Part the First*)' were printed at the conclusion of the 190 lines of 'Saul'—190 lines which correspond to 96 lines of the longer version because, as DeVane points out, the double columns of the *Bells and Pomegranates* pamphlets

---

[16] Browning was always keenly interested in Smart: in 1887 he addressed the third of his *Parleyings with Certain People* to him.

[17] Kintner, i. 173. [18] Ibid. 252.

made it impossible for the poem to be printed as anapaestic pentameters (as it should be): it had to be printed in alternate long and
short lines. 'Saul' is a dramatic monologue spoken by David (a fact
which becomes explicit in the longer version) when he returns
home after ministering to the King:

> Let me tell out my tale to its ending—my voice to my heart
> Which can scarce dare believe in what marvels last night I took
>   part,
> As this morning I gather the fragments, alone with my sheep,
> And still fear lest the terrible glory evanish like sleep!
>
> (199–202)

He describes how he had been greeted, when he arrived to play
to Saul to relieve his melancholy: how he had found him in silent
agony: and how he played him tunes describing his own pastoral
existence[19] and then other tunes appropriate to various occasions in
human life, culminating with a celebration of the goodness of life:

> How good is man's life here, mere living!
>   How fit to employ
> The heart and the soul and the senses
>   For ever in joy!   (153–6)

He ends by telling Saul that all human felicities

> Combine to unite in one creature
>   —Saul!

It is not a very satisfactory conclusion: one can sense that Browning
was running out of subject-matter, and see why Elizabeth Barrett
reassured him that 'the consolation is not obliged to be definite'.

As printed in 1855, 'Saul' is more than three times as long. The
original First Part is revised and improved, as well as being printed
in long lines, while more than 200 lines are added. As Saul begins to
recover, David continues to sing to him, a long song which has
been shown to owe something of its structure to Wyatt's *Seven*

---

[19] In *The Cure of Saul. A Sacred Ode*, by the minor eighteenth-century poet John
Brown—a poem which Browning has not been proved to have known—David 'sings
the Creation of the World, and the happy Estate of our first Parents in Paradise':
'The Argument of the Ode' in *A Dissertation on . . . . Poetry and Music. To which is
prefixed, The Cure of Saul* (1763).

Penitential Psalms.[20] If some parts of this song-sermon are impressive rather than immediately enjoyable, the final words of Section xviii, in which Saul prophesies the coming of Christ, are audacious and striking—

> '. . . O Saul, it shall be
> 'A Face like my face that receives thee; a Man like to me,
> 'Thou shalt love and be loved by, for ever; a Hand like this hand
> 'Shall throw open the gates of new life to thee! See the Christ stand!'

The final section, in which David describes his return through a night of supernatural menace during which he was preserved by 'the Hand [that] impelled me', makes a splendid ending to a poem which is essentially religious and which has an affinity to 'An Epistle of Karshish' and 'Cleon': as in these poems, so here Browning is concerned to render living and vivid a part of the Bible story (though in fact he here goes beyond the story of Saul and David as told in the Bible), rather than to present a particular character.

In 'Up at a Villa—Down in the City (as distinguished by an Italian Person of Quality)' Browning delights in characterizing the speaker,[21] as he delights in describing the Italian scene. The life that appeals to the speaker is the life of the city,[22] where there are

> Houses in four straight lines, not a single front awry;
> You watch who crosses and gossips, who saunters, who hurries by;
> Green blinds, as a matter of course, to draw when the sun gets high;
> And the shops with fanciful signs which are painted properly.

In hot weather the city is no less attractive:

> Is it ever hot in the square? There's a fountain to spout and splash!
> In the shade it sings and springs; in the shine such foam-bows flash

[20] See 'The Shaping of *Saul*', by J. A. S. McPeek, *JEGP* 44 (1945), 360–6.

[21] Almost certainly a man, although Browning may deliberately have left the matter a little uncertain, to suggest that he is a gossiping 'old woman'. Mrs. Sutherland Orr takes it that the speaker is a man: DeVane does not raise the question: while the reviewer in the *Athenæum* (17 Nov. 1855, 1327–8, quoted in Litzinger and Smalley, p. 157) writes: 'Listen only how the Signor or Signora (the latter it must be, we should say, could we forget how Italian men gossip over their cups of water.' A woman would hardly be likely to refer to her own hair as this speaker does in l. 10.

[22] The 'city', as Mrs. Sutherland Orr comments (*Handbook*, p. 284), is more reminiscent of a 'big village' than a metropolis: that is part of the joke.

On the horses with curling fish-tails, that prance and paddle
  and pash
Round the lady atop in her conch—fifty gazers do not abash,
Though all that she wears is some weeds round her waist in a sort
  of sash.

But the most delightful description of the life of the little city occurs
in stanza ix:

Ere you open your eyes in the city, the blessed church-bells begin:
No sooner the bells leave off than the diligence rattles in:
You get the pick of the news, and it costs you never a pin.
By-and-by there's the travelling doctor gives pills, lets blood,
  draws teeth;
Or the Pulcinello-trumpet breaks up the market beneath.

The speaker also describes life in the villa, which bores him to
death, and Browning makes use of this simple device to convey
the tranquillity of life in the Italian countryside as well as the
animation of the town. In stanza v the speaker describes spring in
the country, and in vi the sudden arrival of summer:

'Mid the sharp short emerald wheat, scarce risen three fingers well,
The wild tulip, at end of its tube, blows out its great red bell
Like a thin clear bubble of blood, for the children to pick and sell.

Equally fine is the account of late summer and autumn in stanza
viii. As the speaker dislikes the peaceful landscape which he describes
the effect is amusingly ironical. Nothing but poverty would keep
him in the country, as he makes clear in the opening lines:

Had I but plenty of money, money enough and to spare,
The house for me, no doubt, were a house in the city-square;
Ah, such a life, such a life, as one leads at the window there!

At the beginning of the last stanza he returns to the subject of
money:

But bless you,—it's dear! fowls, wine, at double the rate.
They have clapped a new tax upon salt, and what oil pays passing
  the gate
It's a horror to think of . . .

He rejoices in the multitudinousness of the scene that he is describing, in the fact that something is going on all the time:[23]

> Noon strikes,—here sweeps the procession! our Lady borne smiling and smart
> With a pink gauze gown all spangles, and seven swords stuck in her heart!

An absolute lack of discrimination is characteristic:

> At the post-office such a scene-picture—the new play, piping hot!
> And a notice how, only this morning, three liberal thieves were shot.
> Above it, behold the Archbishop's most fatherly of rebukes,
> And beneath, with his crown and his lion, some little new law of the Duke's!

The speaker is as fascinated by the human scene as is Fra Lippo Lippi, but much less intelligent. We have only to compare Browning's attitude to his lack of discrimination with that in 'Verses on the Death of Dr. Swift', however, to see clearly that the poem is at once simpler and more sophisticated than a direct satire.

Once again we notice Browning's extraordinary metrical resourcefulness. The poem is written in hexameters which rush along in the headlong manner of breathless gossiping conversation, hexameters in which anapaests predominate over iambs. Frequently the expected unstressed syllable or syllables at the beginning of the line are omitted, to give an effect of emphasis:

> ∧ Something to see, by Bacchus, something to hear, at least!

[23] Cf. a passage in a letter from Elizabeth Barrett to her sister, written from Florence in 1847: 'We had a festa on last monday week, the day of S. Leopold, the name-day of our Grand-Duke, and our piazza was nearly brimming over with people. A beautiful sight really! . . . The service extended of course to four and twenty hours, and the nobles armed themselves for the vigil with so many dozens of champagne, cakes, &c., and at twelve at night, and at nine in the morning the Duke paid them a visit. When they came to replace the military, the people who thronged the piazza shouted and clapped their hands—and that clapping of hands is a sound so full of life and mental affirmation to me, (it isn't mere animal life) that it throbs and thrills through me. Then the band played, and a hymn, in congratulation of the Grand Duke, was sung in grand chorus beneath his windows . . . after which he the Duchess and their children came out into the balcony and bowed their thanks to the people': Huxley, pp. 65–6.

In the penultimate line the expected unstressed syllable is omitted at the beginning of the second half of the line, as well as at the beginning of the first half:

$$\overset{/}{\wedge} \overset{/}{Bang}\text{-}\overset{/}{whang}\text{-}\overset{\times}{whang} \overset{\times}{goes} \overset{/}{the} \text{ drum}, \overset{/}{\wedge} \overset{\times}{tootle}\text{-}\overset{\times}{te}\text{-}\overset{/}{tootle} \text{ the fife.}$$

The rhyme scheme is very unusual. In each of the first two stanzas, which consist of three lines each, there is only one rhyme sound, as there is in the third stanza (which contains four lines), in the fourth (which contains six), and in the seventh (which contains five). The use of triplet rhymes at the beginning combines with the rushing versification to enhance the effect of a torrent of chatter. Since Swift wrote 'The Humble Petition of Mrs. Frances Harris' the furniture of a superficial mind has never been so skilfully turned out for our entertainment and delight. This is one of the most light-hearted of all Browning's poems, a poem that is Chaucerian in the skill of the characterization and in the joy that the poet takes in the character whom he is so memorably endowing with a voice.

XI

THE DRAMATIC ROMANCES OF 1855

> The divine art is the story. In the beginning was the story. At the end
> we shall be privileged to view, and review, it—and that is what is
> named the day of judgement.   ISAK DINESEN

> Short-story writing—for me—is only looking closer than normal into
> the human heart. The vagaries and contrarieties there to be found
> have their own integral design.   MARY LAVIN[1]

THREE of the most celebrated poems in the two volumes of *Men
and Women* were later classified by Browning as Dramatic Romances:
'Childe Roland', 'The Statue and the Bust', and 'A Grammarian's
Funeral'. In all there are a dozen Romances in the collection, and
together they constitute a further brilliant exemplification of
Browning's power as a writer of short stories in verse. Although
the character of the speaker is least important in the most successful of these poems, it will be convenient to begin with those in
which this element is most important.

Two otherwise contrasted poems are spoken by men who are
obsessed by love. 'Mesmerism' has never been one of Browning's
best-known poems, and Mrs. Orr's comment on it is unusually far
from the truth:

'Mesmerism' is a fanciful but vivid description of an act of mesmeric
power, which draws a woman, alone, in the darkness, and through
every natural obstacle, to the presence of the man who loves her.[2]

To suggest that the poem is more interesting than Mrs. Orr
realizes it is sufficient to indicate that it is extremely doubtful
whether the action described by the narrator ever takes place at all.

---

[1] Isak Dinesen, 'The Cardinal's First Tale', in *Last Tales*; Mary Lavin, Preface to
Selected Stories.

[2] *Handbook*, p. 305.

The rhythm of the opening lines should surely arouse the suspicion that we are listening to a man whose sanity is not beyond question:

> All I believed is true!
>   I am able yet
>   All I want, to get
> By a method as strange as new:
> Dare I trust the same to you?

We know that while Mrs. Browning believed in mesmerism, her husband did not; yet this external information would hardly be necessary for the right interpretation of this poem. Once again his metrical skill enables Browning to 'place' his speaker, and it is obvious that the mode of speech of the opening stanza is not that of a man whom one should implicitly believe. The rushing movement of the verse of the succeeding stanzas suggests a man who is unhealthily excited, while the variations on the phrase 'have and hold' in the opening lines of stanzas vi–ix contribute to the obsessive effect of the whole. The speaker is feverishly concentrating his will in order to exert a 'mesmeric' influence over his absent mistress:

> Command her soul to advance,
>   And inform the shape
>   Which has made escape
> And before my countenance
> Answers me glance for glance.

The reader's uncertainty about what (if anything) is actually happening is increased by the vagueness of the expression. We come to see that this poem could be classed with 'Porphyria's Lover' and 'Johannes Agricola' as a third 'Madhouse Cell'. Stanza xxiv is particularly reminiscent of the former poem:

> 'Now—now'—the door is heard!
>   Hark, the stairs! and near—
>   Nearer—and here—
> 'Now!' and at call the third
> She enters without a word.

Does she enter? Is it not rather that the speaker imagines that she enters? In the final stanza, with a powerful effect of irony (if my reading of the poem is correct) he prays that he may not abuse his supposed abnormal powers:

> I admonish me while I may,
>   Not to squander guilt,
>   Since require Thou wilt
> At my hand its price one day!
> What the price is, who can say?

The tone in which the speaker tells his story contrasts strikingly with the tone of the speaker in 'A Light Woman' (for example). Whereas the latter is a mature man of the world, describing a complex human situation with an honest and self-depreciatory clarity, the speaker here is clearly deranged, as Porphyria's lover and Johannes Agricola are deranged, and the conclusion is irresistible that his mesmeric powers are in fact a pure delusion.

'The Last Ride Together' is the utterance of another man who is in a sense obsessed by love, but this time the speaker might be described as a triumphant obsessive. The theme of the poem is one of Browning's favourite themes, the importance of striving. Whereas the lovers in 'The Statue and the Bust' have not had the courage to attempt to escape to happiness, the speaker in this poem has done all that he could, and the fact that he has not been successful is of less importance.

> Fail I alone, in words and deeds?
> Why, all men strive and who succeeds?

In the mere fact of striving there is a kind of success—the kind of success that makes a life meaningful. The opening stanza has a theme that is unusual in love poetry, a theme very far from the conventional lover's complaint:

> I said—Then, dearest, since 't is so,
> Since now at length my fate I know,
> Since nothing all my love avails,
> Since all, my life seemed meant for, fails,
>   Since this was written and needs must be—
> My whole heart rises up to bless
> Your name in pride and thankfulness!
> Take back the hope you gave,—I claim

> Only a memory of the same,
> —And this beside, if you will not blame,
>   Your leave for one more last ride with me.

The manner in which the subject is handled suggests that it may be an error to describe the poem as the utterance of an obsessive at all. Riding was often an important imaginative stimulus to Browning,[3] and here it becomes a powerful imaginative symbol:

> What if we still ride on, we two
> With life for ever old yet new,
> Changed not in kind but in degree,
> The instant made eternity,—
> And heaven just prove that I and she
>   Ride, ride together, for ever ride?

From love to hatred, a theme the importance of which in many of Browning's poems has already been emphasized. From one point of view the subject of 'Instans Tyrannus' is the strength of Horace's righteous man, however poor he may be: from another, it is the hatred felt by the speaker, a tyrant who has considered himself all-powerful until he encounters the sort of man whom Horace described as 'iustum et tenacem propositi virum'. Hatred is also the subject of 'The Heretic's Tragedy: A Middle-Age Interlude'. The subject of this poem is the burning of the last Grand Master of the Knights Templar (an event which occurred in the time of Philip IV of France and Pope Clement V), while its form probably owes something to Chatterton, who always fascinated Browning, and on whom he had written at length in 1842 in an article professedly reviewing a book on Tasso.[4] Chatterton's poem, 'The Tournament', is sub-titled 'An Interlude', while his 'Ælla' is sub-titled 'a Tragycal Enterlude'; but it is of the 'Bristowe Tragedie; Or, The Dethe of Syr Charles Bawdin', the first poem in the 1842 edition of Chatterton's *Poetical Works*, that the reader of Browning is reminded. Chatterton's poem begins with a cheerful and

---

[3] Cf. pp. 98–9, above.
[4] The review, of Richard Henry Wilde's *Conjectures . . . concerning . . . Tasso*, appeared in the *Foreign Quarterly Review* for July 1842. It has been reprinted by Donald Smalley, as *Browning's Essay on Chatterton*.

conventional opening that contrasts strongly with the sombre story that he is about to tell:

> The feathered songster chaunticleer,
>   Han wounde hys bugle horne,
> And tolde the earlie villager
>   The commynge of the morne.

The procession that accompanies the condemned man to the place of execution has the same incongruously festive air that is suggested by the singing in Browning's poem:

> Before hym went the council-menne,
>   Ynne scarlett robes and golde,
> And tassils spanglynge ynne the sunne,
>   Muche glorious to beholde:
>
> The Freers of Seincte Augustyne next
>   Appeared to the syghte,
> Alle cladd ynne homelie russett weedes,
>   Of godlie monkysh plyghte:
>
> Ynne diffraunt partes a godlie psaume
>   Moste sweetlie theye dydd chaunt;
> Behynde theyre backes syx mynstrelles came,
>   Who tun'd the strunge bataunt.[5]

In Browning the macabre quality already perceptible in Chatterton is greatly deepened, and the result is a terrifying study of religious hatred. It is prefaced by a prose note rather in the style of Chatterton—

Rosa mundi; seu, fulcite me floribus. A conceit of Master Gysbrecht, Canon-regular of Saint Jodocus-by-the-Bar, Ypres City. Cantuque, *Virgilius*. And hath often been sung at Hock-tide and Festivals. Gavisus eram, *Jessides*

—and by another note informing the reader that the poem 'would seem to be a glimpse from the burning of Jacques du Bourg-Molay, . . . as distorted by the refraction from Flemish brain to brain, during the course of a couple of centuries'. The first stanza, and the

---

[5] Stanzas lxvii–lxix in the edition of 1842, which has a note on 'bataunt': 'The name seems to imply that it was a stringed instrument, like a dulcimer, played on by striking the wires with a piece of iron or wood.'

last line of the poem, are spoken by 'The Abbot Deodaet': the remaining stanzas, which describe the preparations for the burning and the execution itself, are sung by an unnamed singer, with a brief chorus from the other spectators. The third stanza illustrates the nature of the poem:

> In the midst is a goodly gallows built;
> 　'Twixt fork and fork, a stake is stuck;
> But first they set divers tumbrils a-tilt,
> 　Make a trench all round with the city muck;
> Inside they pile log upon log, good store;
> 　Faggots no few, blocks great and small,
> Reach a man's mid-thigh, no less, no more,—
> 　For they mean he should roast in the sight of all.
>
> 　　　　CHORUS
> We mean he should roast in the sight of all.

In stanza v we again note how the horror of the theme is brought out by the easy-going tetrameters of which the song is composed:

> John of the Temple, whose fame so bragged,
> 　Is burning alive in Paris square!
> How can he curse, if his mouth is gagged?
> 　Or wriggle his neck, with a collar there?
> 　Or heave his chest, which a band goes round?
> 　　Or threat with his fist, since his arms are spliced?
> 　Or kick with his feet, now his legs are bound?

The most macabre stanza of all is the ninth:

> Ha ha, John plucketh now at his rose
> 　To rid himself of a sorrow at heart!
> Lo,—petal on petal, fierce rays unclose;
> 　Anther on anther, sharp spikes outstart;
> And with blood for dew, the bosom boils;
> 　And a gust of sulphur is all its smell;
> And lo, he is horribly in the toils
> 　Of a coal-black giant flower of hell!
>
> 　　　　CHORUS
> What maketh heaven, That maketh hell.

In this poem, as so often in Browning, the rhythm is the best clue to his intention. In his work rhythm expresses character. Here he is not characterizing an individual, but a period, or a tradition of maniacal religious hatred; and the versification makes it clear that for the singer and his audience an execution by fire is as exciting a spectacle as a football match to a crowd of modern sports enthusiasts. It is remarkable that this masterpiece of the macabre, which was greatly admired by Swinburne,[6] has recently attracted so little attention from the critics.

Like 'The Heretic's Tragedy', 'Holy-Cross Day' is inspired by an event in the history of the Roman Catholic Church, in this case a recurrent event: the annual sermon in Rome which Jews were compelled to attend. Like the previous poem, this constitutes a mordant satire on religious fanaticism, and does so in a way that reminds us of Browning's perennial interest in the grotesque and in abnormal conditions of the human mind. On this occasion (however) the spirit is that of comedy rather than that of tragedy, while it is not the speaker who is satirized, as in 'The Heretic's Tragedy': on the contrary, the speaker is one of the victims of 'this bad business of the Sermon', and the satire is directed against the Christians who persecute the Jews. With a highly ironical effect, the speaker resolves to inform the Bishop that he will no longer help alleged Christians 'to their sins', since all they do in return is to 'help me to their God': his career as a moneylender is now at an end:

> I meddle no more with the worst of trades—
> Let somebody else pay his serenades.

The abrupt opening of the poem reminds us of 'The Pied Piper' in its robust realism and its remoteness from anything conventionally 'poetical':

> Fee, faw, fum! bubble and squeak!
> Blessedest Thursday's the fat of the week.
> Rumble and tumble, sleek and rough,

---

[6] In 1858 Swinburne 'read [aloud] Browning's essay . . . [on] Shelley; and afterwards repeated, or rather chanted, to his friends a few of Browning's poems, in particular, "The Statue and the Bust", "The Heretic's Tragedy", and "Bishop Blougram's Apology"': *The Life of . . . Swinburne*, by Edmund Gosse (1917), pp. 39–40.

> Stinking and savoury, smug and gruff,
> Take the church-road, for the bell's due chime
> Gives us the summons—'t is sermon-time!

The grotesque description of the Jews huddled together to listen to the sermon reminds one of Browning's father's liking for pictures of Dutch boors:

> Higgledy piggledy, packed we lie,
> Rats in a hamper, swine in a stye,
> Wasps in a bottle, frogs in a sieve,
> Worms in a carcase, flees in a sleeve.
> Hist! square shoulders, settle your thumbs
> And buzz for the bishop—here he comes.

Browning's power as a satirist has never received its due. To find anything comparable to stanza iv—

> Bow, wow, wow—a bone for the dog!
> I liken his Grace to an acorned hog.
> What, a boy at his side, with the bloom of a lass,
> To help and handle my lord's hour-glass!
> Didst ever behold so lithe a chine?
> His cheek hath laps like a fresh-singed swine

—to find anything like that one would have to go back beyond *Hudibras* to Skelton or Dunbar. In the last nine stanzas the poet gives us what professes to be an account of the dying speech of Rabbi Ben Ezra,[7] an eloquent defence of the Jews and their moral position which includes a stanza of satire on the Christian Church:

> By the torture, prolonged from age to age,
> By the infamy, Israel's heritage,
> By the Ghetto's plague, by the garb's disgrace,
> By the badge of shame, by the felon's place,
> By the branding-tool, the bloody whip,
> And the summons to Christian fellowship,—

> We boast our proof that at least the Jew,
> Would wrest Christ's name from the Devil's crew.

[7] Mrs. Melchiori argues that Browning himself probably made up the passage: see the interesting discussion of the poem in her book, *Browning's Poetry of Reticence* (1968), ch. v.

The brevity with which Browning can tell a story is illustrated by 'The Patriot: An Old Story', which describes the reversal of fortune by which a man who had been hailed as his country's hero only a year ago now finds himself on his way to the gallows. Six stanzas of five lines suffice to tell the story. But it is perhaps in 'A Light Woman' that we see Browning's skill as a writer of short stories at its most brilliant. The opening stanza is relaxed in tone— the narrator is obviously a practised raconteur—yet it promises us an account of an interesting human dilemma:

> So far as our story approaches the end,
>   Which do you pity the most of us three?—
> My friend, or the mistress of my friend
>   With her wanton eyes, or me?

The economy of the whole thing is most striking: in fourteen stanzas—fifty-six lines—the characters are sketched in, the story told, and the problem posed. No setting is described, though we may deduce that it is contemporary and upper-class, the sort of society which Henry James was later to describe.[8] No details are given, few adjectives used. Of the 'light woman' we know what the title tells us, and that she has 'wanton eyes'. Of the 'friend' we know that he is young and innocent, with a 'maiden face'. About the character of the narrator we know rather more. He is famous, an 'eagle' compared to his friend, who is a 'wren'. It is clear that he is attractive to women, and fond of his young friend. He is 'noble', probably in the literal sense of the word. He is sophisticated, has quickly understood the character of the woman, and has taken an unusual way of trying to rescue his friend from her clutches. So much we are told—but the main source of our information about the narrator is simply the movement of the verse. If it were not for that, we might begin to speculate about his motives: he has chosen an unusual way of demonstrating the truth to his friend, after all. Is he in fact an honourable man: is there (perhaps) something un-balanced or psychotic about him? The movement of the verse, so

---

[8] Cf. Julia Wedgwood's observation that it seemed to her 'an artistic fault to put James Lee into such a proletarian, to use the horrid new slang, background', and Browning's reply: 'I misled you into thinking the couple were "prolétaire"—but I meant them for just the opposite': (*Wedgwood*, pp. 121 and 123.)

different from what we find in 'Mesmerism', makes it clear that
there is not:

> One likes to show the truth for the truth;
> 　That the woman was light is very true:
> But suppose she says,—Never mind that youth!
> 　What wrong have I done to you?

It is clear that the speaker is experienced, compassionate, and
extremely well balanced. The subject of the poem is not his character, but a human situation and a moral dilemma: an ideal subject
not so much for a 'writer of plays' (as suggested in the last stanza)
as for a writer of short stories. In 'A Light Woman' Browning wrote
a brilliant poem on the sort of subject on which de Maupassant
might have written a brilliant short story.

In the most celebrated of the Dramatic Romances of 1855 the
characterization of the speaker does not appear to be an important
part of Browning's purpose. In 'A Grammarian's Funeral' most of
our attention is certainly focused on the dead man, and the significance of his life: with 'The Statue and the Bust' it hardly seems
worth while to distinguish between the narrator and Browning
himself: while the narrator of 'Childe Roland' has the anonymous
quality characteristic of a dreamer.

'A Grammarian's Funeral' deals with the central subject of
Browning's poetry—success and failure in human life—and stands
in a clear relationship to *Paracelsus* and *Sordello*. Like Paracelsus, the
Grammarian 'aspires' and 'attains', although worldly men may not
realize this:

> He ventured neck or nothing—heaven's success
> 　Found, or earth's failure.

The opening of the prose commentary on the last Book of *Sordello*
might be set as an epigraph to this poem: 'At the close of a day or
a life, past procedure is fitliest reviewed, as more appreciable in its
entirety': while the question asked later in the same commentary—
'may failure here be success also when induced by love?'—could
also be asked of the Grammarian. To worldly men, his career as a
scholar must have appeared Quixotic:

> 'Time to taste life,' another would have said,
> 'Up with the curtain!'
> This man said rather, 'Actual life comes next?
> 'Patience a moment!'

The implausibility of Richard Altick's recent paradox—that although the speaker of the poem unreservedly admires the Grammarian, Browning does not mean the reader to do so[9]—becomes particularly evident when we see 'A Grammarian's Funeral' in relation to the passage in Pope which almost certainly helped to inspire it.

There can be little doubt that one of the germs of the poem was a passage in *An Essay on Criticism* which Johnson had praised eloquently in his *Life of Pope*:

To mention the particular beauties of the *Essay* would be unprofitably tedious; but I cannot forbear to observe that the comparison of a student's progress in the sciences with the journey of a traveller in the Alps is perhaps the best that English poetry can shew. . . . The simile of the Alps has no useless parts, yet affords a striking picture by itself: it makes the foregoing position better understood, and enables it to take faster hold on the attention; it assists the apprehension, and elevates the fancy.[10]

As a young poet Browning must have pondered Johnson's account of this admired comparison, and lines 215–18 of Pope's poem may have helped to suggest lines 95–6 of 'A Grammarian's Funeral':

> A *little learning* is a dang'rous thing;
> Drink deep, or taste not the Pierian spring:
> There shallow draughts intoxicate the brain,
> And drinking largely sobers us again.

Browning also remembered Donne's description of himself as possessed by 'an hydroptic, immoderate desire of human learning and languages':[11]

> Back to his studies, fresher than at first,
> Fierce as a dragon

---

[9] Cf. p. 173, below.
[10] *Lives of the English Poets*, ed. George Birkbeck Hill (1905), iii. 229–30.
[11] Edmund Gosse, *Life and Letters of John Donne* (1899), i. 191.

He (soul-hydroptic with a sacred thirst)
    Sucked at the flagon.

But it is the following lines of Pope's that seem to have 'elevated the fancy' of Browning and to have suggested the structure of his poem:

> Fir'd at first sight with what the Muse imparts,
> In fearless youth we tempt the heights of Arts,
> While from the bounded level of our mind,
> Short views we take, nor see the lengths behind;
> But, more advanc'd, behold with strange surprize
> New distant scenes of endless science rise!
> So pleas'd at first the tow'ring Alps we try,
> Mount o'er the vales, and seem to tread the sky,
> Th'eternal snows appear already past,
> And the first clouds and mountains seem the last:
> But, those attain'd, we tremble to survey
> The growing labours of the lengthen'd way,
> Th'increasing prospect tires our wand'ring eyes,
> Hills peep o'er hills, and Alps on Alps arise!   (219–32)

Browning's father was a great admirer of Pope, and it seems likely that this image remained in his son's imagination throughout his life: we find a particularly clear reminiscence of it in *Pauline*, in the French note to line 811 in which 'Pauline' comments that in the later part of the poem she believes that the poet is alluding to a certain examination of his soul that he had undertaken, 'pour découvrir la suite des objets auxquels il lui serait possible d'atteindre, et dont chacun une fois obtenu devait former une espèce de plateau d'où l'on pouvait apercevoir d'autres buts, d'autres projets, d'autres jouissances qui, à leur tour, devaient être surmontés . . .'. The essential structure of 'A Grammarian's Funeral' is an ascension, a mounting towards the stars:

> Leave we the unlettered plain its herd and crop;
>   Seek we sepulture
> On a tall mountain, citied to the top,
>   Crowded with culture!
> All the peaks soar, but one the rest excels;
>   Clouds overcome it;

No! yonder sparkle is the citadel's
    Circling its summit.
Thither our path lies; wind we up the heights:
    Wait ye the warning?
Our low life was the level's and the night's;
    He's for the morning.

Throughout the poem the way leads upwards, until the mourners leave the corpse at the top of the mountain:

Lofty designs must close in like effects:
    Loftily lying,
Leave him—still loftier than the world suspects,
    Living and dying.

It is almost an apotheosis.

An interesting aspect of the poem is the attitude to old age which it embodies. As a young man, the Grammarian had been strikingly handsome: when his beauty vanished, however, he neither despaired nor grasped greedily at the cruder enjoyments of life. On the contrary:

He knew the signal, and stepped on with pride
    Over men's pity;
Left play for work, and grappled with the world
    Bent on escaping:
'What's in the scroll,' quoth he, 'thou keepest furled?
    'Show me their shaping,
'Theirs who most studied man, the bard and sage,—
    'Give!'—So, he gowned him,
Straight got by heart that book to its last page:
    Learned, we found him.

But the Grammarian is not content. Just as Rabbi Ben Ezra says, in a later poem—

    Therefore I summon age
    To grant youth's heritage,
Life's struggle having so far reached its term:
    Thence shall I pass, approved
    A man, for aye removed
From the developed brute; a god though in the germ
                   (xiii)

—so the Grammarian wishes to plumb learning to its depths before
turning to the ordinary course of living:

> Yes, this in him was the peculiar grace
>   (Hearten our chorus!)
> Still before living he'd learn how to live—
>   No end to learning:
> Earn the means first—God surely will contrive
>   Use for our earning.
> Others mistrust and say, 'But time escapes:
>   'Live now or never!'
> He said, 'What's time? Leave Now for dogs and apes!
>   Man has Forever.'

One is reminded of Yeats's meditation on old age, and in particular
of the second stanza of 'Sailing to Byzantium':

> An aged man is but a paltry thing,
> A tattered coat upon a stick, unless
> Soul clap its hands and sing, and louder sing
> For every tatter in its mortal dress,
> Nor is there singing school but studying
> Monuments of its own magnificence;
> And therefore I have sailed the seas and come
> To the holy city of Byzantium.

The treacherous words 'classic' and 'romantic' have some force
if we wish to contrast the attitude to the scholar expressed in
'A Grammarian's Funeral' with that of Pope, or of Johnson in *The
Vanity of Human Wishes*. Whereas Johnson there sees the life of a
great scholar as one more example of vanity, Browning portrays
his scholar as triumphant, not indeed in any material sense, but in
the sense that he has achieved something of transcendental value—
something (in a humbler way) that may be compared with the
achievement of Adonais in Shelley's poem. Whereas Johnson warns
the young aspirant not to be flattered by 'dreams', Browning
celebrates the Grammarian for having remained faithful to his un-
worldly vision. Browning's attitude to the scholar, in this poem, is
as different as possible from that of the Augustans to critics and
scholars:

> Pains, reading, study, are their just pretence,
>   And all they want is spirit, taste, and sense.[12]

It has recently been argued that in statements about this poem one should not talk of Browning's attitude to the Grammarian, but of that of his narrator; and it is certainly important to note that the speaker lives 'shortly after the revival of learning in Europe'. Altick maintains that Browning 'scarcely means' the Grammarian to be a hero to the reader, as he is to his students—'certainly not to the same uncritical degree'.[13] Such a reading of the poem cannot (of course) be proved to be wrong: it is always possible to argue that the speaker of a dramatic monologue is biased, or mad, or even (simply) a liar. But, as I have tried to show, Browning habitually gives his reader a good deal of guidance about the speaker of a poem by his skilful management of metre and rhythm, and the movement of this poem is celebratory and triumphal:

> Let us begin and carry up this corpse,
>   Singing together.
> Leave we the common crofts, the vulgar thorpes
>   Each in its tether
> Sleeping safe on the bosom of the plain,
>   Cared-for till cock-crow:
> Look out if yonder be not day again
>   Rimming the rock-row!
> That's the appropriate country; there, man's thought,
>   Rarer, intenser,
> Self-gathered for an outbreak, as it ought,
>   Chafes in the censer . . .
> This is our master, famous calm and dead,
>   Borne on our shoulders.

The way in which each confident pentameter is followed by a dimeter composed of the dactyl and spondee which conclude the

---

[12] *An Epistle to Arbuthnot*, ll. 159–60.

[13] '"A Grammarian's Funeral": Browning's Praise of Folly?', *SEL* iii (1963), 449–60. Several critics have opposed Altick, notably Martin J. Svaglic in *VP* v, no. 2 (Summer 1967). I am in general agreement with Svaglic, particularly with his statement that 'The meaning of any poem is communicated . . . by its feeling and tone as well as by its literal statement. The ultimate appeal is to the effect ordinarily produced by a work on a normally qualified reader' (p. 101). But Altick is quite justified, in his introductory comment on Svaglic's article, in insisting on the 'frequent ambivalence' in Browning's dramatic poems.

hexameter line in Greek and Latin verse contributes to the triumphant assertion of the whole poem, and it is difficult to believe
that Browning's own view was very different from that of the
speaker, or that he failed to share his admiration for a man who
might have been portrayed as Mr. Casaubon is portrayed in *Middle-
march*, but who is in fact presented as Browning's heroes are usually
presented:

> That low man goes on adding one to one,
>   His hundred's soon hit:
> This high man, aiming at a million,
>   Misses an unit.
> That, has the world here—should he need the next,
>   Let the world mind him!
> This, throws himself on God, and unperplexed
>   Seeking shall find him.

Whereas the Grammarian has succeeded in saving his soul, in a
sense that has seemed paradoxical to many readers, the lovers in
'The Statue and the Bust' fail to save theirs, in a sense that has
seemed not merely paradoxical but morally objectionable to a
number of critics. In this poem Browning illustrates a characteristic precept—

> Let a man contend to the uttermost
> For his life's set prize, be it what it will!

—by retelling a traditional story connected with Giovanni da
Bologna's equestrian statue of the Grand Duke Ferdinand in the
Annunziata Piazza in Florence. It is a story of love at first sight, and
we notice that loving the lady has a beneficial effect on the lover,
as is required in stories of *l'amour courtois*:

> And lo, a blade for a knight's emprise
> Filled the fine empty sheath of a man,—
> The Duke grew straightway brave and wise.

Browning's conciseness is brilliantly exemplified in the following
tercet:

> He looked at her, as a lover can;
> She looked at him, as one who awakes:
> The past was a sleep, and her life began.

The question is whether the lover will have the courage to play Perseus to his Andromeda. In the event both he and his lady delay, and their opportunity slips away for ever while they console themselves with trivial enjoyments and with the commonplace reflection that

> The world and its ways have a certain worth.

Realizing that her beauty is departing, the lady commissions one of the della Robbias to make a bust of her before it is too late, while the Duke has a statue made of himself which will mislead succeeding generations into thinking of him as a triumphantly successful man.

It is curious to contrast Browning's attitude to sculptured forms in this poem with that of Keats in the 'Ode on a Grecian Urn'. Whereas Keats reflects that the lover on the Urn will love 'for ever', as his beloved will be 'for ever . . . fair', Browning sees the sculptured forms of his lovers as cold and dead, reflecting the futility of a man and woman who have lacked the courage to act. In his tomb the Duke will mock at those who believe that he was a man of determination, while the lady will pass the

> Dreary days which the dead must spend
> Down in their darkness under the aisle

in reflecting:

> . . . 'What matters it at the end?
> 'I did no more while my heart was warm
> 'Than does that image, my pale-faced friend'.

One has only to remember the 'Ode on a Grecian Urn' to be struck by the pace of the verse in Browning's poem. The metre is a shortened form of *terza rima*, with numerous anapaests, and the speed with which it moves contrasts ironically with the failure to act which is the theme of the poem, as well as expressing the impatience of the narrator with that failure to act. The importance of riding to Browning's imagination has already been stressed:[14] it plays a vital part in two of the Dramatic Romances, 'The Flight of the Duchess' and 'The Last Ride Together'. In 'The Statue and the

[14] pp. 98-9, 162, above.

Bust' the lady first sees the Duke (as Criseyde, in Chaucer's great poem, first sees Troilus) as he passes under her window on horseback, and asks:

> 'Who rides by with the royal air?'

When she decides to postpone her escape for a day, for her father's sake—the fatal beginning of the procrastination which is the theme of the poem—she comforts herself with the reflection that

> . . . the Duke rides past, I know;
> We shall see each other, sure as fate.

When the Duke postpones matters further because 'the Envoy arrives from France' there is unconscious irony in his comment:

> To-day is not wholly lost, beside,
> With its hope of my lady's countenance:

> For I ride—what should I do but ride?
> And passing her palace, if I list,
> May glance at its window—well betide!

The question is whether his riding may again prove as 'idle' as it has been in the past (l. 14), and that is precisely what happens. The final irony is contained in his decision to have himself sculpted in the vigorous posture of a man on horseback:

> John of Douay shall effect my plan,
> Set me on horseback here aloft,
> Alive, as the crafty sculptor can,

> In the very square I have crossed so oft:
> That men may admire . . .

Men will believe that he took 'his pleasure once', not suspecting that the imposing figure on the horse was in fact incapable of riding away into happiness, unlike the determined heroine of 'The Flight of the Duchess'.

As has already been mentioned, the rushing speed of the verse expresses the impatience of the narrator with the lovers' failure to act. If we were to take this verse movement as expressive of something rash and unreliable in the character of the narrator, that would do away at a stroke with the difficulty that many readers have found in accepting the apparent moral of the poem, a difficulty indignantly expressed by Berdoe when he wrote:

If every woman flew to the arms of the man whom she liked better than her own husband, and if every governor of a city felt himself at liberty to steal another man's wife merely to complete and perfect the circle of his own delights, society would soon be thrown back into barbarism.[15]

Yet such a solution would not be convincing: except for the fact that he makes him refer to 'our townsmen' (which might be taken to differentiate him from an Englishman), Browning makes no attempt to characterize the speaker, unless he does so through the verse; while the lines that contain the moral of the story occur in a sort of epilogue which is separated from the narrative proper by a line across the page: that the speaker in this epilogue is the poet himself is hardly in greater doubt than that he is the speaker of the epilogue to 'Bishop Blougram's Apology'.

Mrs. Sutherland Orr rightly classifies 'The Statue and the Bust' as one of Browning's few 'Didactic Poems',[16] and it is none the less didactic because he draws 'the non-obvious or inverted moral'.[17] In this poem, as in the poem that he was thinking of writing in his old age, and which he described to Edmund Gosse, Browning had the outline of a story which he could fill in and interpret as he chose. Whereas in the unwritten poem 'the act of spirited defiance was shown to be, really, an act of tame renunciation, the poverty of the artist's spirit being proved in his eagerness to snatch, even though it was by honest merit, a benefit simply material', in 'The Statue and the Bust' what another poet might have interpreted as moral self-restraint is 'shown to be, really, an act of tame renunciation, the poverty of the [lovers'] spirit being proved in [their willingness to be content with] a benefit simply [prudential]'. It hardly seems

---

[15] *The Browning Cyclopaedia* (6th edn., 1909), p. 519: cited by W. O. Raymond in *The Infinite Moment* (2nd edn., Toronto, 1965), p. 217.

[16] *Handbook*, pp. 205–6. The only other poems in this category are 'A Death in the Desert', 'Rabbi Ben Ezra', and 'Deaf and Dumb'; but Mrs. Orr also has a category of 'Critical Poems' which includes a number of poems that contain a marked element of didacticism.

[17] Cf. p. 78, above.

necessary to indulge in subtle casuistry about so successful a poem. It is true that Browning was a little uneasy about the conclusion, as he revised the word 'crime' in the third line from the end—

Though the end in sight was a crime, I say

—to 'vice': a revision that is hardly an improvement, since it might be argued that a 'crime' is a legal concept, whereas a 'vice' is a moral one, so that it might be wrong (from the standpoint of an enlightened morality) to refrain from committing what is technically a crime. But the moral of the poem is not in doubt, and it is interesting to find Browning enforcing it with two Biblical phrases, 'the unlit lamp and the ungirt loin'.[18] His final address to readers who pride themselves on their 'virtue', with the words '*De te, fabula*', may be taken either to mean that they are deterred from 'crime' or 'vice' only by fear, or that they have as much need of courage in pursuing virtue as these lovers had in pursuing 'vice'— and may equally be found wanting, when the test comes.[19]

While one reason why the story appealed to Browning was clearly that it illustrated so well his own belief in the importance of an individual's seizing his great opportunity, and so making (in the true sense) a success of his life, another (closely related to that) must have been the fact that it was a tale of two lovers who had lacked the courage which he and his wife had displayed a few years before.[20] The general parallel between the lovers and the Brownings is unmistakable, with Riccardi playing the part of Mr. Barrett: one notices (in particular) that the lady is a prisoner in her room, as Elizabeth Barrett had been, and that her husband uses her real or

[18] The first phrase refers to Matthew 25, where we read how the foolish virgins were unable to go to the marriage because they had no oil for their lamps. The second refers to 1 Peter 1: 13. 'Gird up the loins of your mind' means 'Let your minds be intent upon, ready, and prepared for your spiritual work': Cruden's *Concordance*, ad loc.

[19] Raymond's chapter in *The Infinite Moment* contains a useful discussion of the morality of the ending. He rightly points out that what Browning 'singles out and dwells upon is the weakness and cowardice of the lovers' procrastination and lack of resolution' (p. 215). He goes on to say: 'Had they repented of their sinful passion and been deterred from eloping by moral considerations, he would have commended them.' No doubt he would, but it is very unlikely that Browning would have chosen to write a poem on such a subject.

[20] DeVane naturally gives the poem a prominent place in his important essay, 'The Virgin and the Dragon' (*Yale Review*, 37 (1947), 33–46, reprinted in Drew).

supposed bad health as an excuse for rejecting the suggestion that a party should be held at Petraja:

> But, alas! my lady leaves the South;
> Each wind that comes from the Appenine
> Is a menace to her tender youth:
>
> Not a way exists, the wise opine,
> If she quits her palace twice this year,
> To avert the flower of life's decline.

No other poem of Browning's has been interpreted so variously as 'Childe Roland to the Dark Tower Came'. It is more than sixty years since Saintsbury described it as an 'admirable thing, on which almost more nonsense has been talked than on anything else even of Browning's',[21] and in these years the amount of 'nonsense' has greatly increased, as has the amount of illuminating commentary. To the first category we must consign the view of a usually intelligent critic who has managed to convince himself that there is 'a neglected social dimension in the symbolism', and that the poem should be read as 'Browning's Industrial Nightmare':[22] in the second we find an outstanding article on the sources of 'Childe Roland' by a scholar partly inspired by the researches of Livingston Lowes on Coleridge.[23] Serious and responsible critics have read the poem in widely differing ways: it is an allegory of dying, or an archetype of rebirth:[24] it 'describes a brave knight performing a pilgrimage, in which hitherto all who attempted it have failed'— or it describes 'the retribution appropriate to [Browning's] own sin: the corruption and sterility that must claim one who has failed, like many another "poor traitor" before him, to deliver to mankind the full burden of the message with which he has been entrusted':[25] it is a poem in which Browning expresses views

---

[21] *A History of English Prosody*, iii (1910), 230. It is remarkable that Saintsbury himself gives an erroneous account of the rhyme scheme, which is abbaab, not aabccb, as he states.

[22] D. V. Erdman, 'Browning's Industrial Nightmare', *PQ* 36, no. 4 (October 1957), 422.

[23] Harold Golder: see pp. 181 ff., below.

[24] Dying: J. Kirkman, *Browning Society Papers*, 1 (1881–4), 21–7: rebirth: C. R. Woodward, 'The Road to the Dark Tower . . .', *Tennessee Studies in Literature* (Knoxville, 1961), pp. 93–9.

[25] Mrs. Sutherland Orr, *Handbook*, p. 273; Miller, p. 168.

characteristic of his thinking as a whole—or it is 'a poem of hate, of the thoughts Browning habitually fought and repressed':[26] it is a poem describing a success, or a poem describing a failure.

One has only to reread 'Childe Roland' to realize why it should have occasioned such a confusion of critics. No sooner is the reader's imagination engaged, as it is from the first line onwards, than he finds himself asking a number of questions: What is the point of the initial reference to *King Lear*? Who is the 'hoary cripple' at the beginning, and why does the narrator follow his directions if he believes that they are false? What is the Dark Tower? Is the narrator's aim in seeking the Tower simply to fail, and so (in his weariness) to find 'some end'? Who were

> The knights who to the Dark Tower's search addressed
> Their steps?

Why should the narrator have to be 'fit' to fail, as the others of the band have failed—particularly as they seem to have failed disgracefully?[27] If the whole aim of the present quest is to die and fail as they have done, then what is the meaning of the words 'Better this present than a past like that'? What (if any) precise significance are we to attach to the details of the nightmare landscape through which the Childe makes his way? What is the meaning of the final scene, in which 'the lost adventurers my peers' watch him from the hillside as he faces the ultimate test? What is that test? What is the 'slug-horn' that plays such an important part in the last stanza? What (above all) is the meaning of the final words of the poem, '*Childe Roland to the Dark Tower came*', which brings us back to the question about *King Lear*? And finally, as a sort of postscript, how much validity is there in the argument that the Childe must

---

[26] Melchiori, p. 139. Mrs. Melchiori immediately qualifies her statement by adding that this 'does not mean that it is to be regarded as a statement of what Browning really believed. It is one-sided.'

[27] Cuthbert was disgraced by one night (l. 95), while Giles died a 'Poor traitor, spit upon and curst' (l. 102): we notice that the stanza describing him (xvii) contains an obvious allusion to *Macbeth*, I. vii. 46:

> What honest men should dare (he said) he durst.
> Good—but the scene shifts—faugh! what hangman-hands
> Pin to his breast a parchment? His own bands
> Read it. Poor traitor, spit upon and curst!

have survived and therefore presumably succeeded, as he has lived to tell his tale?[28]

Little is known about the origin of the poem. It is uncertain whether it was written at the beginning of 1852, as Griffin and Minchin affirm, or during the following year.[29] Much more important, however, is Browning's own statement that it 'came to me as a kind of dream'. 'I had to write it, then and there', he added, 'and I finished it the same day, I believe'.[30] Although he was always impatient with people who interrogated him about the poem, he seems to have told Mrs. Orr that the 'picturesque details' which we find in it 'included a tower which [he] once saw in the Carrara Mountains, a painting which caught his eye years later in Paris; and the figure of a horse in the tapestry in his own drawing-room'.[31] In a letter to a painter who illustrated the poem he gave a little further information:

My own 'marsh' was only made out of my head,—with some recollection of a strange solitary little tower I have come upon more than once in Massa-Carrara, in the midst of low hills.[32]

It is obvious that a number of visual details came together in his mind as he composed the poem, and DeVane is probably correct in suggesting that the chapters in *The Art of Painting* by Gerard de Lairesse describing beauty and ugliness in landscape also influenced its composition.[33]

While visual memories contributed to the inspiration of 'Childe Roland', however, it is clear that literary recollections were of much greater importance, since they provided the story round which the visual images took up their positions. The most remarkable contribution to our understanding of this aspect of the poem's inspiration was made by Harold Golder almost fifty years ago.[34] Starting from

[28] Langbaum has an interesting discussion of this problem, on pp. 197–200 of *The Poetry of Experience*.

[29] See pp. 135n–136n, above.

[30] Lilian Whiting, *The Brownings* (Boston, 1911), p. 261.

[31] *Handbook*, p. 274 n. Mrs. Orr introduces this information by saying that she 'may venture to state' it.   [32] *New Letters*, pp. 172–3.

[33] 'The Landscape of Browning's *Childe Roland*', *PMLA* 40 (1925), 426–32.

[34] 'Browning's *Childe Roland*', *PMLA* 39 (1924), 963–78. It is surprising that the article has not been reprinted by Drew or by Litzinger and Knickerbocker. There is

the words in *King Lear* on which Browning insisted as the inspiration of the poem, Golder reminds his readers of the immediately
succeeding lines—

> His word was still,—Fie, foh, and fum,
> I smell the blood of a British man

—and comments:

The problem lies in establishing a subconscious connection between
Edgar's maudlin words and the material from which Browning
obviously drew; it consists in discovering some threads of association
that will bind them to the great field of romance in so close a way that
the poet would have been conscious of the song and not of the
romances in a frank statement of his sources.[35]

Golder points out that the phrase 'Fie, foh, and fum' is to be
found in such children's tales as 'Hop-o'-my-thumb', 'Jack and the
Bean-stalk', and 'Jack the Giant-killer', and that these must have
lain so deep among Browning's childhood memories that 'he
would be hardly conscious of their presence or see any necessity of
referring to them in citing the song as the germ of his poem'.
Quoting lines 131–3 of 'A Lovers' Quarrel'—

> I would laugh like the valiant Thumb
> Facing the castle glum
> And the giant's fee-faw-fum!

—Golder comments that Browning 'has obviously confused these
tales ['Tom Thumb' and 'Hop-o'-my-Thumb'] with others in
which the main character is a fighting hero'. He points out that

The hero of *Jack and the Bean-stalk* travels, as does Roland, through
a desolate country on his way to the giant's castle. In most chap-book
versions this plain is described as 'a desert, quite barren; not a tree,
shrub, house, or living creature to be seen'; but in some forms of the
tale this description is expanded to include 'scattered fragments of

an interesting footnote to Golder's article (p. 977) in which he comments that 'The
richness of the background in *Kubla Khan* will be more apparent when Dr. J. L.
Lowes' studies in Coleridge are published.' When *The Road to Xanadu* was published,
in 1927, Golder was one of the colleagues and friends whose help was acknowledged in
the preface.

[35] p. 964.

stone; and at unequal distances, small heaps of earth . . . loosely thrown together'.[36]

Golder also reminds us of the last episode in *Jack the Giant-Killer*, with its obvious relevance to Browning's poem. In the evening the hero comes to the foot of a mountain, where he meets a man 'with a head as white as snow':

This man guides him to a castle, shared by a giant and an enchanter, where a host of lost adventurers, who had previously essayed the conquest of the tower, lie imprisoned. On arriving before the gates, Jack finds a golden trumpet hanging suspended by a silver chain, under which is written:

> 'Whoever can this trumpet blow,
> Shall soon the giant overthrow,
> And break the black enchantment straight,
> So all shall be in happy state'.

Whereupon, 'Jack had no sooner read this inscription, but he blew the trumpet.'

As Golder points out, the main features of 'Childe Roland' may be found in one or other of these two stories; while

Both are logically connected with the *Lear* passage through the 'fie-foh-fum' verse and, as the lines from *A Lovers' Quarrel* show, the Dark Tower. . . . But it is obvious that the nursery tale material is only intermediary [he continues]; the larger background for the poem is still to be sought among the romances.

Accordingly Golder goes to Spenser and other romance sources and shows an affinity between the cripple whom the speaker consults and Archimago and the old man whom Prince Arthur encounters in Book I, c. viii, s. 30. He compares the desolate country which Roland has to traverse with 'the frightful battlefield of Roncevaux, with which the name of Roland has a direct connection', and more particularly with the haunts of Friston, in *Don Belianis of Greece*. As a captive damsel describes it, this

may rightly be termed the Desert of Death; for all the Fields are blasted, and continual Mildews burn each plant, the Trees are bare,

---

[36] This and the following quotation are both from p. 966.

and on their naked tops, naught but Owls sit perching and Ravens building, no kindly Sunbeams shed their cheering Lustre, but all as melancholy as the Gloome of Death: here Ghosts do nightly Roam, and the infernal Spirits that obey the great Magitian.[37]

As Golder observes, a final scene in which the hero is watched by sympathetic observers is common, as is the idea of the hero blowing a horn to challenge an enemy in an apparently impregnable tower— this occurs in the *Orlando Furioso*, for example, and also in *The Faerie Queene* (I. viii. 3–4).

Two books which seem particularly closely connected with Browning's poem are *The Renowned History of the Seven Champions of Christendom* and *Palmerin of England*. In the former St. George comes to the country of the Amazons and finds it desolate because a certain necromancer has 'wrought the destruction of this . . . realm and kingdom';

for by his magic arts and damned charms, he raised from the earth a mighty tower, the mortar whereof he mingled with virgin's blood, wherein are such enchantments wrought, that the light of the sun and the brightness of the skies are quenched, and the earth blasted with a terrible vapour and black mist that ascended from the tower, whereby a general darkness overspread our land . . . so this country is clean wasted and destroyed.[38]

Undeterred by warnings, St. George crosses a river as black as pitch, with monstrous birds flying about his head. Golder also quotes two sentences from another episode of *The Seven Champions* which have a suggestive similarity to episodes in 'Childe Roland':

They proceeded toward the island where the knight of the Black Castle had his residence, guided only by the direction of the old man . . . The champions rode to the castle where they espied a pillar of beautiful jaspar stone, at which pillar hung a very costly silver trumpet, with certain letters carved about the same, which contained these words following:
> 'If any dare attempt this place to see,
> By sounding this, the gate shall opened be . . .'

which when St. George beheld, without any more tarrying, he set the silver trumpet to his mouth.[39]

[37] p. 969.   [38] p. 971.   [39] p. 972.

The first part of *Palmerin of England* tells of the rescue of the son of the King of England, who is a prisoner in a remote tower from which almost all the knights of Christendom have tried in vain to rescue him. It becomes known that the victory is reserved for one man, Palmerin: 'Many have and shall attempt, but he alone is ordained to finish this exploit.' It takes him years to find the place. One evening we find him sitting at the foot of a tree, his mind full of 'troublous thoughts' which 'made him the more desirous to be at the castle, where he would prove his fortune, and make an end of the adventure or of himself, as so many others had done'. At length he enters the valley of Perdition, where 'all adventurers were lost', and sees a tower ahead of him. When his enemy emerges for the combat Palmerin, 'seeing the battlement and the windows of the fortress full of his friends, and remembering that they were in captivity, and the confidence which they placed in him, fought with such hardiness and hardihood, that by dint of blows he laid the giant at his feet'.[40]

Only an ignorant reader would fail to notice something of this background to the poem, even on a first reading: only a very learned or complacent one would not feel his understanding of the poem deepened by Golder's article. It becomes clear that the stories Browning read as a boy, and heard told by his father, with his genius for entertaining his son, formed a great reservoir of material on which he was to draw, almost forty years later, as he sat writing this poem in Paris or Florence. We are reminded of a remark of Livingston Lowes about the boy Coleridge, 'the father of the man, if ever this was true',

who used to 'read through all the gilt-cover little books that could be had . . . and likewise all the uncovered tales of Tom Hickathrift, Jack the Giant-killer, etc., etc., etc., etc. And I used to lie by the wall and *mope*, and my spirits used to come upon me suddenly; and in a flood of them I was accustomed to race up and down the churchyard, and act over all I had been reading, on the docks, the nettles, and the rank grass'. So does every child. But the poet is he in whom the Vision does not die away, and in 'The Ancient Mariner' the child grown man was still 'acting over all he had been reading', but now the docks

[40] p. 973.

and nettles and rank grass had given place to the elements which clothe the sea with mystery and terror.[41]

Yet for us the important question still remains: what did Browning make of his materials, and what does his poem mean?

It is clear that the poem has a much greater psychological depth than the stories which helped to inspire it. *Mutatis mutandis*, a comment by Livingston Lowes is again applicable:

Images caught from the pages of Martens and Cook—the shadow of a sail, and a phosphorescent sea, and glowing animalculæ—flashed together . . . and coalesced in a single magical impression. The scattered elements of the picture are present, unmistakable, in the travel-books. But the picture itself is bathed in an atmosphere of which there is no slightest trace in Martens or in Cook.[42]

Whereas in the children's stories that Golder mentions the other adventurers are taken prisoner, or killed by a giant, in Browning's poem they have failed in a deeper, spiritual sense. In his poem, too, the landscape has a psychological significance that it does not have in the children's tales—though it is implicit (at least) in Spenser. DeVane pointed out that 'Childe Roland', 'almost alone of [Browning's] poems . . . depends upon, revolves about, and lives for the sake of the landscape': whereas 'his landscapes are generally brief and entirely subservient to narrative and character', in this poem 'the landscape is everything'.[43] As DeVane of course realized, this is because the landscape in this poem is not an external thing: as we read the poem the dreary and terrifying territory that the narrator describes becomes more and more evidently a landscape of the mind, as we move across the starved plain, with its sinister weeds and frightening horse, in the last stages of starvation, through the 'sudden little river',

> Which, while I forded,—good saints, how I feared
> To set my foot upon a dead man's cheek,
> Each step, or feel the spear I thrust to seek
> For hollows, tangled in his hair or beard!
> —It may have been a water-rat I speared,
> But, ugh! it sounded like a baby's shriek.   (xxi)

[41] *The Road to Xanadu* (edn. of 1930), p. 131.   [42] Ibid., p. 329.
[43] 'The Landscape of Browning's *Childe Roland*', 427.

He moves on, always on foot—the hero in many of the tales is on horseback, but the symbolical connotations of riding for Browning would be quite incompatible with the mood of this poem as a whole: Childe Roland is a pilgrim, making his weary way along with no support but a stick or a sword with which to defend himself—and comes to a place where the state of the ground suggests that there has been a great battle. Images of torture abound here—

> . . . Toads in a poisoned tank,
> Or wild cats in a red-hot iron cage,

'galley-slaves the Turk / Pits for his pastime, Christians against Jews', and a terrifying engine:

> What bad use was that engine for, that wheel,
> Or brake, not wheel—that harrow fit to reel
> Men's bodies out like silk? with all the air
> Of Tophet's tool, on earth left unaware,
> Or brought to sharpen its rusty teeth of steel. (xxiv)

'Tophet's tool' is a powerful image, largely because of its vagueness. Strictly Tophet was 'a place or object in the valley of Hinnom, . . . where human sacrifices were burned by idolatrous Israelites in the worship of Moloch',[44] but the word is often used simply as a synonym for Hell. One critic has oddly argued that although the Childe, 'living of course in some pre-industrial era . . . must think in pre-industrial terms', this is really a reference to the exploitation of labour in the factories,[45] but the true inspiration of this compelling dream goes much deeper than that. The engravings of Piranesi known as the 'Carceri d'Invenzione' may well have contributed to the background, but the frightening bird that appears at line 160 suggests an unmistakable context:

> A great black bird, Apollyon's bosom-friend.

Against this we may set a passage from *The Pilgrim's Progress*:

But now in this Valley of *Humiliation* poor *Christian* was hard put to it, for he had gone but a little way before he espied a foul *Fiend* coming over the field to meet him; his name is *Apollyon*. Then did *Christian*

---

[44] *The Oxford Dictionary of the Christian Church*, ed. F. L. Cross, 1957.
[45] D. V. Erdman, loc. cit., p. 432.

begin to be afraid, and to cast in his mind whether to go back, or to stand his ground. But he . . . resolved to venture, and stand his ground. For thought he, had I no more in mine eye, then the saving of my life, 'twould be the best way to stand.

So he went on, and *Apollyon* met him; now the Monster was hidious to behold, he was cloathed with scales like a Fish . . . he had Wings like a Dragon, feet like a Bear, and out of his belly came Fire and Smoak, and his mouth was as the mouth of a Lion.[46]

The fact that Apollyon's wide wings are 'dragon-penned' confirms the relevance of this passage, which has already been cited by more than one critic.[47]

Browning must have known *The Pilgrim's Progress* from early childhood. In a letter to William Hale White ('Mark Rutherford') written in 1879 Browning expressed his pleasure at receiving a communication from 'a lover of Bunyan . . . the object of my utmost admiration and reverence'.[48] White had probably alluded to the fact that the poem 'Ned Bratts' had been written with 'the story of "Old Tod", as told in Bunyan's "Life and Death of Mr. Badman" . . . distinctly in . . . mind'.[49] When White insisted on giving him a portrait of Bunyan, Browning replied: 'The admirable portrait shall grace this room wherein I write, by the side of Spenser and Milton.' Nothing could have been more appropriate, for Bunyan was clearly one of the major imaginative influences throughout Browning's poetic career.[50]

Two other descriptions in *The Pilgrim's Progress* were probably at the back of Browning's mind as he wrote 'Childe Roland'. The first is the description of 'the Valley of the shadow of Death', and particularly its second part:

for you must note, that tho the first part of the Valley of the shadow of Death was dangerous, yet this second part which he was yet to go,

---

[46] *The Pilgrim's Progress*, ed. J. B. Wharey, rev. R. Sharrock (Oxford, 1960), p. 56.
[47] e.g. by Mrs. Melchiori, p. 128.
[48] *New Letters*, pp. 251–2.   [49] *Letters*, p. 209.
[50] We know that he gave an illustrated edition of *The Pilgrim's Progress* to Pen in 1862, and wrote his name in a folio edition of Bunyan's *Works* in 1878 (*Sale Catalogue*, p. 85). It is tempting to suppose that he knew Thomas Stothard's illustrations for the 1788 edition: 'Apollyon spread forth his dragon's wings and sped him away' (reproduced in *John Bunyan: The Man and his Works*, by Henri Talon, translated into English by Barbara Wall (1951), opposite p. 26) has an obvious relevance to 'Childe Roland'.

was, if possible, far more dangerous: for from the place where he now stood, even to the end of the Valley, the way was all along set . . . full of Snares, Traps, Gins, and Nets here, and . . . full of Pits, Pitfalls, deep holes, and shelvings down there.[51]

The second passage occurs near the beginning of Bunyan's Dream:

I . . . said; Sir, Wherefore, since over this place is the way from the City of *Destruction*, to yonder *Gate*, is it, that *this* Plat is not mended, that poor Travellers might go thither with more security? And he said unto me, this *Miry slow*, is such a place as cannot be mended: It is the descent whither the scum and filth that attends conviction for sin doth continually run, and therefore is it called the *Slough of Dispond*: for still as the sinner is awakened about his lost condition, there ariseth in his soul many fears, and doubts, and discouraging apprehensions, which all of them get together, and settle in this place: And this is the reason of the badness of this ground.

Browning's debt to Bunyan does not provide any kind of master-key to the interpretation of 'Childe Roland': it is simply an important element in the poem—an element that blended well with the romance background which has already been illustrated, for it is clear that Bunyan was indebted both to Spenser and to the various streams of romance tradition which pour into the great ocean of *The Faerie Queene*.[52]

There is a passage on 'The Ancient Mariner' by D. W. Harding which has an obvious relevance to Browning's poem:

The human experience around which Coleridge centres the poem is surely the depression and the sense of isolation and unworthiness which the Mariner describes in Part IV. The suffering he describes is of a kind which is perhaps not found except in slightly pathological conditions, but which, pathological or not, has been felt by a great many people. He feels isolated. . . . At the same time he is not just physically isolated but is socially abandoned, even by those with the greatest obligations. . . . With this desertion the beauty of the ordinary world has been taken away. . . . All that is left, and especially, centrally, oneself, is disgustingly worthless. . . . With the sense of

---

[51] Ed. cit., p. 65: the second quotation is from p. 15.

[52] See, in particular, four articles by Harold Golder: 'John Bunyan's Hypocrisy', *North American Review*, vol. 223 (1926); 'Bunyan's Valley of the Shadow', *MP* 27 (1929–30), 55–72; 'Bunyan and Spenser', *PMLA* 45 (1930), 216–37; and 'Bunyan's Giant Despair', *JEGP* 30 (1931), 361–78.

worthlessness there is also guilt. . . . And enveloping the whole experience is the sense of sapped energy, oppressive weariness. . . . A usual feature of these states of pathological misery is their apparent causelessness. The depression cannot be rationally explained; the conviction of guilt and worthlessness is out of proportion to any ordinary offence actually committed.[53]

But the differences between the two poems are at least as interesting as the similarities. Unlike the Mariner's, the Childe's nightmare journey is a journey by land—Browning was not as fascinated by the sea as many English poets have been—and the Childe is a much more active and striving figure than the Mariner.While it is clear that he is confronting a tremendous challenge, and that he refuses to give up, it is uncertain whether he feels guilty. Near the end (indeed) he certainly feels guilt, when he realizes that he has failed to recognize the ultimate test, for which he has been preparing all his life:

> . . . Dunce,
> Dotard, a-dozing at the very nonce,
> After a life spent training for the sight!

A great noise sounds in his ears at the moment of the final challenge:

> Not hear? when noise was everywhere! it tolled
>   Increasing like a bell. Names in my ears
>   Of all the lost adventurers my peers,—
> How such a one was strong, and such was bold,
> And such was fortunate, yet each of old
>   Lost, lost! one moment knelled the woe of years.
>
> There they stood, ranged along the hill-sides, met
>   To view the last of me, a living frame
>   For one more picture! in a sheet of flame
> I saw them and I knew them all. And yet
> Dauntless the slug-horn[54] to my lips I set,
>   And blew. 'Childe Roland to the Dark Tower came'.

---

[53] *Scrutiny*, 9 (March 1941), 335–6.

[54] Browning found this word, which is bogus English, in Chatterton: see, for example, his 'Battle of Hastings (No. 2)', stanza x:

> Some caught a slughorne, and an onsett wounde;
> Kynge Harolde hearde the charge, and wondred at the sounde.

The word also occurs in 'The Tournament', l. 31, where it is glossed as 'a kind of claryon'.

Few poems can rival this in organic unity: on our interpretation of the last line depends our interpretation of the poem as a whole, or—to put the matter more accurately—our interpretation of the last line grows out of our interpretation of the poem as a whole.

A number of critics have taken the final lines as a record of failure. One of the earliest writers to comment on the connection with Bunyan, R. J. Gratz, believed that Childe Roland finds himself 'at last surrounded by the ugly heights of Doubting Castle, one more victim of Giant Despair'.[55] Betty Miller (in a passage already quoted) tells us that the vision which inspired the poem revealed to Browning 'in a landscape fully as ominous as that of Dante's *Inferno* . . . the retribution appropriate to his own sin'—the failure to deliver his message to mankind. More recently still, Mrs. Melchiori considers that 'Childe Roland's turning-off toward the dark tower is a form of suicide' resulting from despair occasioned by 'the reversal and overturning of all the values which Browning accepted and in which he believed': she finds in the poem 'the triumph of evil which we meet with in Poe's "Metzengerstein" or in Shelley's *Zastrozzi*, and the triumph of despair'.[56] Such readings are very hard to reconcile with the penultimate line of the poem. What happens to the Childe after he has blown the horn we do not know: this is (no doubt) the point at which the dreamer awakes. Yet whatever is about to happen, there is surely a sense in which, by the very act of blowing the horn, 'Dauntless', the dreamer triumphs. Whether we are to suppose that he defeats the giant or other enemy who is to be found inside the Tower, or that he is killed by him, it is hard to believe that he is other than successful, even if death is the condition of his success. We are reminded of the question posed near the end of *Sordello*, as expressed in Browning's own running summary: 'There is a life beyond life, and with new conditions of success, nor such as, in this, produce failure. But, even here, is failure inevitable? Or may failure here be success also when induced by love? Sordello knows: but too late . . . .' The striking similarities between the imagery of 'Childe Roland' and 'Prospice' have been pointed out by several critics, and we recall that the speaker in that poem is so far from committing suicide that he wishes to approach 'the post of the foe' without fear and in full consciousness:

> Where he stands, the Arch Fear in a visible form,
>   Yet the strong man must go:
> For the journey is done and the summit attained,
>   And the barriers fall,
> Though a battle's to fight ere the guerdon be gained,
>   The reward of it all.

The Childe, too, has completed his journey, and when he blows his 'slug-horn' we must suppose that 'the barriers fall', however terrifying the 'Arch Fear' may be with whom he is to do battle, and whatever the outcome of the battle.

If we are at liberty to go as far as that in interpretation, we are certainly unwise to go any further. Such questions as those of the identity of the cripple and of the former colleagues who have some-how proved traitors—and indeed the problem of the significance of the Dark Tower itself—are not susceptible of an exclusive and precise answer. As Robert Penn Warren observed of 'The Ancient Mariner':

If we take the poem as a symbolic poem, we are not permitted to read it in the way which Coleridge called allegorical. We cannot, for instance, say that the Pilot equals the Church, or that the Hermit equals the 'idea of an enlightened religion which is acquainted with the life of the spirit' . . . This allegorical kind of reading makes the poem into a system of equivalents in a discursive sequence. But, as a matter of fact, we must read it as . . . operating on more than one thematic level, as embodying a complex of feelings and ideas not to be differentiated except in so far as we discursively explore the poem itself.[57]

To attempt to provide a literal equivalent for each of the symbols of which the dream consists can only reduce its imaginative power.

To illustrate this point further, we may turn for a moment to Kafka. In his study of that writer Politzer takes the following fragment as the subject of his first chapter: the title of the fragment is 'Gibs auf!'—'Give it up!':

---

[57] 'A Poem of Pure Imagination: An Experiment in Reading', in his *Selected Essays* (edn. of 1958), p. 221.

It was very early in the morning, the streets clean and deserted, I was on my way to the station. As I compared the tower clock with my watch I realized it was much later than I had thought, and that I had to hurry; the shock of this discovery made me feel uncertain of the way, I wasn't very well acquainted with the town as yet; fortunately there was a policeman at hand, I ran to him and breathlessly asked him the way. He smiled and said: 'You asking me the way?' 'Yes', I said, 'since I can't find it myself.' 'Give it up! Give it up!' said he, and turned with a sudden jerk, like someone who wants to be alone with his laughter.[58]

In a brief 'Discourse on Method' Politzer presents various interpretations of this fragment and concludes that they 'are not mutually exclusive. On the contrary, if they are added together they still do not suffice to exhaust the meaning hidden in the anecdote'.[58] The same is true of cut-and-dried interpretations of 'Childe Roland'. When, near the end of his life, Browning was asked whether he accepted one particular allegorical interpretation he replied, in a comment already quoted in part:

Oh, no, not at all. Understand, I don't repudiate it, either. I only mean I was conscious of no allegorical intention in writing it. . . . [It] came to me as a kind of dream. I had to write it, then and there, and I finished it the same day, I believe. But it was simply that I had to do it. I did not know then what I meant beyond that, and I'm sure I don't know now. But I am very fond of it.[59]

With this we may juxtapose a comment of Humphry House's on 'The Ancient Mariner':

It is surely clear that Coleridge never said or meant that the 'Mariner' neither had nor was meant to have a moral meaning or a 'moral sentiment'. He said the fault was *'the obtrusion* of the moral sentiment *so openly* . . . in a work of such pure imagination'.[60]

Mrs. Orr remarks that no 'definite moral' can be extracted from the poem;[61] yet when Browning was asked by J. W. Chadwick whether its meaning could not be expressed in the phrase 'He that endureth

[58] Heinz Politzer, *Franz Kafka: Parable and Paradox* (Ithaca, New York, 1962), p. 14.
[59] Lilian Whiting, *The Brownings*, p. 261.
[60] *Coleridge* (1953), p. 91.
[61] *Handbook*, p. 274.

to the end shall be saved', Browning replied: 'Yes, just about that.'[62] Like so many of Browning's poems, 'Childe Roland' has for its central theme the problem of saving one's soul, of creating something significant out of one's existence on earth. What makes it unique in his work is that it is the only major poem in which he gives such powerful expression to the night-side of his nature. Edwin Muir once wrote:

If we judge Browning by his best work, then it is as absurd to call him an optimist as it would be to call Dante an optimist because the *Divine Comedy* begins in Hell and ends in Heaven. What happened to him when he spoke directly of his hopes was that he forgot the more formidable elements in his imaginative world. He had to to enter into the lives of people quite unlike himself before he could realise all the obstacles to his easy faith in things.[63]

In 'Childe Roland' Browning did not enter into the life of another man, he simply recorded 'a kind of dream' inspired by his deepest fears of failure and spiritual inadequacy.

[62] J. W. Chadwick, 'An Eagle Feather', in *The Christian Register*, lxvii (19 Jan., 1888), 37–8. Quoted in DeVane, p. 231. Cf. Matthew 10: 22.
[63] *Essays on Literature and Society* (1949), p. 105.

XII

THE 'MEN AND WOMEN' POEMS

I have been all my life asking what connection there is between the satisfaction at the display of power, and the sympathy with—ever-increasing sympathy with—all imaginable weakness?[1]

As we have seen, when Browning decided to classify his shorter poems in the edition of 1863 he found that most of them could be described as either (Dramatic) Lyrics or (Dramatic) Romances. For those which fell into neither category he reverted to the title of his great collection of 1855, calling them simply 'Men, and Women'.[2] In 1863 there were twelve poems in this category, in 1868 and subsequently there were thirteen. 'Johannes Agricola', the poem added in 1868, had been published as early as 1836, and four of the other poems had also been published before 1855: 'Artemis Prologizes', 'Pictor Ignotus', 'The Bishop Orders his Tomb', and 'Rudel to the Lady of Tripoli'. While it is easy to see why 'Johannes Agricola', 'Pictor Ignotus', and 'The Bishop Orders his Tomb' were classified in this way, the other two poems do not seem very much at home in the category in which Browning placed them. Three of the 1855 poems have also the air of intruders, three poems (we notice) which relate to Browning's own life and his reflections on his art: in 'Transcendentalism' he imagines a Naddo-like critic[3] objecting to the work of a poet like himself, a man who is not content to 'sing': in 'How It Strikes a Contemporary' the speaker describes an 'objective poet' (to borrow a phrase from Browning's essay on Shelley) who has an obvious affinity to his own view of his role as a poet: while in 'One Word More' he speaks in his own person, celebrating his love for his wife and making incidental

---

[1] Browning to Elizabeth Barrett, 16 Nov. 1845: Kintner, i. 270.
[2] After 1863 the unnecessary comma disappears.   [3] Cf. pp. 47–8, above.

remarks about his poetry. The fact that five of the 'Men and Women' poems have little in common with the remainder suggests that this division of Browning's work is largely a category of residue: the section into which he put those poems which could neither be described as Dramatic Lyrics nor as Dramatic Romances.[4] To a limited extent the remaining eight poems, which include most of the poems now commonly referred to as the best of Browning's 'dramatic monologues', may be regarded as forming a homogeneous division of his work. All but two of them ('Johannes Agricola' and 'Pictor Ignotus') are in blank verse, and they fall naturally into three groups. There are three monologues spoken by churchmen, three spoken by painters, and two verse-epistles. In the monologues spoken by churchmen and painters Browning is not primarily concerned to tell a story (as in a Dramatic Romance) or to describe a mood (as in a Dramatic Lyric): his aim (in general terms) is to depict a man as he is, with such autobiographical flashbacks as may be necessary to explain the character of the speaker. In the two-verse epistles (as I shall try to show) the nature of Browning's purpose has begun to change, and even within the central group of six of these 'Men and Women' poems distinctions and qualifications require to be made. The making of these distinctions will be the business of the present chapter.

Before we consider 'The Bishop Orders his Tomb' and 'Bishop Blougram's Apology', it will be useful to glance back at the first monologue spoken by a man of religion, 'Johannes Agricola in Meditation'. Even if Browning had not at one point yoked this poem with 'Porphyria's Lover' as one of two 'Madhouse Cells', the reader could be in no doubt that he is listening to the reflections of a religious maniac. So much is made clear by the short passage from the *Dictionary of all Religions* prefixed to the first printing of the poem, in which we are reminded that the Antinomians rejected the Law of Moses and believed that salvation was independent of good works.[5] The opening, in which the almost jaunty rhythm perfectly

---

[4] In spite of the title, none of the speakers is a woman—though one is a goddess. Perhaps 'Men, and Women' simply refers to the fact that several of the speakers are much concerned with women.

[5] 'Antinomians, so denominated for rejecting the Law as a thing of no use under the Gospel dispensation: they say, that good works do not further, nor evil works

fits the extraordinary nature of what is said, confirms our expectations:

> There's heaven above, and night by night
> I look right through its gorgeous roof;
> No suns and moons though e'er so bright
> Avail to stop me; splendour-proof
> I keep the broods of stars aloof.

The supernumerary fifth line at the end of each stanza enforces the effect of insane self-confidence. Starting from the premiss that God decided to create him 'ere he fashioned star or sun', Johannes concludes that it is God's will that he should grow,

> Guiltless for ever, like a tree
> That buds and blooms, nor seeks to know
> The law by which it prospers so.

Even if he should 'blend All hideous sins, as in a cup, To drink the mingled venoms up', he is convinced that he has 'God's warrant' that he will be saved.[6] He anticipates looking down from heaven 'on hell's fierce bed',

> And those its waves of flame oppress,
> Swarming in ghastly wretchedness;
> Whose life on earth aspired to be
> One altar-smoke, so pure!—to win

hinder salvation; that the child of God cannot sin, that God never chastiseth him, that murder, drunkenness, &c. are sins in the wicked but not in him, that the child of grace being once assured of salvation, afterwards never doubteth . . . that God doth not love any man for his holiness, that sanctification is no evidence of justification, &c. Pontanus, in his Catalogue of Heresies, says John Agricola was the author of this sect, A.D. 1535': *Dictionary of All Religions* (1704), quoted in the *Monthly Repository*, x (January 1836), 45.

[6] Cf. the reflections of the fanatical Robert Wringhim, in *The Private Memoirs and Confessions of a Justified Sinner*, by James Hogg, ed. John Carey ('Oxford English Novels', 1969), pp. 113–14: 'I had more sense than to regard either my good works, or my evil deeds, as in the smallest degree influencing the eternal decrees of God concerning me, either with regard to my acceptance or reprobation. I depended entirely on the bounty of free grace, holding all the righteousness of man as filthy rags, and believing in the momentous and magnificent truth, that the more heavily loaden with transgressions, the more welcome was the believer at the throne of grace. And I have reason to believe that it was this dependence and this belief that at last ensured my acceptance there.' It would be interesting to know whether this book, which so fascinated André Gide, was known to Browning.

> If not love like God's love for me,
>   At least to keep his anger in;
>   And all their striving turned to sin.
> Priest, doctor, hermit, monk grown white
>   With prayer, the broken-hearted nun,
> The martyr, the wan acolyte,
>   The incense-swinging child,—undone
> Before God fashioned star or sun!

With a powerful effect of dramatic irony, Johannes shies away from the absurdity of his own beliefs and concludes that God is to be praised precisely because his ways are incomprehensible:

> . . . How could I praise,
> If such as I might understand,
> Make out and reckon on his ways,
>   And bargain for his love, and stand,
>   Paying a price, at his right hand?

In sixty lines Browning shows the insane arrogance from which any appearance of humility in such a man must spring. If we are ever prepared to use the word 'satire' of a monologue by Browning, this poem is a satire—whether or not Clarence Tracy is right in conjecturing that Browning printed it in the *Monthly Repository* 'to satirize the Calvinistic doctrines' which may have been attractive to many of its readers.[7]

'The Bishop Orders his Tomb at Saint Praxed's Church' is another monologue spoken by a man of religion of whom Browning cannot be supposed to have approved, yet to describe it as a 'satire' would be to show oneself incapable of appreciating a poem which is as subtle as anything that Browning ever wrote.

We know from his earlier poems that Browning was particularly interested in the vision of life that may present itself to a dying man. Paracelsus reflects that the 'truth And power' of human life are revealed in various situations, and 'oftenest [at] death's approach': as he lies dying his 'varied life Drifts by' and he is able to 'turn new knowledge upon old events'—though with results that he feels he must not communicate to men who have not yet reached

---

7 'Browning's Heresies', *SP* 33 (1936), 618.

their own final hour.[8] The headline at the beginning of the last book of *Sordello* comments that 'At the close of a day or a life, past procedure is fitliest reviewed', while a year or so after the probable date of the composition of 'The Bishop Orders his Tomb' we find Browning translating a passage from Dante for the benefit of Elizabeth Barrett:

> And sinners were we to the extreme hour;
> *Then*, light from heaven fell, making us aware,
> So that, repenting us and pardoned, out
> Of life we passed to God, at peace with him
> Who fills the heart with yearning Him to see.[9]

'Which is just my Sordello's story', he commented. It is not his Bishop's story, by any means. No one should have known better than the Bishop the sort of thoughts appropriate at 'the extreme hour'. Fray Luis de Granada had summed up the teaching of a thousand homilists in the following words:

The house of earth (which is our grave) is the schoole of true wisdome, where almighty God is wont to teach those that be his. There he teacheth them how great is the vanity of this world: There he sheweth unto them the misery of our flesh, and the shortnes of this life. And above all, there he teacheth them to know themselves, which is one of the most highest points of Philosophy that may be learned.[10]

When John Donne had himself painted in his shroud, as when he wrote so compellingly of death in the *Devotions* and in the passage in *The Second Anniversary* which constitutes a 'Contemplation of our state in our death-bed', he was obeying spiritual preceptors whose counsel must be supposed to have been equally available to Browning's imagined Bishop. The opening line of the poem— 'Vanity, saith the preacher, vanity!'[11]—naturally leads us to expect a sermon on the significance of human mortality: leads us to expect that the Bishop, like George Herbert in 'Church-monuments', will compare 'dust with dust, and earth with earth',

---

[8] *Paracelsus*, Part I, ll. 765–9; Part V, ll. 487–8, 507–9.

[9] Kintner, i. 336.

[10] I owe this quotation to *The Poetry of Meditation*, by Louis L. Martz (1954), pp. 135–6.   [11] Ecclesiastes 1: 2.

> [Which] laugh[s] at Jeat and Marble put for signes,
> To sever the good fellowship of dust,
> And spoil the meeting.

But, as Paracelsus had pointed out to Festus:

> Festus, strange secrets are let out by death
> Who blabs so oft the follies of this world.[12]

Our expectation of a religious homily is mocked by every line of the
Bishop's monologue, as his mind drifts from the 'nephews' round
his bed—whose rapacious faces we can almost see, as they cluster
round him—to the mistress who had been their mother—'Your tall
pale mother with her talking eyes'—and to 'old Gandolf', whose
jealousy had added piquancy to the Bishop's delight in possessing so
beautiful a mistress. The most telling moral reflection in the poem
is inspired by Job 7: 6,[13] yet it could equally be a brilliant translation from a chorus of Sophocles:

> Swift as a weaver's shuttle fleet our years:
> Man goeth to the grave, and where is he?

Instead of caring for the salvation of his soul, the Bishop is only
concerned with the destination of his body. His greatest fear has
nothing to do with the Judgement to come: it is simply the nightmare thought that the 'ingratitude' of his illegitimate sons may
lead them to economize in the construction of his tomb. As he
conjures them to obey his wishes, we notice that he does not rely on
their sense of filial duty but solely on their expectation of material
and fleshly rewards:

> And have I not Saint Praxed's ear to pray
> Horses for ye, and brown Greek manuscripts,
> And mistresses with great smooth marbly limbs?

There is a special irony in the fact that the Saint to whom the
Bishop proposes to pray in these terms was a virgin.[14] 'I know no

---

[12] *Paracelsus*, Part III, ll. 109–10.

[13] 'My days are swifter than a weaver's shuttle, and are spent without hope.'

[14] By l. 95, as has often been pointed out, the Bishop's mind is wandering to such
an extent that he refers to Saint Praxed as a man, and as the preacher of the Sermon on
the Mount.

other piece of modern English', Ruskin wrote, 'prose or poetry, in which there is so much told, as in these lines, of the Renaissance spirit,—its worldliness, inconsistency, pride, hypocrisy, ignorance of itself, love of art, of luxury, and of good Latin.'[15]

There has been a great deal of discussion about the tomb. Everyone is agreed that there is no tomb of this sort in the church of Santa Prassede in Rome, while Mrs. Melchiori has pointed out that Browning attributes a dome to 'one of the few Roman churches without a sunny or even a sunless dome'.[16] Various primarily literary sources for the tomb have been suggested, notably passages from Gerard de Lairesse. But surely the important point is so obvious that it has escaped the attention of critics: no tomb corresponding to the Bishop's description exists anywhere. It is one thing to 'order' a tomb, and another to have it erected. The Bishop's fear that his sons will not go to the expense of erecting the tomb he desires is entirely justified. It follows that the search for the tomb is a search for something that never existed except in the imagination of Browning's imaginary Bishop.

It is instructive to compare the Bishop's attitude to religion with Browning's own, almost directly expressed a few years later in *Christmas-Eve and Easter-Day*. As for his thoughts on the disposal of his own body after death, we find him quoting Donne and saying that he had 'no kind of concern as to where the old clothes of myself shall be thrown'.[17]

Since the third monologue spoken by a churchman, 'Bishop Blougram's Apology', was suggested by the elevation of Cardinal Wiseman to be Archbishop of Westminster and head of the Catholic Church in England, the extremely hostile attitude to Catholicism expressed in *Christmas-Eve and Easter-Day* (in which, as we have seen, the speakers are not markedly differentiated from the poet himself) is of particular interest. The traditional view of the origin

[15] *Modern Painters*, vol. iv, ch. xx (*Works*, ed. Cook and Wedderburn (1904), vi. 449).

[16] Melchiori, p. 20. This quiet little church must have been in the news in the 1840s, as the bones of several hundred early martyrs, discovered in 1842, were subsequently buried in a vault under the church. It is also worth mentioning that the church of Santa Prassede is near the great church of Santa Maria Maggiore, which contains a number of ornate tombs.

[17] *Life and Letters*, p. 244. Cf. *The Second Anniversary*, l. 62.

of 'Bishop Blougram's Apology' is that Browning was fascinated by the question of how a man of such ability could profess belief in every article of the Catholic faith, and wrote the poem as a dramatic exploration of an intellectual problem.

Critics who oppose this interpretation of the poem lean heavily on a remark attributed to Browning in the reminiscences of Sir Charles Gavan Duffy. When Duffy taxed Browning with using Wiseman as a model for his 'unfriendly' portrayal of Bishop Blougram, Browning admitted that Blougram 'was certainly intended for the English Cardinal', but added that 'he was not treated ungenerously'.[18] The anecdote has frequently been repeated, sometimes in the inaccurate version given by G. K. Chesterton, and sometimes by critics who forget that Browning was (as a rule) a friendly and polite person. F. E. L. Priestley's observation, that

if Browning drew a portrait of Wiseman as 'a vulgar, fashionable priest, justifying his own cowardice,' yet declared that the portrait was not a satire, and had 'nothing hostile about it,' then Browning was either a hypocrite more brazen than Gigadibs thought Blougram, or incredibly naive[19]

seems overstated. Chesterton's comment, on the other hand, can hardly be improved on. Immediately after (mis)quoting Browning's own words, Chesterton continues:

This is the real truth which lies at the heart of what may be called the great sophistical monologues. . . . They are not satires or attacks upon their subjects, they are not even harsh and unfeeling exposures of them. They are defences; they say or are intended to say the best that can be said for the persons with whom they deal.[20]

This is slightly, but only slightly, overstated on the other side. It is partly a matter of what one means by the word 'satire'. Whereas modern critics insist that there is a marked satirical element in the novels of Jane Austen, old-fashioned critics shrank from using the

[18] Gavan Duffy, *My Life in Two Hemispheres* (1898), ii. 261.
[19] 'Blougram's Apologetics', reprinted from *UTQ* 15 (January 1946) in Litzinger and Knickerbocker, p. 167. Priestley is quoting Chesterton, pp. 201 and 188.
[20] Chesterton, p. 188.

word—although their reading of her books was not always very different. Whether or not one terms 'Bishop Blougram's Apology' a 'satire' depends on one's use of a literary term, but there is little doubt that Chesterton's description of the poem as a defence, a piece which is 'intended to say the best that can be said' for the person with whom it deals, represents what Browning himself must have had in mind as he sat down to describe the great Bishop 'rolling out his mind'.

The skill of the Bishop's casuistry has often been admired: there is no need to retrace here the brilliant evolution of his argument, which is (as the writer of the poem comments at the end) a combination of the Bishop's permanent beliefs and of

> Some arbitrary accidental thoughts
> That crossed his mind, amusing because new.

Although we learn a good deal about Gigadibs in the course of the poem, and he (rather than the Bishop) is the figure on whom the poet's spotlight plays for a moment in the concluding lines, we notice not only that he is never allowed to speak (a necessary concomitant of the monologue form) but that the objections put into his mouth by the Bishop do not allow him any skill as a dialectician. The Bishop is not obliged to defend his position against a trained Protestant theologian, a lawyer, or a man capable of any metaphysical subtlety: his auditor—he can scarcely be termed an antagonist—is an impulsive literary man who can hardly be supposed to be in the habit of marshalling complicated arguments. Gigadibs is simply a foil,[21] although at the end of the poem (unusually for Browning, and perhaps regrettably) his position is suddenly changed.

If we compare this poem with 'The Bishop Orders his Tomb' or 'Fra Lippo Lippi' we find that Browning is less interested in Blougram as a man than he is in the speakers of these other monologues. Whereas we hear a little about the other Bishop's earlier life, and are given a direct account of how Fra Lippo Lippi became

---

[21] As Gigadibs is never in fact allowed to speak, it seems to me that Priestley overstates when he claims that the 'whole course' of the monologue 'is dictated by Gigadibs': Litzinger and Knickerbocker, p. 168.

a monk, we hear nothing of how Bishop Blougram had entered the
Catholic Church, or of the early influences which have made him
what he is. Blougram the man does not engage Browning's imagination as these other men do. His concern is with Blougram's
arguments rather than with his character.

A peculiarity of 'Bishop Blougram's Apology', which is not to be
found in any of the other 'Men and Women' poems, is the postscript of forty-four lines in which the poet himself, or his persona,
comments explicitly on the sincerity of the Bishop, and on the effect
that his defence has had on Gigadibs. It is hard not to feel that these
lines are an artistic flaw: a similar commentary would certainly be
most unwelcome at the end of either of the two other poems just
mentioned. Yet it is essential to ask why Browning wrote the postscript, and the only possible answer appears to be that he feared that
he had given the Bishop such powerful arguments that readers
might take a more favourable view of them and of him than Browning himself intended. As he created the character of the Bishop,
Browning found himself allowing him to give eloquent expression
to certain of his own deepest intuitions and beliefs about human
life, as in lines 693–7:

> . . . when the fight begins within himself,
> A man's worth something. God stoops o'er his head,
> Satan looks up between his feet—both tug—
> He's left, himself, i' the middle: the soul wakes
> And grows. Prolong that battle through his life!

or lines 182–90:

> Just when we are safest, there's a sunset-touch,
> A fancy from a flower-bell, some one's death,
> A chorus-ending from Euripides,—
> And that's enough for fifty hopes and fears
> As old and new at once as nature's self,
> To rap and knock and enter in our soul,
> Take hands and dance there, a fantastic ring,
> Round the ancient idol, on his base again,—
> The grand Perhaps!

Accordingly the opening lines of the postscript 'place' the Bishop
very clearly, and the reader is led to sympathize and identify with

Gigadibs, who has not been allowed to say anything throughout, and who has had such ineffectual arguments put into his mouth by the glib-tongued Bishop:

> Over his wine so smiled and talked his hour
> Sylvester Blougram, styled *in partibus*
> *Episcopus, nec non*—(the deuce knows what
> It's changed to by our novel hierarchy)
> With Gigadibs the literary man,
> Who played with spoons, explored his plate's design,
> And ranged the olive-stones about its edge,
> While the great bishop rolled him out a mind
> Long crumpled, till creased consciousness lay smooth.

The lines which follow are even more unambiguous in their direction:

> For Blougram, he believed, say, half he spoke.
> The other portion, as he shaped it thus
> For argumentatory purposes,
> He felt his foe was foolish to dispute . . .
> While certain hell-deep instincts, man's weak tongue
> Is never bold to utter in their truth
> Because styled hell-deep . . .
> He ignored these,—not having in readiness
> Their nomenclature and philosophy:
> He said true things, but called them by wrong names.

The Bishop's view is that he has justified himself to the sort of 'caviller' who would 'oppugn' his life, defeating his opponent as a skilled fencer defeats a novice. The meaning of the line 'So, let him sit with me this many a year!' is not (as Priestley argues) that 'After Gigadibs has seen the shallowness of his own thinking, then he can start the process of trying to reach firmer ground',[22] but rather: 'This man can dine with me for years, without there being any danger of his getting the better of me in this intellectual game.' To say that the Bishop believes only half of what he says is hardly to present him in a favourable light, while the statements that he ignored 'certain hell-deep instincts' (such as the instinct to save one's own skin, whatever becomes of other people?) and 'said true things, but called them by wrong names', are openly critical.

[22] Litzinger and Knickerbocker, p. 179.

Whereas Priestley argues that 'the victory, unexpected to be sure in its scope, is Blougram's',[23] the final paragraph of the poem makes it clear that Gigadibs has no desire to listen further to the reasonings of this arrogant churchman, or to remain in a society which he seems now to regard as over-sophisticated:

> He did not sit five minutes. Just a week
> Sufficed his sudden healthy vehemence.
> Something had struck him in the 'Outward-bound'
> Another way than Blougram's purpose was:
> And having bought, not cabin-furniture
> But settler's implements (enough for three)
> And started for Australia—there, I hope,
> By this time he has tested his first plough,
> And studied his last chapter of St. John.

Unimpressed by Blougram's argument about the comfortable furnishing of one's cabin for the journey across 'the ocean of this world', Gigadibs has taken the words 'Outward-bound' in their literal sense: he has left London, where Blougram and the Catholic hierarchy are attaining a new prominence, and travelled to the furthest end of the earth. He has abandoned the existence of a minor literary man for the challenge of a practical life in a hard environment, and in his attractive enthusiasm he has bought sufficient settler's implements for three men. So much is clear. The last line is more enigmatic. The syntactical pattern, in which 'his last chapter of St. John' parallels 'his first plough', might seem to suggest the hope that Gigadibs has ceased to study the Bible at the same time at which he has begun working as a farmer: that he has abandoned theological speculation in favour of a purely practical life. Yet Browning had a particular interst in the Gospel according to St. John, and for this and other reasons such an interpretation is clearly unacceptable. The reference to John xxi[24] must express the hope that Gigadibs has now abandoned his scepticism

---

[23] p. 180.
[24] Browning may be including a mischievous reference to Christ's reiterated injunction to his disciples, in the chapter in question: 'Feed my sheep'. For Browning's interest in this Gospel, cf. pp. 234 and 263, below.

not (indeed) in deference to the casuistical arguments of the Catholic Bishop, but in favour of a Christian faith as simple and healthy as his new-found vocation as a farmer.[25]

The decision of Gigadibs to emigrate to Australia recalls an actual decision made by Browning's friend Alfred Domett a few years before. Domett was a minor poet who contributed to *Blackwood's Magazine*, the author of

> . . . sundry jottings,
> Stray-leaves, fragments, blurrs and blottings,
> Certain first steps . . .[26]

which had failed to win very much attention. A friend commented on his 'combativeness' in argument, and referred to his 'morbid disinclination', in spite of a legal training, 'to be employed in the world's work in any prescribed or methodical way'.[27] In New Zealand he continued to undertake some journalism, and it is particularly interesting to find his name being mentioned as that of a possible contributor to a periodical edited by Dickens:

Those 'leaders' are capital [Browning wrote in 1846]—anybody can see that; I commended my last-but-one batch to the notice of Forster, literally on the eve of the publishing that *Daily News* in which he was concerned with Dickens . . . and he, Forster, said they would in all probability secure you for correspondent—but the whole concern went off impotently.[28]

'Of a passionate, fiery nature', Domett was violently opposed to 'the lies, humbug, conventionalities of society', a supporter of schools in which 'no sectarian views whatever should be taught', but where 'the Bible, when read, should be read without note or comment', a man who believed that 'religious faith is a thing more of the heart than of the head'—and an admirer of Browning who was later to include 'long justifications of Browning's metaphysics' in his

---

[25] Cf. the thoughtful discussion of the poem in *The Poetry of Browning: A Critical Introduction*, by Philip Drew (1970), pp. 122–43.

[26] 'Waring', ll. 32–4.

[27] *The Diary of Alfred Domett 1872–1885*, ed. E. A. Horsman (1953), pp. 13–14.

[28] *Domett*, pp. 122–3.

poem *Ranolf and Amohia*.[29] At the end of the first part of 'Waring'
Browning speculates whether Waring is to become 'Some Garrick'
who may

> The heart of Hamlet's mystery pluck,

'Some Junius' or 'Some Chatterton': a man of genius like those to
whom Bishop Blougram tauntingly refers in his monologue with
Gigadibs. In fact, as we know, when Waring 'Chose . . . seafaring'
and went off with his 'Boots and chest',

> Rather than pace up and down
> Any longer London town,

he emigrated to New Zealand, where at first he farmed—no doubt
grazing sheep—and in course of time became Prime Minister.
While Gigadibs is in no sense a portrait of Domett, it is impossible
not to believe that Browning remembered him as he wrote 'Bishop
Blougram's Apology', and this makes it particularly interesting that
Browning used the phrase *'going to New Zealand'* in an openly
symbolical sense in a letter to Domett already quoted.[30] At the end
of the poem Gigadibs makes his escape from an over-sophisticated
London to a supposedly uncorrupted new country where he can
pursue a useful life without worrying his head about the subtle
casuistries of Cardinal Wiseman.

When we turn from the monologues spoken by men of religion
to those spoken by painters we find that one of the three, 'Pictor
Ignotus', is relatively early, while the other two first made their
appearance in *Men and Women*. 'Pictor Ignotus' begins abruptly:

> I could have painted pictures like that youth's
> Ye praise so

—a startling claim, as the youth is clearly Raphael.[31] The speaker
claims that he could have painted, like Raphael,

[29] *The Diary of Alfred Domett*, p. 25, followed by quotations from pp. 28, 23, 24, 17.
[30] Above, p. 72.
[31] The poem is headed 'Florence, 15—'. Raphael lived from 1493 until 1520,
residing in Florence from 1504 to 1508. At ll. 104–5 of 'Andrea del Sarto' Raphael is
referred to as 'that famous youth / The Urbinate who died five years ago'. Lines
13–22 of 'Pictor Ignotus' (quoted above) refer to Raphael's celebrated power in
portraying the Passions.

> Each face obedient to its passion's law,
>   Each passion clear proclaimed without a tongue;
> Whether Hope rose at once in all the blood,
>   A-tiptoe for the blessing of embrace,
> Or Rapture drooped the eyes, as when her brood
>   Pull down the nesting dove's heart to its place;
> Or Confidence lit swift the forehead up,
>   And locked the mouth fast, like a castle braved.

And he acknowledges that he has had moments of yearning for the fame that such pictures would have brought him:

> Nor will I say I have not dreamed (how well!)
>   Of going—I, in each new picture,—forth,
> As, making new hearts beat and bosoms swell,
>   To Pope or Kaiser, East, West, South, or North,
> Bound for the calmly-satisfied great State,
>   Or glad aspiring little burgh, it went,
> Flowers cast upon the car which bore the freight,
>   Through old streets named afresh from the event.

Why did he reject such honours? The poem turns on the words 'But a voice changed it' (his ambitious thought). This voice precipitated a crisis in his development, with the result that he became disgusted with the commercial aspect of the life of a painter outside the cloister: now he limits himself to fresco painting, although he knows that he will never be famous, and that his paintings will decay with the walls on which they are painted.

While 'Pictor Ignotus' relates to the history of Italian painting, it is above all a psychological study of a painter. Our understanding of it has been greatly assisted by Mr. J. B. Bullen's discovery that the main inspiration of the poem, as of Browning's other monologues by artists, is a passage in Vasari's *Lives of the Painters*: in this case the 'Life of Fra Bartolommeo di San Marco'.[32] The first point that this helps to establish is that the Unknown Painter is not a complete self-deluder (as one might have supposed) when he claims that he could have painted like Raphael. Vasari tells us that Raphael 'was constantly in his company, being desirous of acquiring the

---

[32] 'Browning's "Pictor Ignotus" and Vasari's "Life of Fra Bartolommeo di San Marco" ', *RES*, N.S. 23 (1972), 313–19.

monk's manner of colouring': Lanzi remarks that Raphael 'was at
the same time [Fra Bartolommeo's] scholar in colouring, and his
master in perspective': Mrs. Jameson maintains that to the friendship of the two men 'we partly owe the finest works of both': while
Richardson, quoted by Mrs. Jameson, goes so far as to say that 'at
this time Fra Bartolomeo seems to have been the greater man, and
might have been *the* Raphael, had not Fortune been determined
in favour of the other'.[33] The second point, which could not be
answered in terms of the text of the poem itself, is the identity of
the 'voice'. Vasari describes how Fra Bartolommeo 'became closely
intimate with Fra Girolamo' (Savonarola),

and spent almost all his time in the convent, having contracted a
friendship with the other monks also. Girolamo meanwhile continued
to preach daily; and his zeal increasing, he daily declaimed from the
pulpit against licentious pictures, among other things; showing how
these, with music and books of similar character, were calculated to
lead the mind to evil; he also asserted his conviction, that in houses
where young maidens dwelt, it was dangerous and improper to retain
pictures wherein there were undraped figures.[34]

During the Carnival, when it was the custom to light fires in the
public piazza,

Fra Girolamo's exhortations had so powerfully affected the people,
that instead of these accustomed dances, they brought pictures and
works in sculpture, many by the most excellent masters—all which
they cast into the fire . . . a most lamentable destruction. . . . To this
pile brought [Fra Bartolommeo] all his studies and drawings which
he had made from the nude figure, when they were consumed in the
flames.[35]

When the enemies of Savonarola rose against him Fra Bartolommeo
was one of five hundred of his supporters who shut themselves up

---

[33] *Lives of the Most Eminent Painters, Sculptors, and Architects*, by Vasari, trans. Mrs.
Jonathan Foster, ii (1851), 452; *The History of Painting in Italy*, by the Abate Luigi
Lanzi, trans. Thomas Roscoe (edn. of 1847), i. 150; *Memoirs of the Early Italian
Painters*, by Mrs. Jameson (1845), i. 225.
[34] Op. cit., p. 448.
[35] Ibid.

in San Marco, but he became terrified, 'being indeed of a timid and even cowardly disposition', and accordingly he

made a vow, that if he might be permitted to escape from the rage of that strife, he would instantly assume the religious habit of the Dominicans. The vow thus taken he afterwards fulfilled to the letter; for when the struggle was over . . . he assumed the habit of San Domenico on the 26th of July, in the year 1500, as we find recorded in the chronicles of that convent.[36]

For four years he abandoned painting, being exclusively occupied with his attention to the religious services. It was at this point that the young Raphael came to Florence, an event which helped to induce Fra Bartolommeo to resume painting, and led to his visiting Rome:

Having heard much of the excellent works which Michael Angelo and the graceful Raphael were performing in Rome, and being moved by the praises of these masters . . . he . . . repaired to Rome. . . . But the labours undertaken by Fra Bartolommeo in the air of Rome, were not so successful as those executed while he breathed that of Florence; among the vast numbers of works, ancient and modern, which he there found in such overwhelming abundance, he felt himself bewildered and astounded.[37]

When he returned to Florence hostile critics met him with the charge that he was incapable of painting the nude, an episode which no doubt lies behind lines 45–56 of the poem:

> Mixed with my loving trusting ones, there trooped
> . . . Who summoned those cold faces that begun
> To press on me and judge me? Though I stooped
> Shrinking, as from the soldiery a nun,
> They drew me forth, and spite of me . . . enough!
> These buy and sell our pictures, take and give,
> Count them for garniture and household-stuff,
> And where they live needs must our pictures live
> And see their faces, listen to their prate,
> Partakers of their daily pettiness,
> Discussed of,—'This I love, or this I hate,
> 'This likes me more, and this affects me less!'

[36] Op. cit., p. 449.   [37] Ibid., p. 454.

Although Fra Bartolommeo refuted his critics by painting 'a San Sebastian, wholly undraped, by way of specimen',[38] he eventually retreated to a monastery outside Florence and (in Vasari's words) 'While abiding in that place he finally arrived at the wished for power of accompanying the labour of his hands with the uninterrupted contemplation of death':[39] in Browning's words,

> Wherefore I chose my portion. If at whiles
> My heart sinks, as monotonous I paint
> These endless cloisters and eternal aisles
> With the same series, Virgin, Babe and Saint,
> With the same cold calm beautiful regard,—
> At least no merchant traffics in my heart.

He knows that his pictures will 'surely, gently die', as the walls on which they are painted decay,[40] but he asserts that he prefers this, and rhetorically asks Raphael whether worldly fame is worth the price that has to be paid for it.

Browning is little concerned with the 'holiness' for which the biographers praise Fra Bartolommeo, but his general view of the place that he occupies in the development of painting is similar to that of Mrs. Jameson. She introduces her pages on his life and work in the following words:

Before we enter on the golden age of painting—that splendid æra which crowded into a brief quarter of a century (between 1505 and 1530) the greatest names and most consummate productions of the art—we must speak of one more painter justly celebrated. Perugino and Francia (of whom we have spoken at length) and FRA BARTOLOMEO, of whom we are now to speak, were still living at this period; but they belonged to a previous age, and were informed, as we shall show, by a wholly different spirit.[41]

Her view of Fra Bartolommeo's historical position is emphasized by the fact that he is the last painter to be discussed in the first of her two volumes, Leonardo da Vinci and Michael Angelo[42] being the

---

[38] Op. cit., p. 455.   [39] Ibid., p. 457.
[40] ll. 50–2 refer to the rise of easel-painting (as distinct from fresco). The Unknown Painter is horrified by the development whereby a painting has become detachable from its original home, and therefore just another chattel that may be bought and sold.   [41] i. 218, followed by a quotation from ii. 5.
[42] Andrea del Sarto is the third.

first two in her second volume, in which (as she puts it) she is approaching 'the period when the art of painting reached its highest perfection'.

What Browning does is to present us with a dramatic monologue which is in essence a psychological study of the sort of man that Fra Bartolommeo may be supposed to have been. He stresses the painter's timidity, and portrays him as considering 'heaven' and worldly celebrity as mutually incompatible.[43] Browning's 'Pictor Ignotus' is a failure, a man who has retreated from the challenge of life and so failed to give the world the full fruits of which his genius was capable. For all its strangeness, the poem fits squarely into Browning's work as a whole, and we notice that it deals with a theme which had a particular personal relevance for him in the 1840s, when he had so signally failed with *Sordello*, yet had resisted the temptation of withdrawing to the company of the few 'loving trusting ones' who would read and praise his poems without their being subject to the hazards and rigours of published criticism.

Whereas 'Pictor Ignotus' (like 'Andrea del Sarto') is a study in failure, the speaker in 'Fra Lippo Lippi' is a man who is making a success of his life, and his monologue constitutes an eloquent defence of one of the main precursors of the great age of painting in Italy which is informed by a spirit of comedy totally absent from the other monologues spoken by painters.

While the principal source of the poem is undoubtedly Vasari's 'Life of Fra Filippo Lippi',[44] Browning omits, modifies, and adds in accordance with his own poetic purposes. He omits the striking episode near the beginning of the 'Life' in which Lippo is taken prisoner by Moorish pirates and later released because of his skill as a painter—an episode which must have appealed to Browning if (as is probable) he first read the passage as a boy. He is more completely indulgent than Vasari to Lippi's moral lapses. While the 'Life' might be described as sunny—in marked contrast to the

[43] ll. 36-40.

[44] In April 1853, about the time when the poem seems to have been written, Elizabeth Barrett tells a friend that Browning 'is as fond of digging at Vasari as I am at the Mystics, and goes to and from him as constantly, making him a betwixt and between to other writers': Miller, p. 175.

more sombre 'Life of Andrea del Sarto'—Vasari admits that there were 'many circumstances in his life which were very blameable':

It is said that Fra Filippo was much addicted to the pleasures of sense, insomuch that he would give all he possessed to secure the gratification of whatever inclination might at the moment be predominant; but if he could by no means accomplish his wishes, he would then depict the object which had attracted his attention, in his paintings, and endeavour by discoursing and reasoning with himself to diminish the violence of his inclination.[45]

Later we hear how

he one day chanced to see the daughter of Francesco Buti, a citizen of Florence, who had been sent to the Convent. . . . Fra Filippo, having given a glance at Lucrezia, for such was the name of the girl, who was exceedingly beautiful and graceful, so persuaded the nuns, that he prevailed on them to permit him to make a likeness of her, for the figure of the Virgin in the work he was executing for them. The result of this was, that the painter fell violently in love with Lucrezia, and at length found means to influence her in such a manner, that he led her away from the nuns, and . . . bore her from their keeping. By this event the nuns were deeply disgraced, and the father of Lucrezia was so grievously afflicted . . . that he never more recovered his cheerfulness.[46]

Vasari later informs us that the Pope 'offered . . . to give him a dispensation, that he might make Lucrezia . . . his legitimate wife', but that Fra Lippo Lippi, wishing to live 'after his own fashion' and to retain the power of 'indulging his love of pleasure . . . did not care to accept that offer'.[47] While Browning is frank about the amorousness of the painter, in his poem we hear nothing of any woman who suffers as the result of Lippo's propensities, nothing about the father who 'never more recovered his cheerfulness'—and of course nothing of the tradition that 'he was poisoned by certain persons' as a result of one of his libertine love affairs.[48]

---

[45] Vasari, ed. cit., ii. 82, 76. The Italian, which Browning certainly knew (item 1182 in the Catalogue of the possessions of R. W. Barrett Browning as sold in 1913 is a thirteen-volume edition of the *Vite* published in Florence), is more direct in its expression: 'Dicesi ch'era tanto venereo, che vedendo donne che gli piacessero, se le poteva avere, ogni sua facultà donato le arebbe; e non potendo per via di mezzi, ritraendole in pittura, con ragionamenti la fiamma del suo amore intiepidiva.'

[46] Ibid., p. 79.   [47] Ibid., p. 86.   [48] Ibid., p. 85.

The nocturnal escapade which precedes the opening of the poem comes straight from Vasari:

while occupied in the pursuit of his pleasures, the works undertaken by him received little or none of his attention; for which reason Cosimo de' Medici, wishing him to execute a work in his own palace, shut him up, that he might not waste his time in running about; but having endured this confinement for two days, he then made ropes with the sheets of his bed, which he cut to pieces for that purpose, and so having let himself down from a window, escaped, and for several days gave himself up to his amusements.[49]

According to Vasari it was the altarpiece painted for the nuns of Sant' Ambrogio which brought Fra Lippo Lippi to the attention of Cosimo de' Medici, but at the end of the poem this is described as a future project. Browning also differs from Vasari in his account of the relationship between Fra Lippo Lippi and Masaccio (the 'Hulking Tom' of l. 277). Whereas Vasari rightly describes Lippi as an admirer and follower of Masaccio, Browning reverses their roles—an alteration which he defended in a letter: 'I was wide awake when I made Fra Lippo the elder practitioner of Art,' he wrote in 1866, 'if not, as I believe, the earlier born. I looked into the matter carefully long ago . . . from my interest in the Brancacci frescos, indeed in all early Florentine Art.'[50] As Johnstone Parr has recently pointed out, Browning ascribes to Lippi the important historical position that Vasari ascribes to Masaccio in the following words:

Masaccio . . . first attained the clear perception that painting is no other than the close imitation . . . of all the forms presented by nature, exhibiting them as they are produced by her. . . . He it was

---

[49] Ibid., pp. 76–7.

[50] *Letters*, p. 104. This letter makes it clear that Browning knew a number of editions of Vasari, and was aware that different views on his accuracy were current. There can be no doubt that he also knew that Vasari made important revisions in the *Lives*. 'The Brancacci frescos' are the celebrated frescoes, by Masaccio, Filippino Lippi (the son of Filippo Lippi), Masolino, and others in the chapel of the Basilica di S. Maria del Carmine in Florence. Johnstone Parr has pointed out that it was from the Milanesi edition of Vasari, and not from Baldinucci (as Browning later supposed) that the poet derived his false chronology: see 'Browning's *Fra Lippo Lippi*, Baldinucci, and the Milanesi Edition of Vasari', *English Language Notes* (Boulder, Colorado), March 1966, pp. 197–201.

who . . . imparted a life and force to his figures . . . which render them truly characteristic and natural. . . . The works produced before his time should be called paintings; but . . . his performance, when compared with those works, might be designated life, truth, and nature.[51]

Parr illuminatingly juxtaposes the lines in which Lippi describes how as a boy he began joyously painting 'every sort of monk, the black and white . . . then, folk at church' and everyone whom he saw, with the following passage from Vasari's 'Life of Masaccio':

The master painted the portraits of a great number of the citizens . . . clothed in hoods and mantles . . . and not only did he . . . depict the above-named personages from the life, but the door of the convent is also pourtrayed as it stood, with the porter holding the keys in his hand. . . . One distinguishes the short and stout man from the tall and slender figures, as one would if they were living.[52]

As Parr also points out, the contrast drawn in the poem between Fra Lippo Lippi and Fra Angelico is close to that drawn by Mrs. Jameson in her *Memoirs of the Early Italian Painters*.[53] She deals with the two men in a chapter which begins with the following words:

Contemporary with Masaccio lived two painters, both gifted with surpassing genius, both of a religious order, being professed monks; in all other respects the very antipodes of each other. . . . From this period we date the great schism in modern art. . . . We now find, on the one side, a race of painters who cultivated with astonishing success all the mental and mechanical aids that could be brought to

---

[51] Ed. cit. i (1850), 401–2: cf. Johnstone Parr, 'Browning's *Fra Lippo Lippi*, Vasari's Masaccio, and Mrs. Jameson', *ELN*, June 1968, 277–83.

[52] Ed. cit. i. 408–9. Cf. ll. 168–71:

> . . . 'That's the very man!
> 'Look at the boy who stoops to pat the dog!
> 'That woman's like the Prior's niece who comes
> 'To care about his asthma: it's the life!'

[53] It should be noticed, as Mr. Bullen has pointed out to me, that Browning himself did not agree with the black-and-white contrast attributed to the Prior. In 1845 he severely criticized Mary Shelley's view of Fra Angelico in the following words: 'Her remarks on art . . . are amazing—Fra Angelico, for instance, only painted Martyrs, Virgins &.—she had no eyes for the divine *bon-bourgeoisie* of his pictures; the dear common folk of his crowds, those who sit and listen (spectacle at nose and bent into a comfortable heap to hear better) at the sermon of the Saint— and the children, and women,—divinely pure they all are, but fresh from the streets and market place . . .': Kintner, i. 190.

bear on their profession; profoundly versed in the knowledge of the human form, and intent on studying and imitating the various effects of nature in colour and in light and shade, without any other aspiration than the representation of beauty for its own sake. . . ;[54] on the other hand, we find a race of painters to whom the cultivation of art was a sacred vocation—the representation of beauty a means, not an end; by whom Nature . . . was studied . . ., but only for the purpose of embodying whatever we can conceive or reverence as highest, holiest, purest in heaven and earth, in such forms as should best connect them with our intelligence and with our sympathies.[55]

Mrs. Jameson makes it clear that Lippi became a monk 'from necessity rather than from inclination' and mentions that 'he at length broke from the convent', though without giving any date for this event. She tells us that 'the rest of his life is a romance', repeats the story of his capture by pirates, and emphasizes that

This libertine monk . . . adopted and carried on all the improvements of Masaccio, and was the first who invented that particular style of grandeur and breadth in the drawing of his figures, the grouping, and the contrast of light and shade, afterwards carried to such perfection by Andrea del Sarto. He was one of the earliest painters who introduced landscape backgrounds, painted with some feeling for the truth of nature.[56]

Fra Angelico, on the other hand, whom Browning introduces as the admired of 'The Prior and the learned' (ll. 174, 235), is described by Mrs. Jameson as another 'painter-monk, presenting in his life and character the strongest possible contrast' to Filippo Lippi, as 'a man, with whom the practice of a beautiful art was thenceforth a hymn of praise, and every creation of his pencil an act of piety and charity'. Mrs. Jameson tells us that Fra Angelico's 'long life of seventy years presents only one unbroken tranquil stream of placid contentment and pious labours'. She adds, with probably conscious irony, that 'Correct drawing of the human figure could

---

[54] Cf. ll. 283–5, quoted on p. 224, below.   [55] *Memoirs*, i. 110–11.
[56] Ibid. 113–14. With the last sentence cf. ll. 286–90:

> . . . Do you feel thankful, ay or no,
> For this fair town's face, yonder river's line,
> The mountain round it and the sky above,
> Much more the figures of man, woman, child,
> These are the frame to?

not be expected from one who regarded the exhibition of the undraped form as a sin'.[57]

Fra Lippo Lippi had no such inhibitions, and 'flesh' is one of the key words in his monologue. 'Flesh and blood, That's all I'm made of!', he acknowledges near the beginning, a fact which makes it ironical that his official occupation is a painting of St. Jerome

> . . . knocking at his poor old breast
> With his great round stone to subdue the flesh.[58]

His critics urge him to make people 'forget there's such a thing as flesh', telling him:

> 'Your business is to paint the souls of men.'

They say that to 'Fag on at flesh'[59] is all he is capable of, but his reply is that a painter can only paint the soul well by first painting the body well:

> I always see the garden and God there
> A-making man's wife: and, my lesson learned,
> The value and significance of flesh,
> I can't unlearn ten minutes afterwards.   (266–9)

His passion for female beauty is only one manifestation of the fascinated delight that he takes in the human scene, and his keen eye for expressions is vividly illustrated by his comments on the faces of the men who surround him at the beginning of the poem. In 'The Bishop Orders his Tomb' we are able to visualize the Bishop's sons or 'nephews' clustering round him, greedy for his wealth—but we do so largely as an act of the imagination, prompted by one or two vivid hints. Fra Lippo Lippi comments explicitly on the faces that surround him, demonstrating a skill which he has acquired early in life:

> . . . When a boy starves in the streets
> Eight years together, as my fortune was,
> Watching folk's faces to know who will fling
> The bit of half-stripped grape-bunch he desires,

---

[57] *Memoirs*, i. 117, followed by quotations from i. 118 and 120.
[58] ll. 60–1, 73–4.
[59] ll. 182–3, 237.

> And who will curse or kick him for his pains . . .
> Why, soul and sense of him grow sharp alike,
> He learns the look of things.   (112–16, 124–5)

Surrounded by strangers, he instinctively begins to wonder what use he could make of them as models. 'I'd like his face', he exclaims at line 31,

> His, elbowing on his comrade in the door
> With the pike and lantern,—for the slave that holds
> John Baptist's head a-dangle by the hair
> With one hand ('Look you, now,' as who should say)
> And his weapon in the other, yet unwiped!
> It's not your chance to have a bit of chalk,
> A wood-coal or the like? or you should see!

Here Browning is taking a hint from a passage in Vasari describing Fra Lippo Lippi's paintings in the parish church at Prato: 'On the other side of the chapel is the History of St. John the Baptist, his Birth, . . . his Preaching in the Wilderness, his Baptism, the Feast of Herod, and the Decapitation.'[60] Since Fra Lippo Lippi refers to cruelty of expression more than once in the monologue, it is interesting to note that Vasari comments on the 'brutal rage' of the men who stoned St. Stephen to death, a scene portrayed on the other side of the same chapel. One of them in particular is a terrifying study of cruelty of expression.[61] Another vivid glimpse of facial expression is given at line 153 of the poem, where the 'white anger' of the son of a murdered man is described.

Fra Lippo Lippi's frescoes at Prato are usually regarded as the most important work of his career. Browning refers to a part of these which is said to have been destroyed, giving an amusing account of how this came about:

> I painted a Saint Laurence six months since
> At Prato, splashed the fresco in fine style:
> 'How looks my painting, now the scaffold's down?'
> I ask a brother: 'Hugely', he returns—
> 'Already not one phiz of your three slaves
> 'Who turn the Deacon off his toasted side,

---

[60] *Lives*, ed. cit. ii. 82. Cf. Mary Pittaluga, *Filippo Lippi* (Florence, 1949), plate 122.
[61] Pittaluga, plate 131.

'But's scratched and prodded to our heart's content,
'The pious people have so eased their own
'With coming to say prayers there in a rage:
'We get on fast to see the bricks beneath.
'Expect another job this time next year,
'For pity and religion grow i' the crowd—
'Your painting serves its purpose!'[62]

Very different is the painting which gave Browning the idea for the triumphant conclusion of his poem.

To 'make amends' for his escapade Lippi promises to paint a picture for the nuns of Sant' Ambrogio's, adding mischievously that they 'want a cast o' my office':

>   . . . I shall paint
> God in the midst, Madonna and her babe,
> Ringed by a bowery flowery angel-brood,
> Lilies and vestments and white faces, sweet
> As puff on puff of grated orris-root
> When ladies crowd to Church at midsummer.
> And then i' the front, of course a saint or two—
> Saint John, because he saves the Florentines,
> Saint Ambrose, who puts down in black and white
> The convent's friends and gives them a long day,
> And Job, I must have him there past mistake,
> The man of Uz (and Us without the z,
> Painters who need his patience.) Well, all these
> Secured at their devotion, up shall come
> Out of a corner when you least expect,
> As one by a dark stair into a great light,
> Music and talking, who but Lippo! I!—
> Mazed, motionless and moonstruck—I'm the man!
>   (347–64)

This is the 'very beautiful altarpiece' praised by Vasari and already referred to.[63] The lines describing the painter himself are suggested by his kneeling posture in the painting, although of course he has

---

[62] ll. 323–35. Vasari refers to 'a San Lorenzo and other saints' painted by Lippi for the church 'at Vincigliata, on the heights of Fiesole' (p. 84).

[63] Now in the Uffizi in Florence, it is reproduced in Pittaluga and in Griffin and Minchin (facing p. 202).

not come up any stair. From this point onwards Browning allows
his imagination free play:

> Back I shrink—what is this I see and hear?
> I, caught up with my monk's things by mistake,
> My old serge gown and rope that goes all round,
> I, in this presence, this pure company!
> Where's a hole, where's a corner for escape?
> Then steps a sweet angelic slip of a thing
> Forward, puts out a soft palm—'Not so fast!'
> —Addresses the celestial presence, 'nay—
> 'He made you and devised you, after all,
> 'Though he's none of you! Could Saint John there draw—
> 'His camel-hair make up a painting-brush?
> 'We come to brother Lippo for all that,
> 'Iste perfecit opus!' So, all smile . . .   (365–77)

There is no shortage of sweet angelic creatures in the painting (or
in the other 'Coronation of the Virgin' by Lippo Lippi in the Duomo
at Spoleto), and Browning catches a hint from the fact that the
words 'IS[TE] PERFECIT OPUS' seem to be emerging from the lips of
the pretty little angel who is close to Lippi.[64] The description of
this (as yet unpainted) altarpiece ends with an outrageous passage
which is one of the most Chaucerian things that Browning ever
wrote:

> I shuffle sideways with my blushing face
> Under the cover of a hundred wings
> Thrown like a spread of kirtles when you're gay
> And play hot cockles, all the doors being shut,
> Till, wholly unexpected, in there pops
> The hothead husband! Thus I scuttle off
> To some safe bench behind, not letting go
> The palm of her, the little lily thing
> That spoke the good word for me in the nick,
> Like the Prior's niece . . . Saint Lucy, I would say.
> And so all's saved for me, and for the church
> A pretty picture gained. Go, six months hence!

[64] Possibly a favourite of the painter's in real life. Mrs. Jameson observes: 'in the
representation of sacred incidents he was sometimes fantastic and sometimes vulgar;
and he was the first who desecrated such subjects by introducing the portraits of
women who happened to be the objects of his preference at the moment': i. 114.

The swift movement of the blank verse, punctuated by frequent marks of interrogation and exclamation, expresses the volatile character of the speaker, just as the complex and troubled cross-rhyming[65] of the verse of 'Pictor Ignotus' expresses (and helps to create) the timid and inhibited character of that very different painter. With his snatches of song, and his favourite exclamation 'Zooks!', Fra Lippo Lippi is a vivacious man with an imagination that is by no means confined to the world of the senses, as we see when he refers to Christ,

> Whose sad face on the cross sees only this
> After the passion of a thousand years.   (156–7)

More characteristic, however, is his use of such down-to-earth images as 'hip to haunch', and his description of his own stomach as being as 'empty as your hat'.[66] From boyhood onwards he has been an interested observer of animals, as he has of human beings, quickly learning

> . . . which dog bites, which lets drop
> His bone from the heap of offal in the street,   (122–3)

and it is characteristic of him to use animal images in his descriptions of human beings—though we notice that he does so in a manner which is humorous or tender, not brutal in the tradition of Iago or the Elizabethan 'Machiavel'. He is scornful of the officers of the watch who harry out

> Whatever rat, there, haps on his wrong hole,
> And nip each softling of a wee white mouse,
> *Weke, weke,* that's crept to keep him company! (9–11)

A few lines later he bursts out:

> Zooks, are we pilchards, that they sweep the streets
> And count fair prize what comes into their net? (23–4)

He is irresistibly attracted by the scurrying girls, who remind him of 'the skipping of rabbits by moonlight'.[67] He reports the Prior's

---

[65] At a first reading of that poem, one is likely to assume that Browning has simply chosen an unsuitable or unmanageable metrical form.

[66] ll. 44 and 86.

[67] l. 59, followed by l. 137.

remark, about himself: 'Lose a crow and catch a lark'. Later he uses an animal image in self-defence:

> . . . The old mill-horse, out at grass
> After hard years, throws up his stiff heels so,
> Although the miller does not preach to him
> The only good of grass is to make chaff.   (254–7)

The effect of these images is by no means to make him appear a mere 'beast' (a charge he refers to twice,[68] and which harks back to Vasari's reference to his 'animal desires'), but rather to emphasize his delight in the natural world, with which he has a deep instinctive sympathy. In fact these images relate closely to the main argument of his *Apologia pro Vita Sua*: the relations between Body and Soul, Soul and Sense. 'The Prior and the learned' admire Fra Angelico, on the ground that he elevates the soul without paying 'homage to the perishable clay', and urge Fra Lippo Lippi to

> Give us no more of body than shows soul! . . .
> Paint the soul, never mind the legs and arms!
> (188, 193)

Fra Lippo Lippi responds:

> . . . Now, is this sense, I ask?
> A fine way to paint soul, by painting body
> So ill, the eye can't stop there, must go further
> And can't fare worse! . . .
> Can't I take breath and try to add life's flash,
> And then add soul and heighten them threefold?
> Or say there's beauty with no soul at all—
> (I never saw it—put the case the same—)
> If you get simple beauty and nought else,
> You get about the best thing God invents:
> That's somewhat: and you'll find the soul you have missed,
> Within yourself, when you return him thanks.
> 'Rub all out!' Well, well, there's my life, in short,
> And so the thing has gone on ever since.   (198–201, 213–22)

Saint Jerome, Fra Lippo Lippi's present subject,[69] would have been

<hr />

[68] ll. 80 and 270.
[69] Vasari particularly praises this painting, which is 'in Duke Cosimo's wardrobe'.

suited to the taste of Fra Angelico, or to that of the Unknown Painter who preferred 'The sanctuary's gloom' to the light and excitement of the world outside and was content to paint

> These endless cloisters and eternal aisles
> 　　With the same series, Virgin, Babe and Saint,
> With the same cold calm beautiful regard.

Fra Lippo Lippi's reaction has been to make a ladder from his sheets and so to escape, in pursuit not only of 'three slim shapes, / And a face that looked up', but also of the beauty of the world in which man has the good fortune to pass his brief life:

> The beauty and the wonder and the power,
> The shapes of things, their colours, lights and shades,
> Changes, surprises,—and God made it all! 　(283–5)[70]

The comic genius which inspires the opening and the conclusion of the poem is deeply sympathetic, and the Italian painter whom the poet summons from the past, and lends a voice, enables Browning to praise and justify the art of painting, which he himself so deeply loved, as eloquently as he was to praise the art of music, in 'Abt Vogler', a few years later. 'Fra Lippo Lippi' is at once the celebration of a great advance in the art of painting and the celebration of a notable human success.

'Andrea del Sarto', by contrast, is a study in failure, and the tone is correspondingly muted.[71] A tradition connects the poem with a painting in the Pitti Palace in Florence. According to DeVane it 'grew out of Browning's attempt to describe the painter's portrait of himself and his wife . . . to John Kenyon'. Kenyon 'desired a photograph of the picture, and when one was not available, Browning wrote the poem and sent it instead'. DeVane's source is an article contributed to the periodical *Temple Bar* by Mrs. Andrew Crosse in 1890. Mrs. Crosse makes it clear that what Kenyon had asked for was a copy of the painting, not a photograph:

---

[70] Cf. p. 217, above.

[71] A failure, although he perfected techniques which had been pioneered by Fra Lippo Lippi: Mrs. Jameson, for example, remarks that the latter 'was the first who invented that particular style of grandeur and breadth in the drawing of his figures, the grouping, and the contrast of light and shade, afterwards carried to such perfection by Andrea del Sarto': *Memoirs*, i. 113–14.

When the Brownings were living in Florence, Kenyon had begged them to procure for him a copy of the portrait ... of Andrea and his wife. Mr. Browning was unable to get the copy made, with any promise of satisfaction, and so—wrote the exquisite poem of Andrea del Sarto—and sent it to Kenyon! No mean compensation for the doubtful copy of what some art critics declare is a doubtful picture, both as to the authenticity of the portraiture and the painter's name![72]

Behind Mrs. Crosse's account of the matter there lies a letter in which we find Browning hesitating to comply with Kenyon's request because 'The business of copying is carried on with remarkable rascality here.'[73] He urges Kenyon to commission him, rather, to purchase an original painting, which will not entail a wait of months and which will not cost very much more: 'Unless you liked, more than I am altogether sure that you do, Ghirlandaio & Frater Philippus [Fra Lippo Lippi]'—why not empower him to buy Pontormo's "Venus and Cupid"? Browning makes no reference to writing a poem about Andrea del Sarto, so that the statement that he later sent the poem to Kenyon in 'compensation' for being unable to send him a copy of the painting seems to rest wholly on the authority of Mrs. Crosse. It by no means follows that it is false: Mrs. Crosse may have had the information from Kenyon himself. In any event, Mrs. Crosse is right in stating that the portrait in question is 'doubtful': modern experts point out that the picture is in fact two portraits joined together, and add that there is no reason to suppose that it represents Andrea and his wife, or even to attribute it to Andrea at all. As Browning was probably ignorant of such un-certainties, however, and certainly knew the picture well, these matters do not concern us here: what does concern us is that the poem is in no sense a description of the painting. While it is likely that his knowledge of the picture played some part in inspiring 'Andrea del Sarto', it is a gross exaggeration to term the result 'a "translation into song" of the picture'.[74] As usual, the principal source of Browning's inspiration was not visual but literary, and the all-important literary source that lies behind the poem (as has always

---

[72] Vol. 88 (1890), p. 489.
[73] Unpublished letter, now at Wellesley College.   [74] Symons, p. 92.

been acknowledged) is Vasari's long and censorious *Life of Andrea del Sarto*.

The theme of the poem is clearly enunciated near the beginning of the *Life*:

Had this master possessed a somewhat bolder and more elevated mind, had he been as much distinguished for higher qualifications as he was for genius and depth of judgment in the art he practised, he would beyond all doubt, have been without an equal. But there was a certain timidity of mind, a sort of diffidence and want of force in his nature, which rendered it impossible that those evidences of ardour and animation, which are proper to the more exalted character, should ever appear in him; nor did he at any time display one particle of that elevation which, could it but have been added to the advantages wherewith he was endowed, would have rendered him a truly divine painter.[75]

The situation at the beginning of 'Andrea del Sarto' is brilliantly realized, and more unusual (in a monologue) than the death-bed scene found in 'The Bishop Orders his Tomb' and elsewhere in Browning's work. We are reminded fleetingly of Pauline, whose long hair overhangs the young poet at the beginning of that poem —but much more interestingly (as already noted)[76] of the scene in *Pippa Passes* where the young sculptor addresses a long monologue to the beautiful Phene, not realizing the truth about her past:

> . . . Sit here—
> My work-room's single seat. I over-lean
> This length of hair and lustrous front; they turn
> Like an entire flower upward: eyes, lips, last
> Your chin—no, last your throat turns: 't is their scent
> Pulls down my face upon you . . .   (Part II, ll. 3–8)

As he muses on the girl's beauty, on his future work as a sculptor, and on the books and other meagre contents of his room, Jules reveals the whole of his soul and of his aspirations. Whereas this scene between Jules and Phene is the work of the optimistic, Shelleyan Browning, 'Andrea del Sarto' reminds us (rather) of Gogol's 'Nevsky Avenue', in which a man who has been deceived in the nature of the woman whom he loves is drawn by her to his

---

[75] Ed. cit. iii (1851), 180–1.   [76] Above, pp. 66–7.

own destruction. Obliged to choose 'Perfection of the life, or of the work',[77] Andrea has chosen 'perfection of the life', only to find that his life is deeply unhappy while it is his work that is 'perfect'—too perfect, cripplingly perfect, 'perfect' in a sense which implies (for a man so richly endowed) downright failure. Whereas de Musset, in his slight dramatic piece on the subject, portrays Andrea as a simple cuckold outwitted by the youthful Cordiani, who escapes with Lucrèce at the end, leaving an absurd and unattractive André tippling with his friends, Browning penetrates much deeper into the psychology of failure and the nature of unhappiness.

If Andrea were of tragic stature, there would be no doubt about the nature of his tragic flaw. Vasari had been a pupil of Andrea's, and in the first edition of the *Lives* he treats Lucrezia with great severity.[78] Even in the second edition his attitude to Lucrezia remains extremely hostile, and his account of the part that she played in the painter's life is unambiguous:

Having fallen in love with a young woman whom on her becoming a widow he took for his wife, he found that he had enough to do for the remainder of his days, and was subsequently obliged to work much more laboriously . . . for . . . he was now tormented by jealousy, now by one thing, now by another; but ever by some evil consequence of his new connection.[79]

Painter-like, Browning's Andrea lives in the eye, and it is the beauty of Lucrezia's body that holds him prisoner. He is fascinated by the curves of her form, not least by the rounded outline of her hands and ears:

---

[77] W. B. Yeats, 'The Choice', in *The Winding Stair and Other Poems* (1933).

[78] In the words of John Shearman, 'Vasari's squalid account of the private life of Andrea del Sarto in the first edition of the *Vita* has been enormously influential; factually, a good deal of it is untrue. As we have seen, the artist did not marry beneath him, and he was not reduced to miserable circumstances by demands to subsidize his in-laws. It seems improbable that he neglected to support his own parents. . . . There is no sign that he lost any friends or professional reputation by marrying her. Finally, it is certain that Lucrezia did not abandon him on his deathbed': John Shearman, *Andrea del Sarto* (1965), i. 9–10. Shearman points out that 'Most of the gossip disappears' in the second edition, 'and is replaced, if at all, by more criticism of the man as an artist; this helps to explain why the first edition was more popular in the nineteenth century, and the second edition in ours': ibid.

[79] Ed. cit. iii (1851), 193–4.

> Your soft hand is a woman of itself,
> And mine the man's bared breast she curls inside. (21–2)

We do not have to wait long to find the perfectly revealing epithet:

> My serpentining beauty, rounds on rounds!   (26)

Lucrezia is not only reminiscent of the serpent who led to the Fall of Man: she is also an embodiment of the moon, whom she resembles in her inconstancy:

> My face, my moon, my everybody's moon,
> Which everybody looks on and calls his,
> And, I suppose, is looked on by in turn,
> While she looks—no one's.   (29–32)

There is irony in the very perfection of her beauty; for her 'perfect brow',

> And perfect eyes, and more than perfect mouth   (123)

are uninformed by soul, and it is this (as Andrea sometimes speculates) that has made of him no more than a 'perfect' painter. The most revealing image of all occurs immediately after his reference to the perfection of her beauty:

> And the low voice my soul hears, as a bird
> The fowler's pipe, and follows to the snare.   (124–5)

Her 'hair's gold' has also been a snare to him, but in the end we find that the woman who proved a 'fowler's pipe' to Andrea obeys 'the Cousin's whistle' no less unquestioningly.

Andrea thinks in colour, as well as in form, and in lines 35–40 he sees his own life (appropriately) in the most subdued of colours:

> A common greyness silvers everything,—
> All in a twilight, you and I alike
> —You, at the point of your first pride in me
> (That's gone, you know),—but I, at every point;
> My youth, my hope, my art, being all toned down
> To yonder sober pleasant Fiesole.

Browning introduces a landscape here just as a painter often does, and it is a background as carefully painted and as appropriate to the

portrait which is his main concern as the background of some great
Renaissance painting:

> There's the bell clinking from the chapel-top;
> That length of convent-wall across the way
> Holds the trees safer, huddled more inside;
> The last monk leaves the garden; days decrease,
> And autumn grows, autumn in everything.
> Eh? the whole seems to fall into a shape
> As if I saw alike my work and self
> And all that I was born to be and do,
> A twilight-piece.   (41–9)

The same colour characterizes his painting, and symbolizes its
limitations:

> . . . All is silver-grey
> Placid and perfect with my art: the worse!   (98–9)

He feels that it is appropriate that Lucrezia's whim should have
lured him away from the French court, and from his 'kingly days';

> . . . 't was right, my instinct said;
> Too live the life grew, golden and not grey,
> And I'm the weak-eyed bat no sun should tempt
> Out of the grange whose four walls make his world.
>   (167–70)

It is appropriate that we last see the painter as the light fades into
darkness:

> See, it is settled dusk now,

and leave him to sit

> The grey remainder of the evening out,
> Idle, you call it, and muse perfectly
> How I could paint, were I but back in France,
> One picture, just one more.   (227–30)

Sombre as the poem is, it is not a tragedy, and it would be untrue
to say that the protagonist comes to self-knowledge as the monologue progresses. Andrea sees the truth, with a sad lucidity, from
the opening lines. He knows that he is a cuckold, and he knows that
he is a failure. The fact that Lucrezia remains 'very dear, no less' is

due not to magnanimity but to uxoriousness. His sense of his own
lack of freedom is expressed in three significantly alliterating lines:

> . . . Love, we are in God's hand.
> How strange now, *l*ooks the *l*ife he makes us *l*ead;
> So *f*ree we seem, so *f*ettered *f*ast we are!
> I *f*eel he *l*aid the *f*etter: *l*et it *l*ie!   (49–52)

The central passage occurs just after Andrea has been telling the
uninterested Lucrezia how easy it is for him to excel most of his
contemporaries:

> Well, less is more, Lucrezia: I am judged.
> There burns a truer light of God in them,
> In their vexed beating stuffed and stopped-up brain,
> Heart, or whate'er else, than goes on to prompt
> This low-pulsed forthright craftsman's hand of mine.
> Their works drop groundward, but themselves, I know,
> Reach many a time a heaven that's shut to me . . .
> Ah, but a man's reach should exceed his grasp,
> Or what's a heaven for?   (78–84, 97–8)

Andrea lacks the elevation of soul that would enable him to aspire
greatly. For a moment he is disposed to blame Lucrezia:

> Had you enjoined [more] on me, given me soul,
> We might have risen to Rafael, I and you!   (118–19)

Yet almost at once he reverts to the truth. Even if she had urged him
to aim for 'God and the glory! never care for gain', he is by no
means sure that he would have responded:

> Perhaps not. All is as God over-rules.
> Beside, incentives come from the soul's self;
> The rest avail not. Why do I need you?
> What wife had Rafael, or has Agnolo?
> In this world, who can do a thing, will not;
> And who would do it, cannot, I perceive.   (133–8)

Browning brings out clearly the timidity which Vasari stresses as
a central weakness in the character of Andrea, and we see that this
is part of the general moral weakness which has made him a failure.
We now hear of the financial dishonesty into which his uxoriousness

has led him, and have a glimpse of his 'golden' period which reminds us of the (unrealized) vision of success in 'Pictor Ignotus':

> A good time, was it not, my kingly days?
> And had you not grown restless . . . but I know—
> 'T is done and past; 't was right, my instinct said;
> Too live the life grew, golden and not grey,
> And I'm the weak-eyed bat no sun should tempt
> Out of the grange whose four walls make his world.
> How could it end in any other way?
> You called me, and I came home to your heart.
> The triumph was—to reach and stay there; since
> I reached it ere the triumph, what is lost?   (165–74)

Men will excuse him, when they see pictures of his wife and realize how beautiful she was. He is determined to believe that he is a more fortunate man than Raphael—if he can:

> . . . I am glad to judge
> Both pictures in your presence; clearer grows
> My better fortune, *I resolve to think*.[80]   (180–2)

Towards the end of the poem the fact that Andrea is a failure becomes (if possible) even more evident. When he is telling Lucrezia how he had once been praised by Michelangelo, to Raphael one of the most memorable incidents in his whole life—he finds her attention wandering to such a degree that she has forgotten of whom he is talking:

> What he? why, who but Michel Agnolo?
> Do you forget already words like those?   (199–200)

Begging for her smiles, he has to descend to her low level:

> If you would sit thus by me every night
> I should work better, do you comprehend?
> I mean that I should earn more, give you more.   (205–7)

Her only reply to his plea for love is to insist that she must go down to her waiting lover:

> That Cousin here again? he waits outside?
> Must see you—you, and not with me? Those loans?

[80] My italics.

> More gaming debts to pay? you smiled for that?
> Well, let smiles buy me! have you more to spend?
> While hand and eye and something of a heart
> Are left me, work's my ware, and what's it worth?
> I'll pay my fancy.   (220–6)

This is the prostitution of an artist. Even the offer of a bribe does
not suffice to retain Lucrezia for this one evening. Andrea does not
have character enough to be indignant or rebellious about what is
happening to him. He is resigned, as a weak man may be resigned:

> I am grown peaceful as old age to-night.
> I regret little, I would change still less.
> Since there my past life lies, why alter it?   (244–6)

He recurs to his dishonest treatment of his patron and to his failure
to be a good son in abandoning his parents and allowing them to
die in want. He speculates idly that perhaps he will be given another
chance in heaven, a chance to compete with the three great masters,
Leonardo, Raphael, and Michelangelo. Here on earth these men
may have 'overcome' him,

> Because there's still Lucrezia,—as I choose.

He is not even convincing, when he makes the claim: such is the
measure of his failure as a 'soul'—a key word in this poem, as
everywhere in Browning.

Andrea is one of the most passive of all Browning's speakers, and
this makes it interesting to remember that the poem was probably
written in the very year in which Matthew Arnold excluded
Empedocles on Etna from his collected *Poems* on the ground that it
presented a situation 'in which the suffering finds no vent in action'
—only to reprint it at the request of Browning.[81] The passivity of
Andrea is brilliantly expressed by the verse, from the opening lines
onwards:

> But do not let us quarrel any more,
> No, my Lucrezia; bear with me for once:
> Sit down and all shall happen as you wish . . .
> I often am much wearier than you think,
> This evening more than usual.

[81] Cf. p. 239, below.

Throughout we notice the simplicity of the diction, and the occurrence of an unusual number of monosyllabic lines, like line 4—.

> You turn your face, but does it bring your heart?

—and line 172:

> You called me, and I came home to your heart.

Andrea speaks like an old man,[82] and the contrast between the verse in which his character is created and that of 'Fra Lippo Lippi' points forward to the contrasting verse spoken by the Pope and Dominus Hyacinthus de Archangelis in *The Ring and the Book*.

Whereas 'Fra Lippo Lippi' ends with the dawn breaking, 'Andrea del Sarto' is a 'twilight piece'. Lippi has escaped into the street, with its unruly vivacity: Andrea sits quietly at the window, in his own house, while his unfaithful wife goes to join her lover in the street. Lippi is full of life and movement—as the verse which he speaks makes evident: Andrea is resigned, languid, immobile— and this is just as brilliantly conveyed by the slow-moving verse of his monologue. The one man is free, the other 'fettered'. The one poem is full of colour: in the other the colours are muted. The one painter is sociable and Chaucerian: the other solitary. The one painter talks of what he will do, scurrying off at the end after promising to paint a fine new picture: the other talks of what he has done, and even more of what he might have done—or might he? Whereas the ranging amorousness of Lippi leaves him free, uxoriousness has reduced Andrea to the condition of a slave. The very 'perfection' of his art is a sign of his limitations, and of his ultimate failure. One is reminded of two passages in Ruskin. In the first, which occurs in *Modern Painters*, he states that 'in order to receive a *sensation* of power, we must see it in operation. Its victory, therefore, must not be achieved, but achieving, and therefore imperfect.' In the second, in *The Stones of Venice*, Ruskin claims that two 'great truths . . . belonging to the whole race' are 'the confession of Imperfection, and the confession of Desire of Change'.[83]

---

[82] The historical Andrea died at the age of forty-four.

[83] *Modern Painters*, Part i. sect. ii, ch. i (Cook-Wedderburn, iii, 118); *The Stones of Venice*, vol. ii, ch. vi, sect. 40 (Cook-Wedderburn, x, 214).

The contrast between the two painters is drawn at a point beyond the commonplaces of conventional morality: it might be argued (after all) that Andrea is faithful to an undeserving wife, while Lippi is clearly incapable of fidelity to any woman. It is much more important that Fra Lippo Lippi is faithful to the requirements of his art, while Andrea is not. The parable of the talents, which was never far from Browning's mind, is highly relevant to these two poems.

Browning's remarkable fertility, his extraordinary ability to create a new idiom for a new speaker, to be used only once and then discarded, is brilliantly exemplified by 'An Epistle containing the Strange Medical Experience of Karshish, the Arab Physician'. As he had already shown in *Christmas-Eve and Easter-Day*, Browning was deeply concerned by the religious controversies of the day, and in this poem he concentrates on a miracle described only in the Gospel according to Saint John, a Gospel which had already been under attack for a number of years and which he was again to defend in 'A Death in the Desert'. He takes the story of the raising of Lazarus from the dead and considers how it might have 'struck a contemporary'. Whereas the painters who have chosen the story of Lazarus have concentrated on the moment of his raising from the dead, Browning is concerned with his later experiences, and with the impression that he might have made on an inquisitive observer who encountered him. 'Karshish' is thus a poem with a double psychological interest: there is psychological interest in the portrayal of Lazarus, and psychological interest in the characterization of the narrator of the story, Karshish.

The choice of an intelligent medical man as narrator was a stroke of genius. Karshish has a speculative and wide-ranging intellect, and is particularly interested in the relations between the flesh and the soul—once again key-words in this poem.[84] Medical men have always been fascinated by the apparent connection between mystical experiences and epilepsy, and Karshish's official view of what has happened in this case is that

> 'T is but a case of mania—subinduced
> By epilepsy, at the turning-point
> Of trance prolonged unduly some three days. (79–81)

---

[84] 'Flesh': 3, 10, 24, 106, 114, 140 ('fleshly'), 270: 'Soul': 6, 114, 141, 142, 191, 207.

Yet his attitude to human experience is essentially reverent, as is emphasized in the opening lines:

> Karshish, the picker-up of learning's crumbs,
> The not-incurious in God's handiwork
> (This man's-flesh he hath admirably made,
> Blown like a bubble, kneaded like a paste,
> To coop up and keep down on earth a space
> That puff of vapour from his mouth, man's soul).

There is a consistency in the fact that he is devoted to his teacher Abib, 'all-sagacious in our art', and that he should be portrayed as writing to him a regular account of his travels. We are given the 'twenty-second' of his letters. Browning was always attracted by Jewish lore, and he had a natural sympathy with scholars, pedants, and enthusiasts of all kinds. We can sense his sympathy as he makes Karshish tell his old teacher that he is sending him

> Three samples of true snakestone—rarer still,
> One of the other sort, the melon-shaped,
> (But fitter, pounded fine, for charms than drugs).   (17–19)

Garrulous as he is—his garrulity is conveyed by the twenty-line opening sentence of the poem and by the presence of several other unusually long sentences, which contrast dramatically with the shorter and almost staccato sentences in which he describes his first meeting with Lazarus—Karshish is a highly intelligent man with a passion for medical observation which makes it natural for him to use a medical image to describe the distance between Bethany and Jerusalem:

> This Bethany, lies scarce the distance thence
> A man with plague-sores at the third degree
> Runs till he drops down dead.   (36–8)

He is interested in the 'viscid choler' which is 'observable In tertians', excited that he has heard of a new cure for 'falling-sickness', fascinated by the strange medicinal properties of a kind of spider that he has discovered. He is eager to tell Abib of his other observations, but cannot rely on the Syrian messenger who has promised to deliver his letter in gratitude for treatment of his

'ailing eye'. Yet Karshish has had one experience that he is burning
to share with his old master, and reflecting (ironically enough) that
no harm will be done even if his account of this particular case
should fall into the wrong hands, he sets out to give an account of
it, confessing that Lazarus has touched him with 'peculiar interest
And awe indeed'.

    As a trained observer, Karshish is at first at pains not to seem to
be exaggerating in any way the unusual nature of the case. He is as
interested in the psychological condition of his patients as in their
physical symptoms. Taking it for granted that Lazarus simply
passed three days in some sort of trance, he is fascinated not only by
the medical importance of discovering how this sort of healing
trance can be induced, but also by the effect that it has had on the
patient:

> This grown man eyes the world now like a child. (117)

Karshish finds himself wondering whether this child's view of life
may not have a greater validity than that of the ordinary adult:
perhaps this is a case of

> Heaven opened to a soul while yet on earth,
> Earth forced on a soul's use while seeing heaven:
> The man is witless of the size, the sum,
> The value in proportion of all things,
> Or whether it be little or be much.   (141–5)

Perhaps (he reflects) Lazarus has had experience of

> The spiritual life around the earthly life:
> The law of that is known to him as this,
> His heart and brain move there, his feet stay here.
>   (183–5)

Lazarus appears so obedient to God's will that he does not even
preach about his experiences, having no inner prompting to do so:

> Hence, I perceive not he affects to preach
> The doctrine of his sect whate'er it be,
> Make proselytes as madmen thirst to do:
> How can he give his neighbour the real ground,
> His own conviction?   (213–17)

By using his narrator so skilfully, Browning is able to present Lazarus in the most favourable light without making his story sound incredible:

> The man is apathetic, you deduce?
> Contrariwise, he loves both old and young,
> Able and weak, affects the very brutes
> And birds—how say I? flowers of the field—
> As a wise workman recognizes tools
> In a master's workshop, loving what they make.
> Thus is the man as harmless as a lamb. (226–32)

The introduction of Christ into the poem is most skilfully managed. So far from regarding Christ as an impostor, Karshish takes it for granted that he was a brilliant medical man, feels a sympathy for him, and only wishes that he were still alive, so that he could consult with him:

> Thou wilt object—why have I not ere this
> Sought out the sage himself, the Nazarene
> Who wrought this cure, enquiring at the source,
> Conferring with the frankness that befits?
> Alas! it grieveth me, the learned leech
> Perished in a tumult many years ago,
> Accused,—our learning's fate,—of wizardry,
> Rebellion, to the setting up a rule
> And creed prodigious as described to me. (243–51)

Karshish believes that Christ was killed by 'the mad people' because he was unable to prevent an earthquake (presumably the earthquake that is said to have followed His death). 'The other imputations must be lies', he continues, yet he feels obliged to tell Abib that Lazarus regards his physician

> As—God forgive me! who but God himself,
> Creator and sustainer of the world,
> That came and dwelt in flesh on it awhile! (268–70)

Having narrated this, Karshish apologizes for writing

> . . . of trivial matters, things of price
> Calling at every moment for remark,

and tells his old master how

> I noticed on the margin of a pool
> Blue-flowering borage, the Aleppo sort,
> Aboundeth, very nitrous. It is strange!

Feeling that some further apology is called for, for detaining a busy man with 'this long and tedious case', he goes on to describe how he first saw Lazarus, in lines that recall 'Childe Roland to the Dark Tower Came' and which are among the most remarkable that Browning ever wrote. Perhaps (Karshish speculates) it was because he was tired that the incident had struck him so strangely:

> . . . I met him thus:
> I crossed a ridge of short sharp broken hills
> Like an old lion's cheek teeth. Out there came
> A moon made like a face with certain spots
> Multiform, manifold and menacing:
> Then a wind rose behind me. So we met
> In this old sleepy town at unaware,
> The man and I.   (290–7)

The epistle ends with a sort of postscript which makes it clear that Karshish cannot get the strange opinion of 'the madman' out of his mind:

> The very God! think, Abib; dost thou think?
> So, the All-Great, were the All-Loving too—
> So, through the thunder comes a human voice
> Saying, 'O heart I made, a heart beats here!
> 'Face, my hands fashioned, see it in myself!
> 'Thou hast no power nor mayst conceive of mine,
> 'But love I gave thee, with myself to love,
> 'And thou must love me who have died for thee!'
> The madman saith He said so: it is strange.

It is a successful poem, and a complicated one. While Browning's original aim was no doubt to describe how the story of Lazarus might have sounded to an observer who heard it at first hand, he clearly took delight in creating the character of the observer, and in describing how the extraordinary experience might have affected the man who was raised from the dead. The merit of the poem is partly due to the absence of direct theological argument, partly to the fact that the fictitious character of Karshish appealed to Browning's imagination, and partly to the fact that the poet was given an opportunity of expressing a visionary view of life that had a deep appeal for him. Karshish is no atheistical physician like Chaucer's, but a man who is as conscious of 'The beauty and the wonder and the power' of the world as Fra Lippo Lippi himself, although the idiom in which he expresses this awareness is not that of an artist but that of a physician.

The supposed author of the other verse-epistle in the collection of 1855 is a man of a very different character. The idea for 'Cleon' came to Browning as a result of reading *Empedocles on Etna*, a work which so interested him that (as already mentioned) he persuaded Matthew Arnold to reprint it in 1867. In 1853, commenting on the work that he had excluded, Arnold had written as follows:

I intended to delineate the feelings of one of the last of the Greek religious philosophers, one of the family of Orpheus and Musaeus, having survived his fellows, living on into a time when the habits of Greek thought and feeling had begun fast to change, character to dwindle, the influence of the Sophists to prevail. Into the feelings of a man so situated there entered much that we are accustomed to consider as exclusively modern; how much, the fragments of Empedocles himself which remain to us are sufficient at least to indicate. What those who are familiar only with the great monuments of early Greek genius suppose to be its exclusive characteristics, have disappeared; the calm, the cheerfulness, the disinterested objectivity have disappeared: the dialogue of the mind with itself has commenced; modern problems have presented themselves; we hear already the doubts, we witness the discouragement, of Hamlet and of Faust.[85]

Arnold omitted *Empedocles* not 'because I had, in my own opinion, failed in the delineation which I intended to effect', but because he believed that poetry should 'inspirit and rejoice the reader', and that this work could not have that effect. There is clear evidence that Arnold himself sympathized with Empedocles and his dilemma: so much is evident not only from the drama itself, but also from the

[85] *The Poems of Matthew Arnold*, ed. Kenneth Allott (1965), p. 591. The manuscript notes are printed on p. 148 of the same edition.

notes about his protagonist which are preserved in a manuscript
at Yale:

He is a philosopher.

He has not the religious consolation of other men, facile because
adapted to their weaknesses, or because shared by all around and
charging the atmosphere they breathe.

He sees things as they are—the world as it is—God as he is: in their
stern simplicity.

The sight is a severe and mind-tasking one: to know the mysteries
which are communicated to others by fragments, in parables.

The impression made by Cleon, on the other hand, is that of an
unsympathetic man: a man with whom Browning himself does not
sympathize, and with whom the reader is not intended to sympathize. The poem contains fine lines and passages, such as the description of the beautiful slave whom Protus has sent Cleon as a gift—

> One lyric woman, in her crocus vest
> Woven of sea-wools, with her two white hands (15–16)

and the reference to

> . . . the little chant,
> So sure to rise from every fishing-bark
> When, lights at prow, the seamen haul their net.
>
> (48–50)

For all his sensibility and his power of words, however, Cleon is
above all an arrogant and self-centred man:

> It is as thou hast heard: in one short life
> I, Cleon, have effected all those things
> Thou wonderingly dost enumerate.   (44–6)

Protus has sent to ask Cleon certain questions about the meaning
of human life and the true nature of human happiness, and Cleon
replies at some length, with the comment:

> Nay, thou art worthy of hearing my whole mind. (181)

Cleon believes in Progress, but this does not lead him to adopt a
cheerful interpretation of human life, because he has concluded that
Zeus is indifferent:

. . . If care—where is the sign? I ask,
And get no answer, and agree in sum,
O king, with thy profound discouragement,
Who seest the wider but to sigh the more.
Most progress is most failure: thou sayest well.

(268–72)

He rejects with impatience the Tyrant's suggestion that a poet or
a musician 'survives' because his work survives:

I can write love-odes: thy fair slave's an ode.
I get to sing of love, when grown too grey
For being beloved: she turns to that young man
The muscles all a-ripple on his back.   (296–9)

His vision of his own old age is almost Struldbruggian in its
intensity:

. . . Thou diest while I survive?
Say rather that my fate is deadlier still,
In this, that every day my sense of joy
Grows more acute, my soul (intensified
In power and insight) more enlarged, more keen;
While every day my hairs fall more and more,
My hand shakes, and the heavy years increase—
The horror quickening still from year to year,
The consummation coming past escape
When I shall know most, and yet least enjoy. (308–17)

Cleon's philosophical speculations have repeatedly brought him to
the threshold of Christianity, to a point at which he feels that life is
meaningless without Divine concern and Divine intervention:

And thus our soul, misknown, cries out to Zeus
To vindicate his purpose in our life:
Why stay we on the earth unless to grow?
Long since, I imaged, wrote the fiction out,
That he or other god descended here
And, once for all, showed simultaneously
What, in its nature, never can be shown,
Piecemeal or in succession;—showed, I say,
The worth both absolute and relative
Of all his children from the birth of time,
His instruments for all appointed work.   (112–22)

Near the end of the epistle, after his horrifying vision of the meaning-
lessness of old age and death, he returns to this speculation:

> . . . It is so horrible,
> I dare at times imagine to my need
> Some future state revealed to us by Zeus,
> Unlimited in capability
> For joy, as this is in desire for joy,
> —To seek which, the joy-hunger forces us . . . (323–8)

The irony of the poem lies in the fact that Protus has asked Cleon
for news of Christ and of 'one called Paulus', and has sent a letter to
Paulus, for Cleon to redirect. Yet Cleon, in his cold arrogance,
turns away from the small group of men to whom the secret for
which he thirsts has been revealed:

> Thou canst not think a mere barbarian Jew
> As Paulus proves to be, one circumcized,
> Hath access to a secret shut from us?
> Thou wrongest our philosophy, O king,
> In stooping to inquire of such an one,
> As if his answer could impose at all!
> He writeth, doth he? well, and he may write.
> Oh, the Jew findeth scholars! certain slaves
> Who touched on this same isle, preached him and Christ;
> And (as I gathered from a bystander)
> Their doctrine could be held by no sane man. (343–53)

'Cleon' is a good poem, and the fact that Browning mentions it
in 'One Word More' may suggest that he regarded it as one of the
best in his two-volume collection of 1855. If we can hardly agree
with that estimate today, it is not because Cleon is an unsympathetic character but because we sense that he failed to engage
Browning's imagination, as Fra Lippo Lippi and the Bishop in
Saint Praxed's Church engaged his imagination. There is not the
slightest hint of pathos in the poem, as there well might be: Cleon
is (after all) a man who has devoted his life to the most arduous
pursuits and who, faced with the horror of a nihilistic interpretation of human existence, understandably turns away in contempt
from the unpersuasive form in which the teaching of Christ has

been reported to him. Browning portrays him as spiritually blind in his arrogance, and the resultant poem is nearer to satire than the greatest of the Men and Women poems. Cleon's view of human life is close to that of many men today, yet we read the poem with admiration rather than enthusiasm because we feel that Browning is getting at us—a feeling that we often have as we read his later work.

XIII

DRAMATIS PERSONÆ

It is probable that no man of our times has written so much and so well without general acknowledgment as Robert Browning.[1]

Men and Women, to the contents of which the last three chapters have been devoted, is the most distinguished collection of poetry to appear at any time in the Victorian Age. When, a few weeks before publication, Browning read 'Fra Lippo Lippi' to Tennyson and a few other friends, he had every reason to hope that full recognition was at last about to be accorded him. With a very few exceptions, however, the reviewers completely failed to rise to the occasion, and 'the reception of *Men and Women* was probably the deepest literary disappointment Browning ever experienced'.[2] Praise came from George Eliot, David Masson, Joseph Milsand, and a handful of others; but this praise must have been small compensation for the storm of abuse and misunderstanding to which Browning found himself subjected, and it is possible that the openly hostile reviews were less disconcerting than the fact that he was obliged to struggle to explain and justify his 'obscurity' and poetic aims to men as intelligent and well disposed as Carlyle and Ruskin.[3]

In 1865 Browning informed Isabella Blagden that most of the poems in *Dramatis Personæ* had been 'written a long time ago', and

[1] From an anonymous review of *Selections from the Poetical Works of Robert Browning* (1863), in *Chambers's Journal*, 19 (7 Feb. 1863), 91–5: quoted in Litzinger and Smalley, p. 205.

[2] Litzinger and Smalley, p. 16. Their extracts from reviews and other contemporary comments omit Milsand's outstanding critiques, for example his long and penetrating review of *Men and Women* in the *Revue contemporaine*, 27 (15 Sept. 1856), 511–46.

[3] Carlyle's letter of criticism and advice is given by Litzinger and Smalley on pp. 198–200: they also print the greater part of Browning's letter to Ruskin (pp. 14–15), which is to be found entire in *The Life and Work of John Ruskin*, by W. G. Collingwood (1893), i. 199–202.

that some of them had been seen by his wife,[4] but we have little further information about the date of their composition. In August 1857 he had told Isabella Blagden that he had 'begun to write poetry again'.[5] In May 1860 his wife reported that 'he has been writing a good deal this winter—working at a long poem which I have not seen a line of, and producing short lyrics which I *have* seen, and may declare worthy of him'.[6] That summer, however, he wrote little if anything, and about the end of March 1861 his wife told his sister that 'Robert waits for an inclination—works by fits and starts—he can't do otherwise he says. . . . I wanted his poems done this winter very much.'[7] The 'long poem' which Mrs. Browning did not see was probably 'Mr. Sludge', which her husband would have hesitated to show her because of her belief in the reality of clairvoyance, but as we do not know the precise date of composition of most of the poems in the volume we must tread warily in attributing such characteristics of the new poems as their emphasis on separation and failure in love to Browning's own experiences. The one thing that is clear is that he reacted to his wife's death with characteristic courage. He told Story that he intended to 'break up everything, go to England and live and work and write'.[8] During the next two and a half years he worked extremely hard, taking great pains about his son's education, editing two volumes by his wife, and publishing a three-volume edition of his own *Poetical Works*, as well as preparing *Dramatis Personæ* for the press.

The fact that the contents of *Dramatis Personæ* are essentially similar to those of the volumes of 1855 is emphasized by Browning's reference to the forthcoming book in October 1862: 'I hope to print a new book of "Men & Women" (or under some such name) in April or May.'[9] It is clear that he was speculating about possible categories of his shorter poems at this time, since in *The Poetical Works* of 1863 all the poems published in 1855 and in the two earlier pamphlets of shorter poems were divided into the three categories already mentioned.[10] Although he did not classify the contents of the *Dramatis Personæ* volume in the six-volume *Poetical*

[4] *Dearest Isa*, p. 212.
[5] Ibid., p. 3.
[6] *E.B.B.* ii. 388.
[7] Ibid. 435.
[8] *Story*, ii. 66.
[9] *Dearest Isa*, p. 128.
[10] See p. 77, above.

Works of 1868, as consistency would have demanded, it may be useful for us to make the attempt. 'A Death in the Desert', 'Caliban upon Setebos', and 'Mr. Sludge' are 'Men and Women' poems: 'James Lee', 'Gold Hair', 'Dîs Aliter Visum', 'Youth and Art' and 'Too Late' are Dramatic Romances: while the remaining poems, or at least the majority of them, are clearly Dramatic Lyrics.

One of the first things that strikes the reader is the absence of the conciseness which makes the best of the poems of 1855 so impressive. Several of the new poems retain this quality—notably 'Confessions', 'Prospice', and 'Youth and Art'—but as a rule Browning now requires more room, and at times the length of a poem is not justified by its significance. While the ninety-six lines of 'Abt Vogler' are full of matter, 'Mr. Sludge' becomes tedious long before the end of its 1,525 lines (for comparison, 'The Bishop Orders his Tomb' is 125 lines long, 'Fra Lippo Lippi' 392). This lapse from conciseness is well illustrated by the opening poem—or rather, sequence of poems —'James Lee'.[11]

In telling a story by stages, rather than revealing it as it presents itself to the speaker at a single moment in time, 'James Lee' is unusual in Browning's work. The speaker throughout is a woman who has lost the love of her husband, and the different metres of the nine sections express the moods through which she passes. In the sixth section it is interesting to find Browning incorporating a lyric which he had written almost thirty years before, long before he had met Elizabeth Barrett. One is reminded of *Maud*, of which the germ was a lyric which Tennyson had written more than twenty years before he wrote his 'little Hamlet', and while it would be wrong to describe Browning's early lyric as the 'germ'[12] of his sequence the term 'Monodrama' is as applicable to it as to *Maud*. As DeVane points out, 'the scenery of Brittany is everywhere in the poem', and it is likely that Browning wrote it during his holiday there in 1862: it is also probable that it was influenced by *Modern Love*, on receiving which Browning expressed himself 'astounded at the originality, delighted with the naturalness and beauty' of

---

[11] Renamed 'James Lee's Wife' in 1868.
[12] Cf. *The Poems of Tennyson*, ed. Christopher Ricks (1969), p. 1037.

Meredith's sequence of sonnets describing the course of an unhappy love.[13]

The plot of the poem was outlined in a letter to Julia Wedgwood: 'people newly-married, trying to realize a dream of being sufficient to each other, in a foreign land (where you can try such an experiment) and finding it break up—the man being tired *first*,—and tired precisely of the love.'[14] Without this letter one would hardly have guessed that the couple were newly married, while the wife's description of her skin as 'this bark of a gnarled tree' in the last stanza suggests a woman no longer young. It is inevitable that Browning should have thought of his own lost love as he wrote the poem, yet we find the usual divergence between the situation which he imagines and any actual situation which he had experienced: the speaker is a woman, and it is not death that has robbed her of the person she loved. In spite of fine passages, such as the opening of the last section—

> There is nothing to remember in me,
>   Nothing I ever said with a grace,
>   Nothing I did that you care to see,
>   Nothing I was that deserves a place
> In your mind, now I leave you, set you free

—in spite of occasional felicities the work is hardly successful as a whole, and it cannot stand comparison with earlier poems in which a woman is the speaker: the opening section, for example, can only lose from comparison with 'In A Year'. Browning was aware of this, and told Julia Wedgwood that he had 'expressed it all insufficiently, and [would] break the chain up, one day, and leave so many separate little round rings to roll each its way, if it can'.[15]

In August 1862 Browning told Isabella Blagden that he 'wrote a poem yesterday of 120 lines', adding that he meant 'to keep writing, whether I like it or no'.[16] Whether he was referring to part

---

[13] *The Letters of George Meredith*, ed. C. L. Cline (1970), i. 148 (9 June 1862). The case for the influence has recently been argued by F. E. Faverty in 'Browning's Debt to Meredith in *James Lee's Wife*' (*Essays in American and English Literature Presented to Bruce Robert McElderry, Jr.*, ed. M. F. Schulz, Athens, Ohio, 1967).

[14] *Wedgwood*, p. 123.   [15] Ibid.

[16] *Dearest Isa*, p. 119.

of 'James Lee' or to 'Gold Hair' (as seems more likely) it cannot be doubted that his comment describes the mood in which a number of the poems in *Dramatis Personæ* were written: a mood of determination rather than inspiration.

Of the other five poems in the collection which deal with love, the only one which portrays it as a source of happiness is 'Confessions', an unusual and gay little poem in which a dying man refuses to repent of a youthful love affair, surrounded though he is by 'physic bottles' and besieged by a pious minister of religion. His mind drifts back many years to a certain summer's day:

> At a terrace, somewhere near the stopper,
>   There watched for me, one June,
> A girl: I know, sir, it's improper,
>   My poor mind's out of tune.

There was a lane he could creep down, keeping close to the wall, so that however vigilant her parents were they

> [Could] never catch her and me together,
>   As she left the attic, there,
> By the rim of the bottle labelled 'Ether',
>   And stole from stair to stair,
>
> And stood by the rose-wreathed gate. Alas,
>   We loved, sir—used to meet:
> How sad and bad and mad it was—
>   But then, how it was sweet!

The poem is a good example of Browning's love of telling the truth about human nature, a truth which is not (after all) invariably sombre.

The other four poems all tell stories of failure in love, and in each the speaker is middle-aged. The two which are certainly successful are both Dramatic Romances. In 'Dîs Aliter Visum' the speaker is a woman who is addressing an elderly poet who had been 'le Byron de nos jours' ten years before. The two have met at a fashionable gathering, and the poem opens strikingly, in mid conversation:

> Stop, let me have the truth of that!
>   Is that all true? I say, the day
> Ten years ago when both of us
>   Met on a morning, friends—as thus
> We meet this evening, friends or what?

Browning has at once attained the aim of every storyteller, whether he writes in verse or in prose: he has caught our interest, and we wonder what has been said to occasion the woman's outburst, and what is to happen next. We soon find that the man is much older than the woman, and that when he met her as a young beauty, a decade ago, he was already sure of an eventual seat in the Academy and 'Famous . . . for verse and worse'. She has never forgotten the short walk they took together, by the side of the sea:

>   . . . The church
>   With spire and sad slate roof, aloof
> From human fellowship so far,
>   Where a few graveyard crosses are,
> And garlands for the swallows' perch.

She imagines what must have passed through his mind, as he made the 'prudent' decision not to snatch at the adoring young girl and so seize the brief renewal of youth which she could have brought him:

> Now I may speak: you fool, for all
>   Your lore! WHO made things plain in vain?
> What was the sea for? What, the grey
>   Sad church, that solitary day,
> Crosses and graves and swallows' call?

She points out that the great opportunity for them both had been missed:

> Was there nought better than to enjoy?
>   No feat which, done, would make time break,
> And let us pent-up creatures through
>   Into eternity, our due?
> No forcing earth teach heaven's employ?

If anyone is disposed to criticize the speaker's argument as betraying an over-simplification which is often thought to be characteristic of Browning it is sufficient answer to point to the level-headedness which she actually displays: in stanzas xiv–xx she faces the fact that the 'perfect . . . hour' would have passed, for both of them. One can hardly accuse the woman of being a simple-minded romantic, any more than one can accuse Browning of any lack of psychological insight when at the end of the poem the woman tells the poet that he might have 'saved two souls: nay, four', adding—

> For Stephanie sprained last night her wrist,
>   Ankle or something. 'Pooh', cry you?
> At any rate she danced, all say,
>   Vilely; her vogue has had its day.
> Here comes my husband from his whist.

This little tale of a French poet reminds the reader of de Maupassant and other masters of the nineteenth-century short story.[17]

'Youth and Art' is a simpler variation on a similar theme. A middle-aged woman looks back regretfully to the days when she was a poor student of music, and when the interesting young sculptor in the garret opposite failed to pay court to her. Since then each of them has succeeded in life, in the vulgar sense; but each of them has failed, in the real sense:

> But you meet the Prince at the Board,
>   I'm queen myself at *bals-paré*,
> I've married a rich old lord,
>   And you're dubbed knight and an R.A.
>
> Each life unfulfilled, you see;
>   It hangs still, patchy and scrappy:
> We have not sighed deep, laughed free,
>   Starved, feasted, despaired,—been happy.
>
> And nobody calls you a dunce,
>   And people suppose me clever:
> This could but have happened once,
>   And we missed it, lost it for ever.

---

[17] ' A Likeness' is a fragmentary study that reads like a sketch for a short story in verse or prose.

The same theme of the missed opportunity, which was of almost
obsessive interest to Browning, recurs in 'Too Late'. As in the two
previous poems, the man has failed to seize an opportunity, years ago;
but this time the man himself is the speaker, and the lady is dead.
The poem opens well:

> Here was I with my arm and heart
>   And brain, all yours for a word, a want
> Put into a look—just a look, your part . . .

The speaker has just received news of the lady's death, and the
verse recreates his sense of dramatic loss:

> But, dead! All's done with; wait who may,
>   Watch and wear and wonder who will   (37–8)

The poem is emphatically a Dramatic Romance, though the details
of the story are left uncertain. Perhaps he proposed to the lady once;
but if so, he now reflects that he should have tried harder. He
behaved prudently: the lady was not beautiful: in danger of being
'laid on the shelf', she married a popular poet—a man who is
now, as the speaker bitterly reflects, 'tagging your epitaph'. The
last lines make explicit what a sensitive reading of the poem may
already have suggested to the reader: that the speaker is drinking
as he muses, drowning the sorrows of a disappointed man. The
movement of the verse indicates this: with the straightforward
directness of the opening, we may compare the more hectic tone at
the beginning of stanza vii:

> Handsome, were you? 'T is more than they held,
>   More than they said; I was 'ware and watched:
> I was the 'scapegrace, this rat belled
>   The cat, this fool got his whiskers scratched.

As he continues to drink, the speaker becomes bitter. He proclaims
that he will live a 'successful' life of the most worldly kind, at the
cost of his own soul:

> Go on with the world, get gold in its strife,
>   Give your spouse the slip and betray your friend!
> There are two who decline, a woman and I,
>   And enjoy our death in the darkness here.   (117–20)

There is powerful dramatic irony in the concluding stanza:

> But I turn my back on the world: I take
> Your hand, and kneel, and lay to my lips.
> Bid me live, Edith! Let me slake
> Thirst at your presence!

Whereas he means that he should have slaked the thirst of his soul by loving her, in fact he is merely becoming maudlin as he reflects on the opportunity that he has missed:

> . . . There you stand,
> Warm too, and white too: would this wine
> Had washed all over that body of yours,
> Ere I drank it, and you down with it, thus!

Like 'Porphyria's Lover' and 'Mesmerism', 'Too Late' is a poem in which the speaker is a man whose mental balance has been upset.[18]

There is less story in 'The Worst of It', in which the focus of interest is again the mood of the speaker. He has idolized his wife, and she has been false to him. Almost perversely chivalrous, he argues that it is his fault that she has ruined herself:

> Yes, all through the speckled beast that I am,
> Who taught you to stoop; you gave me yourself,
> And bound your soul by the vows that damn:
> Since on better thought you break, as you ought,
> Vows—words, no angel set down, some elf
> Mistook,—for an oath, an epigram!

He himself is eager to forgive her. In the words of a sentence in Mrs. Orr which may well be Browning's own, 'Her account is not with him who absolves her, but with the world which does not; with her endangered womanhood, her jeopardized hope of Heaven'.[19] Regarding it as inevitable that she should be punished, he hopes that the punishment will come during her lifetime, and not afterwards. The most memorable stanzas are those in which he muses on her possible remorse when he is dead and she herself is old:

---

[18] I cannot agree, however, with the suggestion of Laurence Perrine that the speaker is on the point of committing suicide: cf. *VP* 7 (1969), 339–45.

[19] *Handbook*, p. 236. Mrs. Orr gives the sentence in inverted commas, citing no source.

It will come, I suspect, at the end of life,
  When you walk alone, and review the past;
And I, who so long shall have done with strife,
  And journeyed my stage and earned my wage
  And retired as was right,—I am called at last
When the devil stabs you, to lend the knife.

The very narrowness of the speaker's religious views emphasizes
the magnanimity that is particularly apparent in the following
stanza:

He stabs for the minute of trivial wrong,
  Nor the other hours are able to save,
The happy, that lasted my whole life long:
  For a promise broke, not for first words spoke,
  The true, the only, that turn my grave
To a blaze of joy and a crash of song.

A stanza or two later his naïve but generous casuistry brings him to
the proposition that 'truth is not as good as it seems!', a proposition
demonstrated by his own misfortune:

Far better commit a fault and have done—
  As you, Dear! for ever; and choose the pure,
And look where the healing waters run,
  And strive and strain to be good again,
  And a place in the other world ensure,
All glass and gold, with God for its sun.

There is more than a hint of ambiguity about the description of
heaven in that last line, as there is in the last two lines of the poem:

I knew you once: but in Paradise,
  If we meet, I will pass nor turn my face.

The only poem in *Dramatis Personæ* which does not deal with love
but is certainly to be regarded as a Dramatic Romance is 'Gold
Hair: A Story of Pornic'. The local legend on which it is based is the
sort of tale that would more often fire the imagination of a short-
story writer than a poet. It is a traditional story about a beautiful and
aristocratic girl who died in her youth and who came to be regarded
almost as a saint. Her only fault seemed to be a pardonable vanity

about 'her great gold hair', for as she lay dying she insisted that
it should not be disturbed. Many years later, when her grave
was opened, a treasure of gold coins was revealed—coins she had
hidden under her hair because she was a miser. The poem is not
one of Browning's finest, yet it is interesting because it is so unlike
the work of most poets, and because it vividly reveals his characteristic preoccupation with the truth. The concluding stanzas are
remarkably explicit:

> Why I deliver this horrible verse?
> As the text of a sermon, which now I preach:
> Evil or good may be better or worse
> In the human heart, but the mixture of each
> Is a marvel and a curse.
>
> The candid incline to surmise of late
> That the Christian faith proves false, I find:
> For our Essays-and-Reviews' debate
> Begins to tell on the public mind,
> And Colenso's words have weight:
>
> I still, to suppose it true, for my part,
> See reasons and reasons; this, to begin:
> 'T is the faith that launched point-blank her dart
> At the head of a lie—taught Original Sin,
> The Corruption of Man's Heart.

In 'Gold Hair', as in all his finest poetry, Browning is concerned
(as a novelist is concerned)[20] with the truth about human nature
although we may object that he is here expressing that truth in too
didactic a form.

   Whereas the visual arts play practically no part in the inspiration
of the poems in *Dramatis Personæ*, the collection contains the most
brilliant poem that Browning ever wrote on the subject of music.

   As a young man he was known among his associates 'as a musician

---

[20] It is appropriate that George Eliot should be responsible for the addition of
three stanzas (xxi–xxiii) in the second and subsequent editions. 'The great novelist
remarked upon reading the poem that its motive was not made sufficiently clear at
the point where the money is discovered. Browning took away her copy of the book
. . . and brought it back . . . with . . . three stanzas added': *Literary Anecdotes of the
Nineteenth Century*, ed. W. Roberston Nicoll and Thomas J. Wise ([i], 1895), p. 377.

and artist rather than as a poet',[21] and his passionate interest in
music went back to his early childhood. We are told that as a small
boy 'he stole downstairs from bed to listen to his mother at the
piano, and, as she ceased, flung himself into her arms, whispering,
amid sobs, "Play, play" '.[22] Looking back on his early life, he regarded such experiences as so important that he made an obscure
composer called Charles Avison his interlocutor in one of the
Parleyings with Certain People of Importance, printing the music of a
march of his at the end of the poem. 'I was studying the grammar of
music', he once remarked, 'when most children are learning the
multiplication table, and I know what I am talking about when I
speak of music'.[23] He was well taught, with the result that he could
set songs to music, compose fugues, and contemplate writing an
opera.[24] Among his masters was John Relfe, a man of note in his day
who wrote *The Principles of Harmony* and other works with the aim of
teaching 'not only Thorough Bass, but the whole arcana of the
science, so as completely to analyze any regular composition'.[25]

It is not surprising that music plays a very prominent part in
Browning's writings. In *Pauline* he asserts that music

> . . . is earnest of a heaven,
> Seeing we know emotions strange by it,
> Not else to be revealed.   (365–7)

In *Paracelsus* he makes the poet Aprile speak as follows:

> This done, to perfect and consummate all,
> Even as a luminous haze links star to star,
> I would supply all chasms with music, breathing
> Mysterious motions of the soul, no way
> To be defined save in strange melodies.   (ii. 475–9)

Passages in two of his letters to Elizabeth Barrett are equally
revealing. On 6 May 1846 he describes 'A large party at Chorley's'

[21] Sharp, *Life of Robert Browning*, p. 54.
[22] Griffin and Minchin, p. 17.   [23] Ibid., p. 16.
[24] He set Donne's 'Go, and catch a falling star' and Peacock's 'The mountain
sheep are sweeter' (DeVane, *Parleyings*, p. 255): for the idea of an opera, cf. p. 11,
above. It should be added that Browning probably exaggerated a little when talking
about his musical expertise: cf. H. E. Greene, 'Browning's Knowledge of Music',
PMLA 62 (1947), 1095–9.
[25] Griffin and Minchin, p. 17.

where there was 'admirable music . . . A Herr Kellerman told a
kind of crying story on the violoncello, full of quiet pathos, and
Godefroi . . . harped like a God harping,—immortal victorious
music indeed!'[26] It was natural to him to use a musical metaphor to
express the transformation which Elizabeth Barrett had wrought in
his own life, as he did when he referred to 'octaves and octaves of
quite new golden strings you enlarged the compass of my life's
harp with'.

She herself was less musical, and although there was a piano at
Casa Guidi, while Browning attended such concerts as he could,
music played a less prominent part in his life during his Italian years
than it had done before. Two poems in *Men and Women*, however,
'A Toccata of Galuppi's' and 'Master Hugues'—the one about a
real composer, the other about an imaginary one—remind us that
stories about composers and musicians appealed to Browning, as did
stories about painters and sculptors. From his father's books and
conversation, and from the talk of John Relfe, Browning had early
nourished his imagination with information about composers and
their work—as we are reminded by a brilliant image in 'Bishop
Blougram's Apology':

> Like Verdi when, at his worst opera's end
> (The thing they gave at Florence,—what's its name?)
> While the mad houseful's plaudits near out-bang
> His orchestra of salt-box, tongs and bones,
> He looks through all the roaring and the wreaths
> Where sits Rossini patient in his stall.   (381–6)

On his return to England music once again became one of the
principal delights of Browning's life. Mrs. Orr tells us that it now
grew 'into a passion, from the indulgence of which he derived, as he
always declared, some of the most beneficent influences of his life.
It would be scarcely an exaggeration to say that he attended every
important concert of the season.'[27] It was in these years that he
wrote 'Abt Vogler'.

As John Relfe's system of musical theory derived from that of
Vogler and Schicht, we may take it as certain that Browning heard

---

[26] Kintner, ii. 681–2, followed by i. 32.   [27] *Life and Letters*, p. 290.

about Vogler from his own master. Browning himself loved to extemporize, just as he loved to model in clay, and he must have heard from Relfe of Vogler's extraordinary gift for extemporizing, a gift so remarkable that when Vogler and Beethoven extemporized alternately at a musical party in 1803, one observer awarded the palm to Vogler. We are told that 'his extempore playing never failed to create an impression, and in the elevated fugal style he easily distanced all rivals'.[28] The fact that he was sometimes accused of being a charlatan would not have lessened his appeal for Browning.

While the facts in 'Abt Vogler' fit the historical personage admirably, Browning's main aim in this poem is not to characterize the speaker but to express the effect of music on the human soul. Here, as elsewhere, we notice the association of music and religion in Browning's imagination, an association that went back to his childhood memories. The poem is a profoundly religious utterance, and it is appropriate that the first stanza should refer to Solomon. In the opening lines Browning is probably remembering Prospero's great speech in *The Tempest*, and he is certainly playing with the old idea of architecture as 'frozen music', since the music that has been rising from his organ, and which has already faded, leaving 'not a rack behind', reminds him of the Temple of Solomon: Abt Vogler wishes that his music could remain, as the Temple did.

The verse movement of 'Abt Vogler' proclaims the difference between it and the two earlier poems about music. Unlike them, this is a soliloquy. Whereas the speaker in 'A Toccata' addresses the composer to whose work he has been listening, and the speaker in 'Master Hugues' addresses the composer whose work he has been playing, 'Abt Vogler' has been extemporizing the music which moves him to utterance. There is the strongest possible contrast between the colloquial opening of the earlier poems and the soaring opening of this, which is in a high lyrical style which recalls the ode:

> Would that the structure brave, the manifold music I build,
> Bidding my organ obey, calling its keys to their work,
> Claiming each slave of the sound, at a touch, as when Solomon
> willed,

[28] *Grove's Dictionary of Music and Musicians*, 3rd edn., ed. H. C. Colles (1928), v. 563b.

Armies of angels that soar, legions of demons that lurk,
Man, brute, reptile, fly,—alien of end and of aim,
    Adverse, each from the other heaven-high, hell-deep
        removed,—
Should rush into sight at once as he named the ineffable Name,
  And pile him a palace straight, to pleasure the princess he loved!

Such a stanza is most inadequately described, in DeVane's words, as consisting of 'eight alexandrine lines'. As George Saintsbury and others noticed long ago, the suggestion of the opening lines is strongly classical: lines 1 and 3 may be read as accentual equivalents of the classical hexameter (lacking the last syllable), while lines 2 and 4 correspond precisely to the even lines in elegiac metre.[29] While the first four lines open with dactyls, lines 5 and 6 (and arguably line 7) open with spondees, while in the last two lines, after the first foot of line 7, 'falling' rhythm gives way to 'rising'.[30] The effect is brilliant, since the rush of anapaests and iambs in lines 7–8 expresses the triumph of Solomon in the past, and the wished-for triumph of the composer in the present or future.

The first half of the second stanza echoes that of the first,[31] but the rising metrical pattern of line 13—

  x   /   x   / x x /   x x /   /   / x /
And one would bury his brow with a blind plunge down to hell

contrasts strongly with the 'elegiac' suggestion of line 14. Lines 15 and 16 also contrast with each other, the former (after the initial spondee) being in rising metre, the latter in falling:

/ / x   /   x x /   x x /   x   x / x   /
Then up again swim into sight, having based me my palace well,
/ x x / /   x /   / x   x / x /
Founded it, fearless of flame, flat on the nether springs.

As we consider the third stanza, which is more difficult to scan, we

---

29   /   x x   / /   /   x   / x x / x x   /
      Would that the structure brave, the manifold music I build,
      / x   x   / x x / / x   /   x x
      Bidding my organ obey, calling its keys to their work,
      /   x   x   / x x   /   x x /   x x   / x x   /
      Claiming each slave of the sound, at a touch, as when Solomon willed
      / x x / x x   / / x x   /   x   x
      Armies of angels that soar, legions of demons that lurk.

Cf. *A History of English Prosody*, iii (1910), 233–4.
30 Iambs and anapaests 'rise', trochees and dactyls 'fall'.
31 But for the second half of l. 11.

realize that what Browning is doing is to 'improvize' metrically with a brilliance that matches and recreates the brilliance of Abt Vogler improvizing on his instrument. The poem consists of twelve eight-line stanzas, rhyming ababcdcd, but the number of syllables in a line varies from twelve—

> Sorrow is hard to bear, and doubt is slow to clear[32]

—to seventeen:

> Up, the pinnacled glory reached, and the pride of my soul was in sight.[33]

Within the pattern of the poem we find a combination of rising and falling lines[34] bound together with a most intricate network of alliteration that recalls Hopkins.

In the fifth stanza dream-figures appear, as often happens when writers try to express in words the effect of music. In the 'Parleying with Charles Avison' Browning was to remember how in his boyhood his mother's playing created an army in his mind:

> Dream-marchers marched, kept marching, slow and sure,
> In time, to tune, unchangeably the same,
> From nowhere into nowhere,—out they came,
> Onward they passed, and in they went.   (iii)

In 'Abt Vogler' a commonplace becomes major poetry:

> Nay more; for there wanted not who walked in the glare and glow,
>   Presences plain in the place, or, fresh from the Protoplast,
> Furnished for ages to come, when a kindlier wind should blow,
>   Lured now to begin and live, in a house to their liking at last;
> Or else the wonderful Dead who have passed through the body
>   and gone,
> But were back once more to breathe in an old world worth
>   their new:
> What never had been, was now; what was, as it shall be anon;
>   And what is,—shall I say, matched both? for I was made
>   perfect too.

---

[32] l. 85: cf. l. 5 (quoted above), l. 23, and the first line of the last stanza (quoted below).   [33] l. 24: cf. l. 18.

[34] Rising lines are roughly twice as numerous as falling, the latter being most prominent in the first twelve lines of the poem. Saintsbury rightly remarks on 'that inevitable tendency of English dactylic metres to the anapaest' (p. 234).

In the seventh stanza the praise of music reaches a climax, as its supremacy over painting and poetry is asserted:

> But here is the finger of God,[35] a flash of the will that can,
>   Existent behind all laws, that made them and, lo, they are!
> And I know not if, save in this, such gift be allowed to man,
>   That out of three sounds he frame, not a fourth sound, but a star.
> Consider it well: each tone of our scale in itself is nought;
>   It is everywhere in the world—loud, soft, and all is said:
> Give it to me to use! I mix it with two in my thought:
>   And, there! Ye have heard and seen: consider and bow the
>   head!

As the speaker philosophizes in the last five stanzas we are reminded of Shelley's particular blend of Platonism:

> All we have willed or hoped or dreamed of good shall exist;
>   Not its semblance, but itself; no beauty, nor good, nor power
> Whose voice has gone forth, but each survives for the melodist
>   When eternity affirms the conception of an hour.

It is significant that Browning should have chosen a musician for the utterance of some of his own deepest convictions about life. The final stanza brings the poem back to everyday life:

> Well, it is earth with me; silence resumes her reign:
>   I will be patient and proud, and soberly acquiesce.
> Give me the keys. I feel for the common chord again,
>   Sliding by semitones, till I sink to the minor,—yes,
> And I blunt it into a ninth, and I stand on alien ground,
>   Surveying awhile the heights I rolled from into the deep;
> Which, hark, I have dared and done, for my resting-place is found,
>   The C Major of this life: so, now I will try to sleep.

The first line reminds us of the 'elegiac' lines in the first stanza: the spondee at the beginning of the penultimate line has the triumphant effect of emphatic notes on the piano or organ, proclaiming the achievement of the work: while in the last line we return from vision to common experience. It is interesting to recall that Vogler's most distinguished works were his Requiem and his Symphony in C,

---

[35] Cf. Hopkins, 'The Wreck of the Deutschland', l. 8:
  Over again I feel thy finger and find thee.

and that 'His system of harmony was founded on acoustics, and its fundamental principle was that not only the triad (common chord), but also the discords of the seventh, ninth and eleventh could be introduced on any degree of the scale without involving modulation.'[36] Although there does not seem to be any correspondence between the twelve stanzas of the poem and the constituent parts of Vogler's Requiem, 'the occupation of his last days', the poem itself is a sort of Requiem written by a poet who believed that

> There is no truer truth obtainable
> By Man than comes of music.[37]

The remaining shorter poems in the volume of 1864 need not detain us long. 'Rabbi Ben Ezra' and 'Prospice' are both lyrics, the former nominally dramatic in form, the latter making no pretence to be other than the poet's own direct utterance. The stanza-form of 'Rabbi Ben Ezra' may have been suggested by that of Praed's 'Cassandra', of which I quote stanza viii:

> Lo, where the old man stands,
> Folding his palsied hands,
> And muttering, with white lips, his querulous prayer:
> 'Where is my noble son,
> My best, my bravest one—
> Troy's hope and Priam's—where is Hector, where?'[38]

DeVane and others have argued that Browning is in a sense replying to the hedonistic philosophy of *The Rubáiyát of Omar Khayyám*, which could have been brought to his attention by Rossetti. In their turn, Arnold's sombre lines, 'Growing Old', are probably a reply to Browning, or a commentary on his poem.[39] Little as it may be to the taste of the present day, 'Rabbi Ben Ezra' is a much better poem than Arnold's, but we notice that Browning is hardly concerned at all to characterize the speaker. 'Prospice' remains an impressive utterance, and an utterance which throws light on 'Childe Roland'. It is instructive to compare the active tone of this poem with the elegiac and almost passive tone of 'Crossing the Bar'.

---

[36] Grove, v. 564b.   [37] 'Parleying with Charles Avison', section vi.
[38] The possible influence of Praed is implied by Fuson, p. 40.
[39] Cf. *The Poems of Matthew Arnold*, ed. cit., p. 538.

As a sort of antidote to the aspect of Browning which appealed to
the Browning Societies more than it does to us today we may take
'Apparent Failure', a little poem equally characteristic of Browning
which is tucked away just before the end of the volume. The
announcement that the Morgue was soon to be demolished must
have prompted many memories and macabre reminiscences in the
minds of Parisians, and this news item, which might have prompted
another writer to produce a short story, led Browning to write a
poem. The third stanza describes the scene:

> First came the silent gazers; next,
>   A screen of glass, we're thankful for;
> Last, the sight's self, the sermon's text,
>   The three men who did most abhor
> Their life in Paris yesterday,
>   So killed themselves: and now, enthroned
> Each on his copper couch, they lay
>   Fronting me, waiting to be owned.

The last stanza begins with an irony reminiscent of Clough's 'The
Latest Decalogue', yet concludes with a serious affirmation of faith:

> It's wiser being good than bad;
>   It's safer being meek than fierce:
> It's fitter being sane than mad.
>   My own hope is, a sun will pierce
> The thickest cloud earth ever stretched;
>   That, after Last, returns the First,
> Though a wide compass round be fetched;
>   That what began best, can't end worst,
> Nor what God blessed once, prove accurst.

The title of the poem is peculiarly revealing, reminding us (as it
does) of Browning's constant attempt to probe the true meaning of
the word 'success', as applied to a human life.

'A Death in the Desert' is the first of the three long monologues
in blank verse which account for the greater part of the second half
of the volume. Like 'Karshish' and 'Cleon' in *Men and Women*, and
'Caliban upon Setebos' in *Dramatis Personæ*, it was clearly inspired
by Browning's interest in the religious controversies of the day.

DeVane argues convincingly that it was conceived as an answer to Strauss's celebrated work, *Das Leben Jesu*, translated by Mrs. Charles Hennell and George Eliot in 1846 as *The Life of Jesus Critically Examined*, although before the poem was published Browning had also read *La Vie de Jésus*, by Renan, and Strauss's *New Life of Jesus*.

After the introductory lines, describing the parchment roll from which the greater part of the poem is supposed to be transcribed, the narrative begins with an account of the means used to restore Saint John to consciousness, as he lies on the threshold of death. The setting is vividly imagined:

> This did not happen in the outer cave,
> Nor in the secret chamber of the rock
> Where, sixty days since the decree was out,
> We had him, bedded on a camel-skin,
> And waited for his dying all the while;
> But in the midmost grotto, since noon's light
> Reached there a little, and we would not lose
> The last of what might happen on his face.

The greater part of the poem consists of the words spoken by John himself, so that once again we are presented with a monologue spoken by a dying man. What distinguishes the present poem—as its title, which is not its speaker's name, might suggest—is that Browning is not concerned with the character of the speaker, but with the speaker's message to mankind and his defence of his own faith against hostile argument: the account of the work given by Arthur Symons is essentially correct:

A Death in the Desert is an argument in a dramatic frame-work. . . . Delicately as the verisimilitudes are preserved, it is as a piece of ratiocination—suffused, indeed, with imagination—that the poem seems to have its *raison d'être*.[40]

'Caliban upon Setebos', too, is in a sense 'an argument in a dramatic frame-work': its sub-title, 'Natural Theology in the Island',

[40] Symons, p. 124. In 1882 Frederick W. Farrar dedicated *The Early Days of Christianity* 'To Robert Browning, Esq., Author of "A Death in the Desert", and of many other poems of the deepest interest to all students of Scripture.'

proclaims as much. Yet it is a much more remarkable poem, and a poem which brilliantly illustrates Browning's flair for the grotesque.[41] Johnson's rhetorical question—'Who but Donne would have thought that a good man is a telescope?'—might be adapted to the present case: 'Who but Browning, wishing to comment on the theological speculation of his day, would have recalled Shakespeare's strangest creation from the past, and made him deliver a lecture in an idiom especially created for the purpose?'

Theological argument in verse has a long and curious history, and the tradition of endowing a non-human being with a reasoning voice goes back beyond Dryden and Spenser to the Middle Ages. What makes 'Caliban upon Setebos' unique is the imaginative power which renders it truly dramatic. Unlike the Hind and the Panther, in Dryden's remarkable poem, Caliban neither speaks nor thinks like an intelligent human being. The clue to his mode of speculation is given by the epigraph, from Psalm 50: 21: 'Thou thoughtest that I was altogether such an one as thyself'. At the end of 1859, as C. R. Tracy has pointed out, the Brownings met Theodore Parker, the American Unitarian, and were much struck by his conversation about *The Origin of Species*. Parker maintained that

A man rude in spirit must have a rude conception of God. He thinks the deity like himself. If a buffalo had a religion, his conception of deity would probably be a buffalo, fairer limbed, stronger, and swifter than himself, grazing in the fairest meadows of heaven.[42]

---

[41] 'Grotesque art ... takes the type, so to say, *in difficulties*. It gives a representation of it in its minimum development, amid the circumstances least favourable to it, just while it is struggling with obstacles, just where it is encumbered with incongruities. It deals, to use the language of science, not with normal types but with abnormal specimens; to use the language of old philosophy, not with what Nature is striving to be, but with what by some lapse she has happened to become. This art works by contrast. It enables you to see, it makes you see, the perfect type by painting the opposite deviation. It shows you what ought to be by what ought not to be; when complete, it reminds you of the perfect image, by showing you the distorted and imperfect image': Walter Bagehot, 'Wordsworth, Tennyson, and Browning; or, Pure, Ornate, and Grotesque Art in English Poetry', reprinted from the *National Review*, xix (Nov. 1864) in *Literary Studies*, ed. R. H. Hutton (1902), ii. 366. Isobel Armstrong has continued the discussion of 'Browning and the "Grotesque" Style' in an essay in *The Major Victorian Poets: Reconsiderations*, ed. Isobel Armstrong (1969).

[42] 'Caliban upon Setebos', *SP* 35 (1938), 497. Mrs. Melchiori has a useful discussion of the relevance of the Psalm in her ch. vii.

Caliban's reasoning follows the same lines. He believes that
Setebos,[43] whom he conceives after his own image, lives in the
moon, being the creator of all sublunary things:

> 'Thinketh, He made thereat the sun, this isle,
> Trees and fowls here, beast and creeping thing.
> Yon otter, sleek-wet, black, lithe as a leech;
> Yon auk, one fire-eye in a ball of foam,
> That floats and feeds; a certain badger brown
> He hath watched hunt with that slant white-wedge eye
> By moonlight; and the pie with the long tongue
> That pricks deep into oakwarts for a worm.   (44–51)

Caliban believes that Setebos created him because:

> He could not, Himself, make a second self
> To be His mate; as well have made Himself:
> He would not make what he mislikes or slights,
> An eyesore to Him, or not worth His pains:
> But did, in envy, listlessness or sport,
> Make what Himself would fain, in a manner, be—
> Weaker in most points, stronger in a few,
> Worthy, and yet mere playthings all the while,
> Things He admires and mocks too, that is it. (57 65)

Like Hardy's President of the Immortals, Setebos is morally in
different:

> 'Thinketh, such shows nor right nor wrong in Him,
> Nor kind, nor cruel: He is strong and Lord.
> 'Am strong myself compared to yonder crabs
> That march now from the mountain to the sea,
> 'Let twenty pass, and stone the twenty-first,
> Loving not, hating not, just choosing so.
> 'Say, the first straggler that boasts purple spots
> Shall join the file, one pincer twisted off;
> 'Say, this bruised fellow shall receive a worm,
> And two worms he whose nippers end in red;
> As it likes me each time, I do: so He.   (98–108)

Caliban is not very good at thinking, and we notice that he
sometimes becomes most confused when his intuitions take him

[43] In *The Tempest*, I. ii. 373, Setebos is the god of Caliban's dam, Sycorax.

nearest to a higher truth. Immediately after the passage just quoted, in which Setebos is said to be 'Nor kind, nor cruel', Caliban is prepared to believe that he

> 'is good i' the main, . . .
> But rougher than His handiwork, be sure!'

Envy is one of Caliban's ruling passions: he envies Prospero, and when he plays at being Prospero he keeps 'a sea-beast, lumpish, which he snared', blinded and mutilated,

> In a hole o' the rock and calls him Caliban;
> A bitter heart that bides its time and bites. (166–7)

Accordingly at one point Caliban accounts for the attitude of Setebos to his creatures by supposing that he is envious of them. Perhaps (he speculates) there is another and greater power, whom he terms the Quiet:

> This Quiet, all it hath a mind to, doth.   (137)

Caliban believes that Setebos envies the Quiet, as he himself envies Setebos: here he disagrees with his dam, Sycorax:

> His dam held that the Quiet made all things
> Which Setebos vexed only: 'holds not so.
> Who made them weak, meant weakness He might vex . . .
> (170–2)

Unlike his dam, he does not believe in a heaven or a hell:

> 'Believeth with the life, the pain shall stop.
> His dam held different, that after death
> He both plagued enemies and feasted friends.
> (250–2)

The whole poem is a brilliant exploration of the primitive mind in its attempts to fathom the unfathomable. There is little point in talking of Manicheism or the Gnostic Demiurge (with whom Caliban's conception of Setebos has a good deal in common), or discussing whether Sycorax is closer to the Hebraic tradition than Caliban himself. The thought is confused and muddy, and it is meant to be so.

The vitality of the poem is due to the fact that the figure of Caliban made a deep appeal to Browning's imagination. He early acknowledged to Elizabeth Barrett his curious interest in insects and other creeping things:

I suspect . . . you have found out by this time my odd liking for 'vermin'—you once wrote '*your* snails'—and certainly snails are old clients of mine . . . never try and catch a speckled gray lizard when we are in Italy . . . because the strange tail will snap off, drop from him and stay in your fingers. . . . What a fine fellow our English water-eft is; 'Triton paludis Linnaei'—*e come guizza* (*that* you can't say in another language; cannot preserve the little in-and-out motion along with the straightforwardness!)—I always loved all those wild creatures God '*sets up for themselves*' so independently of us, so successfully, with their strange happy minute inch of a candle, as it were, to light them; while we run about and against each other with our great cressets and fire-pots . . .[44]

As Keats could identify himself with the sparrow on his window ledge, so Browning identifies himself with the creature which he describes in the opening lines of the poem:

'Will sprawl, now that the heat of day is best,
Flat on his belly in the pit's much mire,
With elbows wide, fists clenched to prop his chin.
And, while he kicks both feet in the cool slush,
And feels about his spine small eft-things course,
Run in and out each arm, and make him laugh:
And while above his head a pompion-plant,
Coating the cave-top as a brow its eye,
Creeps down to touch and tickle hair and beard,
And now a flower drops with a bee inside,
And now a fruit to snap at, catch and crunch,—
He looks out o'er yon sea which sunbeams cross
And recross till they weave a spider-web
(Meshes of fire, some great fish breaks at times)
And talks to his own self, howe'er he please,
Touching that other, whom his dam called God.

It is none the less true that Caliban is presented as (essentially)

a comic character. He is profoundly superstitious, and is terrified
that Setebos should discover the truth about him:

> Wherefore he mainly dances on dark nights,
> Moans in the sun, gets under holes to laugh,
> And never speaks his mind save housed as now:
> Outside, 'groans, curses. If He caught me here,
> O'erheard this speech, and asked 'What chucklest at?'
> 'Would, to appease Him, cut a finger off,
> Or of my three kid yearlings burn the best . . .
> Hoping the while, since evils sometimes mend,
> Warts rub away and sores are cured with slime,
> That some strange day, will either the Quiet catch
> And conquer Setebos, or likelier He
> Decrepit may doze, doze, as good as die.   (266–72, 279–83)

Suddenly a storm breaks out, and Caliban attributes this to the supposition that a raven has told Setebos of his wicked speculations:

> . . . Fool to gibe at Him!
> Lo! 'Lieth flat and loveth Setebos!
> 'Maketh his teeth meet through his upper lip,
> Will let those quails fly, will not eat this month
> One little mess of whelks, so he may 'scape!   (291–5)

It is clear that Browning is here using his dramatic genius, as he is
giving rein to his delight in the grotesque, for a definite and deliber-
ate purpose. He is satirizing any purely 'Natural Theology' by
giving us the reflections on the nature of God of a creature much
inferior to man, yet supposedly man's ancestor. The clear implication is that although mankind has progressed far beyond the
point at which Caliban was produced, men are still incapable of
giving a full and reasoned account of the deity, and of all the
mysteries of human life. The poem is therefore much more complicated than 'A Death in the Desert'. Whereas we are to accept the
reasoning of Saint John, we are to reject the reasoning of Caliban.
Although 'Caliban upon Setebos' is concerned with 'ratiocination',
therefore, it is concerned with it in a very different manner from
that which obtains in 'A Death in the Desert', and the result is a
much more imaginative poem.

In Browning's own day 'Mr. Sludge, "The Medium" ', was greatly admired, but with the passage of time what has become apparent is its marked inferiority to the best of his 'Men and Women' poems. It is very long, half as long again as 'Bishop's Blougram's Apology', with which it has something in common. It is the only monologue inspired by a man whom Browning had met, and the only one attributed to a man whom he despised and hated. That is the root of the trouble. Home made no appeal whatever to Browning's imagination: on the contrary, he had been the cause of one of the very few serious disagreements Browning had ever had with his wife, and her letters to her sister provide a suitable commentary on the poem. If, as seems likely, 'Mr. Sludge' was retouched or revised after Mrs. Browning's death, that would have been the worst possible time for Browning to have felt any imaginative sympathy for Home. Browning had no illusions about the possibility of communing with his wife through the assistance of a 'Medium', and the poem, so far from being an Apology, is simply a satire in the form of a dramatic monologue. Whereas Browning had no personal animus against Cardinal Wiseman, and the point of view that Blougram defends is in some respects a very sound one (as the reviewer in the Catholic *Rambler* pointed out),[45] there is really nothing at all to be said for Mr. Sludge, or if there is, Browning fails to make him say it. For this reason the length of the poem, which occupies more than a quarter of the volume, is quite indefensible: after a hundred lines or so we have learned all that we are to learn about Mr. Sludge: the rest is repetition.

The fact that Browning is more deeply concerned, throughout the volume, to comment on the Victorian crisis of faith than to give life to imaginary men and women, is emphasized by the 'Epilogue'. Since readers of the first edition of *Dramatis Personæ* were understandably confused about the identity of the speakers of the three parts, Browning subsequently identified the first as David and the second as Renan. The third, who, remains unnamed, is obviously the poet himself. The emphatic and confident rhythm of the first

[45] The old belief that *Men and Women* was reviewed by Wiseman himself has now been shown to be mistaken: see the article by Esther Rhodes Houghton in *Victorian Newsletter*, 33 (Spring 1968), 46. The reviewer was one of the editors of the *Rambler*, Richard Simpson.

part is an admirable expression of an Age of Faith. The hesitant rhythm of the second part forms a sharp contrast:

> Gone now! All gone across the dark so far,
>   Sharpening fast, shuddering ever, shutting still,
> Dwindling into the distance, dies that star
>   Which came, stood, opened once!

The two heavy spondees in the first line, followed by the increasing pace of the second, give a variety to the underlying pentameter norm which is extremely effective. In the Age of Faith, Renan says,

>   . . . We gazed our fill
> With upturned faces on as real a Face
>   That, stooping from grave music and mild fire,
> Took in our homage, made a visible place
>   Through many a depth of glory, gyre on gyre,
> For the dim human tribute.

Later, for a while, men were able to catch sight of

> Some vestige of a Face no pangs convulse,
> No prayers retard; then even this was gone,
> Lost in the night at last.

The rhythm of the third speaker's voice is again quite different:

> Witless alike of will and way divine,
> How heaven's high with earth's low should intertwine!
> Friends, I have seen through your eyes: now use mine!

The simple device of using pentameter triplets, with the emphatic alliteration of the opening line, lends emphasis to the poet's own statement of faith. Browning uses the image of the whirlpool more brilliantly than that of the potter and his wheel (in 'Rabbi Ben Ezra') to explain the uniqueness of each individual human life:

> Take the least man of all mankind, as I;
> Look at his head and heart, find how and why
> He differs from his fellows utterly.

Browning never wrote more revealingly about the philosophical basis of his interest in the individual.

And yet *Dramatis Personæ* contains far fewer vividly portrayed men and women than his previous collection: none of the three 'Men and Women' poems is primarily inspired by interest in the character of the speaker, while only one or two of the Dramatic Romances have any real claim to distinction. There is also a certain falling off in lyrical power: although 'Abt Vogler' is a triumph, most of the remaining Dramatic Lyrics are markedly inferior to those published in 1855. But the 'reading public' was becoming less shy of Browning, and *Dramatis Personæ* was—ironically enough—the first of his publications to reach a 'genuine second edition'.[46]

It is tempting to say that when Browning left Italy he left his genius behind him. Of course it is an exaggeration, and when we try to account for the relative decline in his work we are puzzled by the difficulty of distinguishing between his debt to Italy and his debt to his wife. As we have already noted, Italy had inspired some of his finest work (notably 'My Last Duchess') before he met Elizabeth Barrett, while he wrote little in the years immediately after his marriage. That he wrote most of his greatest shorter poems during the years when he lived in Italy with his wife is undeniable, but if (as he himself stated) most of the poems in *Dramatis Personæ* had been written 'a long time ago', and if 'Mr. Sludge' was the 'long poem' that he did not show her,[47] then it seems likely that the decline had begun while they were still together in Italy. What happened (we may conjecture) is that during the period when he was still discouraged by the miserable reception accorded to *Men and Women* he had also to face the heaviest blow of his life and to leave Italy with the feeling that he was no longer young and that his 'kingly days'[48] had come to an end.

Italy had provided ideal working conditions for him, but perhaps that was only because he took Italy very much on his own terms. There is a curiously revealing passage in a letter to Isabella Blagden written five years after his wife's death:

I agree with you [Browning wrote] & always did, as to the un-interestingness of the Italians individually, as thinking, originating souls: I never read a line in a modern Italian book that was of use to

---

[46] DeVane, p. 283.   [47] See p. 245, above.   [48] 'Andrea del Sarto', l. 165.

me,—never saw a flash of poetry come out of an Italian *word*: in art, in action, *yes*,—not in the region of ideas: I always said, they *are* poetry, don't and can't *make* poetry ... my liking for Italy was always a selfish one,—I felt alone with my own soul there.[49]

Precisely. Italy provided Browning in his prime with what he needed as a poet, a refuge from the distracting pressures of Victorian England from which Tennyson was fated never to escape. Italy saved Browning from becoming just another Eminent Victorian. As soon as he returned to the England of *The Origin of Species* and Bishop Colenso and 'our Essays-and-Reviews' debate'[50] he was inevitably caught up in the fog of Worry that pervaded the age. In England there was no shortage of people for him to talk to: 'here', as he told Isabella Blagden, 'there are fifties and hundreds, even of my acquaintance, who do habitually walk up & down in the lands of thought I live in, . . . and I never saw footprint of an Italian there yet'.[51] It is most doubtful whether this intellectual hubbub was beneficial for his poetry. What is certain is that the play of his imagination round the drama of human existence was never again to be so untrammelled or so audacious as it had been when he wrote 'The Bishop Orders his Tomb' and 'Fra Lippo Lippi', although it blazes up here and there in his later work, most notably in the more successful of the monologues in *The Ring and the Book*, an Italian story inspired by an old book he had found in Florence.

[49] *Dearest Isa*, pp. 238–9.   [50] 'Gold Hair', l. 143.   [51] *Dearest Isa*, p. 239.

XIV

THE RING AND THE BOOK

There, we say, is the grand peculiarity; the immeasurable one; distinguishing, to a really infinite degree, the poorest historical Fact from all Fiction whatsoever. Fiction, 'Imagination', 'Imaginative Poetry,' etc. etc., except as the vehicle for truth, or *fact* of some sort . . . what is it? Let the Minerva and other Presses respond!

CARLYLE

The Ring and the Book is serious experimentation.

EZRA POUND[1]

The Ring and the Book marks the end of Browning's major period. Although he lived for another twenty years, and continued to write prolifically, the genius which had blazed out in *Men and Women* appears only fitfully in his later volumes, obscured (too often) by a dense smog of verbal pollution. In his longest and most ambitious poem he attempted to build a series of dramatic monologues into a great work which should stand as the crowning masterpiece of his career. The result is certainly the most impressive long poem of the Victorian Age,[2] yet its limitations are very marked and it is appropriate that its structure should so markedly recall the unfunctional elaboration of Victorian Gothic.

As we have seen, Browning early conceived the ambition of writing a long poem. It was only after the relative failure of *Paracelsus*, the absolute failure of *Sordello*, and the slow dawning of the realization that he was not destined to be a successful playwright, that he was prepared to give sustained attention to the writing of shorter poems. During his courtship of Elizabeth Barrett he insisted (in a passage already quoted)[3] that he had

---

[1] *Past and Present*, Book ii, ch. 1, penultimate paragraph; *Literary Essays of Ezra Pound*, ed. T. S. Eliot (1954), p. 33.
[2] If we exclude *In Memoriam*, as being (rather) a sequence of elegiac lyrics.
[3] p. 116, above.

'never . . . begun, even, what I hope I was born to begin and end,—
"R. B. a poem" ', and told her that when he began to plan his
'great building' he would want her 'to come with me and judge it
and counsel me before the scaffolding is taken down'.[4] The idea of
writing a long poem was associated with the idea of speaking out in
his own voice, an ambition of which, as we have seen,[5] Elizabeth
Barrett strongly approved. It is a paradox thoroughly characteristic
of Browning's strange career that the nearest he was ever to come to
fulfilling his ambition was to be in a poem written after his wife's
death, on a subject in which 'she never took the least interest . . .
[even] so much as to wish to inspect the papers'.[6]

It is not difficult to see why the subject which failed to appeal to
Elizabeth Barrett so fascinated her husband:

Do you remember once [Julia Wedgwood asked him, with reference to
this poem] saying to me that your Wife was quite wanting in . . . the
scientific interest in evil?—I think you said, the physiology of wrong.
I feel as if that interest were in you unduly predominant. . . . I know
that we can only discern the white against the black. But hatred and
scorn of evil, though it be inseparable from the love of good, ought
not surely to predominate over it?[7]

'In this case, I think you do correctly indicate a fault of my nature',
Browning replied: '. . . I believe I do unduly like the study of
morbid cases of the soul';[8] but he maintained that in this poem (at
least) he had found a rich and legitimate field for the kind of study
of 'moral science' which so appealed to him:

I was struck with the enormous wickedness and weakness of the
main composition of the piece, and with the incidental evolution of
good thereby—good to the priest, to the poor girl, to the old Pope,
who judges anon, and, I would fain hope, to who reads and applies my
reasoning to his own experience, which is not likely to fail him. The
curious depth below depth of depravity here—in this chance lump
taken as a sample of the soil—might well have warned another from
spreading it out,—but I thought that, since I could do it, and even
liked to do it, my affair it was rather than another's.[9]

[4] Kintner, i. 17, 123.   [5] Cf. p. 118, above.   [6] *Wedgwood*, p. 168.
[7] Ibid., pp. 152–3.   [8] Ibid., p. 158.
[9] Ibid., p. 159. Cf. a remark of Dostoevsky's, who introduced a series of accounts of
notorious trials in his periodical, *Vremya* (February 1861), as 'More interesting than

It is a very Italian story, the dramatis personæ being recognizable descendants of the men and women of the Renaissance who had already inspired some of Browning's greatest poetry. At the structural centre he found a trial, which gave him an opportunity for a full deployment of his casuistical skill: at the psychological centre, behind all the evil and the squalor, he found—or thought he found —a chivalrous man and a woman of the type which had already been prominent in a number of his earlier poems: a young girl as innocent as Pippa yet fated to live through experiences as terrible as those of the Duke's first wife in 'My Last Duchess'.

Or of Beatrice in *The Cenci*. Eleven years after Browning's death a third account of the Franceschini trial was discovered in a volume that turned up in Rome, and it is appropriate that the same volume contains an account of the trial of Beatrice Cenci. One of the most exciting things about the story that Browning found in The Old Yellow Book must have been the fact that it had so much in common with the story dramatized by the idol of his youth in one of the most remarkable of his productions. In the Preface to *The Cenci* Shelley describes how 'A Manuscript was communicated to me during my travels in Italy, which was copied from the archives of the Cenci Palace at Rome, and contains a detailed account of . . . horrors' in which a beautiful and innocent young woman was involved in a hideous situation by a grossly evil older man, a situation involving murder and an execution, in spite of appeals to the Pope:[10]

Such a story [Shelley had commented], if told so as to present to the reader all the feelings of those who once acted it, their hopes and fears, their confidences and misgivings, their various interests, passions, and opinions, acting upon and with each other, yet all conspiring to one tremendous end, would be as a light to make

any kind of novel, since they throw light on such dark aspects of the human soul as art does not like to touch on, and, even if it does, it does so only in passing': see Katharine Strelsky, 'Lacenaire and Raskolnikov', *The Times Literary Supplement*, 8 Jan. 1971. Like Dostoevsky, Browning refused to deal with such manifestations of the human personality 'only in passing'.

[10] In *The Cenci*, of course, Beatrice herself is guilty, because she is driven to join in murdering her father, who has made her the victim of his incestuous passion.—The similarities between certain aspects of *The Cenci* and *The Ring and the Book* have been noticed by a number of critics, notably Betty Miller (pp. 231-3).

apparent some of the most dark and secret caverns of the human heart.

Shelley observes later:

I have endeavoured as nearly as possible to represent the characters as they probably were, and have sought to avoid the error of making them actuated by my own conceptions of right or wrong, false or true: thus under a thin veil converting names and actions of the sixteenth century into cold impersonations of my own mind.

In dramatizing this story of Catholics who were yet capable of 'perseverance in enormous guilt' Shelley adds that he has avoided 'what is commonly called mere poetry', writing instead in 'the familiar language of men'. In all these respects—though not in any avoidance of 'what is vulgarly termed a moral purpose'—Browning's poem recalls Shelley's drama, and it is no surprise to find that at one point he intended to entitle it simply *The Franceschini*.[11]

Browning bought the Old Yellow Book in June 1860, but the old belief that he immediately settled the plan of the poem is clearly mistaken.[12] William Rossetti gives a more nearly accurate account of the matter:

He began it in October '64. Was staying at Bayonne, and walked out to a mountain-gorge traditionally said to have been cut or kicked out by Roland, and there laid out the full plan of his twelve cantos, accurately carried out in the execution.[13]

The delay of four years between the time when the germ of the poem came to Browning and the time when he began writing it was in accordance with his usual habit of composition. As Rossetti

---

[11] Miller, p. 233.

[12] Here I agree with DeVane. In a passage in *An Artist's Reminiscences*, by Rudolf Lehmann (1894), Browning is quoted as saying: 'When I had read it, my plan was at once settled' (p. 224).

[13] *Rossetti Papers 1862 to 1870*, ed. William Michael Rossetti (1903), p. 302. Part of the passage is quoted by William O. Raymond in an important essay reprinted in *The Infinite Moment*. Raymond points out that Browning visited *le pas de Roland* 'about August 20', not in October (p. 85). Thinking again about Roland would have stimulated his imagination. On 3 October he told Julia Wedgwood: 'I have got the whole of [the] poem . . . well in my head, shall write the Twelve books of it in six months, and then take breath again': *Wedgwood*, p. 95.

records, 'he seldom or never, unless in quite brief poems, feels the inspiring impulse and sets the thing down into words at the same time—often stores-up a subject long before he writes it'.[14] The story had never been long absent from his mind, and on several occasions he offered it to friends as an eligible subject. It is understandable that he saw it as possible material for a novelist, but the fact that he offered it to Trollope is more surprising than the fact that the author of *Barchester Towers* 'couldn't manage it'. Even more surprisingly, perhaps, Browning also offered it to Tennyson.[15] By 1862, however, he had decided to write about the Franceschini affair himself. In September of that year he asked Isabella Blagden to borrow for him 'a M.S. account of the trial of Count Francesco Guidi [*sic*] for the murder of his wife,—which I am anxious to collate with my own collection of papers on the subject'.[16] A month later, acknowledging receipt of the papers, he added: 'I am going to make a regular poem of it . . . which shall be a strong thing, if I can manage it.'[17] William Allingham records a curious fact about the early development of the poem, in Browning's own words: 'I began it in rhymed couplets, like *Laurence Bloomfield*, but thought by and by I might as well have my fling, and so turned to blank verse.'[18] He wrote remarkably fast: at the beginning of November 1865 Tennyson told Allingham that Browning's 'new poem has 15,000 lines',[19] and DeVane is probably right in concluding that the greater part of the poem was written between October 1864 and November 1865. Before its completion there were 'spaces of interruption, months at a time',[20] but Browning told Rossetti that it was 'all [written] consecutively—not some of the later parts before the earlier'.[21]

He wanted it read consecutively, too, as he explained to Allingham:

I want people not to turn to the end, but to read through in proper

[14] *Rossetti Papers*, p. 302.

[15] *William Allingham: A Diary*, ed. H. Allingham and D. Radford (1907), pp. 180, 326.

[16] *Dearest Isa*, p. 124.   [17] Ibid., p. 128.

[18] *William Allingham: A Diary*, p. 181 (26 May 1868). *Laurence Bloomfield in Ireland: A Modern Poem*, by Allingham, was published in 1864.

[19] Ibid., p. 128.   [20] *Wedgwood*, p. 140.   [21] *Rossetti Papers*, p. 302.

order. Magazine, you'll say: but no, I don't like the notion of being
sandwiched between Politics and Deer-Stalking, say. I think of
bringing it out in four monthly volumes, giving people time to read
and digest it, part by part, but not to forget what has gone before.[22]

This procedure, reminiscent (like other features of the poem) of
the novels of the time, was adopted, and the poem appeared in four
volumes between November 1868 and February 1869. Its success
was beyond question, and critics who were beginning to realize
that they had been unjust to Browning's earlier volumes vied with
each other in lavishing praise on his latest publication. The reviewer
in the *Athenæum* recorded his conviction 'not merely that "The
Ring and the Book" is beyond all parallel the supremest poetical
achievement of our time, but that it is the most precious and
profound spiritual treasure that England has produced since the
days of Shakspeare'.[23] Such hyperbole invites contradiction, and
there have been many critics with grave reservations about Browning's 'Roman Murder Story'. 'This is no way to tell a story',
David Daiches observes, while Edmund Wilson seemed to grudge
the admission that '*The Ring and the Book* still has some claims to
distinction'.[24] Recently, however, there has been a marked revival
of interest, and the detailed 'Reading' by Richard D. Altick and
James F. Loucks is only the most thoroughgoing of a number of
reappraisals.[25] Any critic attempting a reassessment of Browning's
work as a whole is bound to make his own estimate of the place in it
occupied by his most ambitious poem.

It will be best to begin with a brief account of the structure.
Browning was seldom happy in the openings of his long poems,
and that of *The Ring and the Book* is abrupt in a manner more appropriate to a Dramatic Romance or Lyric than to a poem of great
length:

Do you see this Ring?

---

[22] *William Allingham: A Diary*, p. 181 (26 May 1868).

[23] *Athenæum*, 20 Mar. 1869 (Litzinger and Smalley, p. 317). The writer was
Robert Williams Buchanan.

[24] David Daiches, *A Critical History of English Literature* (1960), ii. 1007; Edmund
Wilson, *The Shores of Light* (1952), p. 36.

[25] *Browning's Roman Murder Story: A Reading of 'The Ring and the Book'* (Chicago
and London, 1968).

The Ring is a symbol for the poem which he is about to construct from the

> . . . pure crude fact
> Secreted from man's life when hearts beat hard,
> And brains, high-blooded, ticked two centuries since.
>
> (i. 35–7)[26]

Browning's Miltonic sense of being constantly in the sight of God comes out very clearly when he describes how

> . . . a Hand,
> Always above my shoulder, pushed me once,   (40–1)

in the direction of the stall where he found the book. As a ring is made from gold, so his story is made from the fact contained in the Book. Although the opening is less confusing than that of *Sordello*, the symbol of the Ring is not very helpful and it is a relief to reach the preliminary outline of the story. This makes it clear that Pompilia is innocent, Guido an unmitigated scoundrel, and Caponsacchi a chivalrous priest who came to the rescue of Pompilia 'in a glory of armour like Saint George'.[27] As if trying to reply to Carlyle's doubts about the validity of poetry and fictional writing, the poet meditates on the nature of imaginative truth:

> Is fiction which makes fact alive, fact too?
> The somehow may be thishow.   (705–6)

He then introduces the speakers whom (as in *Sordello*) he is about to summon from the grave, ending Part I with the celebrated invocation to 'lyric Love, half angel and half bird'.

Having been told the truth in Part I, we are presented (in Parts II–IV) with three perversions of the truth. It is as if we found ourselves back in Chaucer's House of Rumour, listening to three versions of an ancient *cause célèbre*. The first speaker, 'Half-Rome', is a great believer in the rights of husbands, and therefore a strong supporter of Guido. His introductory lines give a vivid impression of the glee of the crowd as they gaze at the public exposure of the

---

[26] Repeated at ll. 86–8. Quotations are from vols. viii–x of *The Poetical Works* of 1888–9.
[27] i. 585. As DeVane points out, Browning changes the date of Pompilia's flight from her husband to 23 April, St. George's Day.

bodies of Pompilia's parents. This man sees Guido as Adam, Pompilia as Eve, and Caponsacchi as Lucifer.[28] Although Browning makes him a long-winded gossip, we notice that he is made to pass over the murder itself in half a dozen lines because Browning wants to leave that for other narrators. Half-Rome's view is simply that Guido is a wronged husband who

> Revenged his own wrong like a gentleman. (ii. 1529)

We already know that this is a prejudiced and absurd interpretation of what has happened.

'The Other Half-Rome' is as violently pro-Pompilia as the previous speaker is pro-Guido. In the early paragraphs of his speech Browning seems less concerned to characterize his speaker than he usually is, no doubt because the view of Pompilia as 'a saint and martyr both' is less remote from the poet's own than that presented in most of the other monologues. 'Tertium Quid', by way of contrast, is admirably characterized, from his opening words onwards:

> True, Excellency—as his Highness says,
> Though she's not dead yet, she's as good as stretched
> Symmetrical beside the other two;
> Though he's not judged yet, he's the same as judged,
> So do the facts abound and superabound:
> And nothing hinders that we lift the case
> Out of the shade into the shine, allow
> Qualified persons to pronounce at last,
> Nay, edge in an authoritative word
> Between this rabble's-brabble of dolts and fools
> Who make up reasonless unreasoning Rome.

The speaker, a Superior Person who is affected in his speech, is particularly shocked by the substitution trick played by Pompilia's pretended mother because it affects the rights of property, and 'the mode':

> A crime complete in its way is here, I hope?
> Lies to God, lies to man, every way lies
> To nature and civility and the mode. (iv, 215–17)

[28] ii. 167–9.

He despises 'these cits', and thinks of marriage as a mere commercial transaction in which (in this instance) each side partly
cheated the other. He is very cynical about Violante, and takes
the view that Guido deliberately engineered the affair between
Pompilia and Caponsacchi to get his revenge on her parents. This
sophisticated man is in fact too clever by half, and in the end he has
to admit that he has not got anywhere near the truth, any more
than he has succeeded in holding the attention of the high-born
lady whom he has been addressing:

> Her Excellency must pronounce, in fine!
> What, she prefers going and joining play?
> Her Highness finds it late, intends retire?
> I am of their mind: only, all this talk talked,
> 'T was not for nothing that we talked, I hope?
> Both know as much about it, now, at least,
> As all Rome: no particular thanks, I beg!
> (You'll see, I have not so advanced myself,
> After my teaching the two idiots here!)

After the first four parts, therefore, one third of the way through
the poem, we have been told the truth in a full outline, and we have
heard three versions of what happened which are completely
inaccurate, and which we know to be completely inaccurate.
Whatever they throw light on, it is not the truth about the events
in question. We now come to the accounts given by the three chief
actors in the drama, Guido, Caponsacchi, and Pompilia.

Part V begins more completely in the manner of a 'dramatic
monologue' than any of the preceding parts:

> Thanks, Sir, but, should it please the reverend Court,
> I feel I can stand somehow, half sit down
> Without help, make shift to even speak, you see,
> Fortified by the sip of . . . why, 't is wine,
> Velletri,—and not vinegar and gall,
> So changed and good the times grow!

Claiming as he does to be an aristocrat, Guido senses that the
court will be on his side: from his opening sentence onwards he
never allows it to forget that a nobleman has been put to the
torture. As a plea for pity, made by a man with whom we have no

sympathy whatever, this monologue may be compared with 'Mr. Sludge', and it comes well out of the comparison. It is astonishing that so bad a case can be put so well. Guido's task is to convince the court that it was entirely reasonable that he should have married a very young girl with a good dowry as a compensation for the disappointments of his life, entirely natural that his lust should have turned to hatred when he discovered that her birth and dowry were not what he had supposed. His tone is that of a man of the world who makes no pretence of having loved Pompilia, and who finds that he has been cheated:

> I have paid my pound, await my penny's worth,
> So, hoodwink, starve and properly train my bird,
> And, should she prove a haggard,—twist her neck!
> (v. 708–10)

The cold callousness of his tone contrasts sharply with the passionate jealousy of the speech in *Othello* which helped to inspire the passage.[29] Guido has even the effrontery to maintain that if Pompilia herself had come to the door, when he turned up with his hired assassins, his heart would have been softened, and he might have held his hand: an audacious piece of special pleading which completely fails to convince us. He ends, with the same cynicism which has prompted his insistence on 'honour' throughout his speech, by expressing his confidence in the members of the court, his faith that they

> Shall see truth yet triumphant, justice yet
> A victor in the battle of this world!   (v. 2024–5)

Like Guido's, Caponsacchi's monologue begins abruptly:

> Answer you, Sirs? Do I understand aright?
> Have patience! In this sudden smoke from hell,—
> So things disguise themselves,—I cannot see
> My own hand held thus broad before my face
> And know it again.

For Caponsacchi Pompilia is

> The glory of life, the beauty of the world,
> The splendour of heaven,   (vi. 118–19)

---

[29] III. iii. 264–7.

and the overwhelmingly important fact, hardly referred to by most
of the speakers, is that

> Pompilia is bleeding out her life belike,
> Gasping away the latest breath of all,
> This minute, while I talk—not while you laugh?   (vi. 61–3)

There is a touch of the dash and bravado of Renaissance man
about Caponsacchi, yet in his conduct to Pompilia he has been
completely innocent. He did not write the love-letters which she
received, but he gradually came to see it as his Christian duty to
save her from her monster of a husband, though without any design
of taking her to himself. His monologue is a great deal more manly
than Guido's. Realizing that Guido is a real dragon, he accepts the
role of Saint George,[30] and insists that he stands before the court
'guiltless in thought, word and deed'. There is a good deal of
Browning himself in Caponsacchi, and he enunciates the poet's
own belief in the occasional need for the Hero:

> Here's the exceptional conduct that should claim
> To be exceptionally judged on rules
> Which, understood, make no exception here.   (vi. 1851–3)

A highly intelligent man, he points out that Guido has told two
different stories to the two courts before which he has been
summoned. His speech ends well, with the assertion that 'priests
Should study passion', but his claim that he will now resume the
quiet life appropriate to his vocation breaks off as he utters a last
passionate cry of despair—

> O great, just, good God! Miserable me!

After the cold casuistry of Guido and the passionate appeal for
justice of Caponsacchi, we hear the quiet voice of a girl, caught up
in a nightmare which she has difficulty in comprehending. Pompilia's opening words, as slow moving as Caponsacchi's have been
rapid, are among the unforgettable things in the poem:

> I am just seventeen years and five months old,
> And, if I lived one day more, three full weeks;

[30] vi. 1771–2.

'T is writ so in the church's register,
Lorenzo in Lucina, all my names
At length, so many names for one poor child,
—Francesca Camilla Vittoria Angela
Pompilia Comparini,—laughable!
Also 't is writ that I was married there
Four years ago: and they will add, I hope,
When they insert my death, a word or two,—
Omitting all about the mode of death,—
This, in its place, this which one cares to know,
That I had been a mother of a son
Exactly two weeks.

Pathos is the keynote of Pompilia's speech, but a dignified pathos
which only occasionally falls into sentimentality:

. . . I do not suffer much—
Or too much pain,—and am to die to-night.   (vii. 39–40)

We are reminded of the last words of Beatrice Cenci, in Shelley's
play. It is characteristic of Pompilia that she should think so much
about her child, whom she has hardly seen, and will never see
again. She recalls how, when she heard the knock on the door on
the night of the murder, her heart leapt up with expectation:

Still, I half fancied when I heard the knock
At the Villa in the dusk, it might prove she—
Come to say 'Since he smiles before the time,
'Why should I cheat you out of one good hour?'   (59–62)

She hopes that her son will be told, when he is grown up, that she
had become a woman before she died, young as she was:

Therefore I wish someone will please to say
I looked already old though I was young;
Do I not . . . say, if you are by to speak . . .
Look nearer twenty?   (72–5)

Because she is so proud of her own baby, Pompilia is clear that
Violante did wrong to pretend to be her mother:

If one should take my babe, give him a name,
Say he was not Gaetano and my own,

But that some other woman made his mouth
And hands and feet,—how very false were that! (275-8)

The Archbishop himself had told her that she must sleep with her husband:

But I did wrong, and he gave wrong advice
Though he were thrice Archbishop,—that, I know!—
Now I have got to die and see things clear. (731-3)

She sees Caponsacchi as pure virtue and innocence:

The first word I heard ever from his lips,
All himself in it,—an eternity
Of speech, to match the immeasurable depth
O' the soul that then broke silence—'I am yours'
(1444-7)

A 'Soldier-saint', he has

The broad brow that reverberates the truth. (1796)

Now that she is on her death-bed, Pompilia wants to

Begin the task, I see how needful now,
Of understanding somewhat of my past,—
Know life a little, I should leave so soon. (1664-6)

Of Browning's death-bed monologues this is the only one spoken by a young woman, and the only one spoken by a person of complete innocence and purity.[31] It is well done, if just bordering (from time to time) on *simplesse*. The words that recur, as one seeks to describe it, are Pathos, Pity, and Innocence. Julia Wedgwood described Pompilia as 'a lovely Snowdrop growing out of that dunghill', as a 'dainty, lovely, pathetic little picture . . . like some sudden snatch of melody breaking in on the din of tumult and clamour'.[32] More than a year later she wrote again to tell Browning the view of 'a beautiful soul' of her acquaintance:

I cannot help writing to try to pass on the impression made by Pompilia on a beautiful soul, among my friends. She said it made an impression on her that no work of art had ever approached, that she woke after reading it wondering what had made the world so

---

[31] Unless we wish to add the Pope.
[32] *Wedgwood*, p. 170, followed by a quotation from p. 205.

different and feeling as if she must write to you to express her gratitude. She said it seemed to her the only thing that could approach it
in its effect was a beautiful sunset, that no music even was so pure
and aspiring, that the character shone before her eyes like an upward
flame.

One is reminded of Dickens's rapturous response to *A Blot in the
'Scutcheon*. It is not surprising that Pompilia's monologue made a
particular appeal to the Victorian public, whose attitude to Browning changed as the poem was coming out.[33] The monologue is a
trifle 'Victorian', indeed, in a limiting sense, and lacks the penetrating psychological insight of Browning's greatest monologues;
yet the final emphasis should be on its success, in its own mode.

Part of Browning's intention, in the design of the poem, was
clearly to contrast the various dramatis personæ, as Chaucer had
done—or begun to do—in *The Canterbury Tales*; and the contrast
between Pompilia and Dominus Hyacinthus de Archangelis is as
striking as that between any two of Chaucer's characters. Nor did
Browning ever create a more Chaucerian personage than the
'Pauperum Procurator' charged with the task of defending Guido.
Although we are given scraps of the oration which Archangelis is
preparing for the court, the greater part of his monologue consists
of his own musings as he works on it, and the opening lines are
sufficient to reveal that his heart is not in his work:

> Ah, my Giacinto, he's no ruddy rogue,
> Is not Cinone? What, to-day we're eight?
> Seven and one's eight, I hope, old curly-pate!
> —Branches me out his verb-tree on the slate,
> *Amo-as-avi-atum-are-ans,*
> Up to *-aturus*, person, tense, and mood,
> *Quies me cum subjunctivo* (I could cry)
> And chews Corderius with his morning crust!

His motto is concisely stated at line 18:

> Dispose, O Don, o' the day, first work then play!

---

[33] As acknowledged in the course of the poem: cf. i. 410—
> Well, British Public, ye who like me not,
and i. 1379–80 with xii. 835:
> So, British Public, who may like me yet.

Throughout his mind is more on the evening's birthday party than on the speech that he is preparing, and in his paternal infatuation he expresses the hope that his son's grandfather will die soon (perhaps as a result of overeating at the party) and leave the boy his fortune. While he welcomes the case as an opportunity of displaying his forensic skill, the truth of the matter does not concern him in the slightest. The way in which the monologue is laced with passages from his Latin speech reminds us of Browning's Renaissance characters, and their concern with good Latinity:

> *Sed etiam assassinii qualitate*
> *Qualificatos,* people qualified
> By the quality of assassination's self,
> Dare I make use of such neologism,
> *Ut utar verbo.* (viii. 1572–6)

Very soon his mind has drifted back to the birthday party, and to his astonishment at the life led by people like his legal adversary:

> How the ambitious do so harden heart
> As lightly hold by these home-sanctitudes,
> To me is matter of bewilderment—
> Bewilderment! Because ambition's range
> Is nowise tethered by domestic tie,
> Am I refused an outlet from my home
> To the world's stage?—whereon a man should play
> The man in public, vigilant for law,
> Zealous for truth, a credit to his kind . . . (1773–81)

Of course the effect is highly ironical, as Archangelis is completely cynical about the true facts of the case. He is interested in the law, but not at all in justice, and he bases his case on the ground of Honour,

> . . . a gift of God to man
> Precious beyond compare. (459–60)

He is not concerned about Guido's treatment of his wife, nor does it even occur to him that Pompilia and Caponsacchi may be innocent of adultery. One of his finest pieces of special pleading occurs when he has to oppose a powerful argument brought by his opponent: the

fact that Guido's delay in taking his revenge weakens the contention
that he was passionate in the defence of his honour:

> Object not, 'You reached Rome on Christmas-eve,
> 'And, despite liberty to act at once,
> 'Waited a whole and indecorous week!'
> Hath so the Molinism, the canker, lords,
> Eaten to our bone?[34] Is no religion left?
> No care for aught held holy by the Church?
> What, would you have us skip and miss those Feasts
> O' the Natal Time, must we go prosecute
> Secular business on a sacred day?   (1071–9)

He has the effrontery to defend Guido by maintaining that he went
to the Sistine Chapel, like a good Catholic, before proceeding with the
plans for his multiple murder. It is characteristic of Archangelis
to state that he sees only 'one sole and single knotty point' in the
whole fabric of the defence—the defence, as one might well suppose,
of the indefensible—and no less characteristic that he sees this
highly technical point particularly vividly with reference to his
own little son. By an extraordinary twist of argument, he proclaims
the 'rectitude' of Guido's hired accomplices, and Guido's own
'integrity'.[35] The assassins did their work purely for money, and
when Guido absent-mindedly refrained from paying them they
innocently schemed to murder him to gain the wages due to them.
One of the most striking things about the whole monologue is the
manner in which his love for his little son (which is instinctive
rather than rational or moral) coexists with a callous indifference
to Pompilia and the vile crime that has been committed. He is a
cynical man, with nothing admirable about him; yet he is human,
and the conclusion of his monologue is somehow appealing:

> Into the pigeon-hole with thee, my speech!
> Off and away, first work then play, play, play!
> Bottini, burn thy books, thou blazing ass!
> Sing 'Tra-la-la, for, lambkins, we must live!'

---

[34] Almost every character refers to Molinism, usually in a highly characteristic
manner. On Molinism in the poem see A. K. Cook, *A Commentary upon Browning's
'The Ring and the Book'* (1920), Appendix viii, and William Coyle, 'Molinos: "The
Subject of the Day" in *The Ring and the Book'*, *PMLA* 67 (1952), 308–14.

[35] viii. 1604.

There is absolutely nothing that is appealing about Juris Doctor Johannes-Baptista Bottinius, whose monologue, but for a few lines at the beginning and the end, consists of the text of the speech which he will shortly be making in court. The only thing that he and his opponent have in common is a complete indifference to the truth: later in the poem, indeed, Bottinius complains that he is always given the easy side in a case, so that he has no opportunity of displaying his skill in making the worse appear the better cause. He opens with an elaborate simile or story by way of exordium, and throughout makes frequent appeals to antiquity, 'Our one infallible guide'. His attitude to Pompilia is merely condescending, and when he refers to

> . . . melting wiles, deliciousest deceits,
> The whole redoubled armoury of love,   (ix. 231–2)

we realize how far he is from comprehending the nature of innocence. The innocence of Pompilia hardly occurs to him as a possibility, nor is it at all interesting to him. His concern is with his own rhetoric, and the nice selection of his figures of speech:

> The Pope, we know, is Neapolitan
> And relishes a sea-side simile.   (372–3)

He regards 'impudence' as of the essence of the feminine character, and addresses the court as one cynic addressing others:

> . . . What i' the way
> Of wile should have allowance like a kiss
> Sagely and sisterly administered,
> *Sororia saltem oscula?*   (678–81)

Although Bottinius claims to be defending a saint, in fact Pompilia is besmirched by every word that he speaks.

When the Pope speaks, a man of wisdom succeeds two men who are merely clever. The musings of an old man rendered lonely both by his position and by his great age form a perfect contrast to the legalistic wrangling of the lawyers, and the verse which the Pope is given to speak is the perfect expression of his character:

> Like to Ahasuerus, that shrewd prince,
> I will begin,—as is, these seven years now,

My daily wont,—and read a History
(Written by one whose deft right hand was dust
To the last digit, ages ere my birth)
Of all my predecessors, Popes of Rome . . .

In striving to reach a just view of the case, he harks back to his own earlier life and experience:

My ancient self, who wast no Pope so long
But studiedst God and man, the many years
I' the school, i' the cloister, in the diocese
Domestic, legate-rule in foreign lands,—
Thou other force in those old busy days
Than this grey ultimate decrepitude . . .   (x. 384–9)

Old as he is, the directness and lucidity of his reasoning give the lie to the rumour, credited by Archangelis and others, that the Pope is senile. On the contrary, his summing up is both shrewd and just, as he reaches the conclusion that Pompilia is 'First of the first, Perfect in whiteness'. In the latter part of his monologue he muses on matters suggested by the Franceschini affair—the vogue of Molinism, the historical importance of Euripides, and the fact that an age of beneficial scepticism (clearly the Enlightenment) will soon dawn on mankind. It is a relief when the Pope gets back to the case, and the verse tautens and improves as he does so, at the end of his monologue:

For the main criminal I have no hope
Except in such a suddenness of fate.
I stood at Naples once, a night so dark
I could have scarce conjectured there was earth
Anywhere, sky or sea or world at all:
But the night's black was burst through by a blaze—
Thunder struck blow on blow, earth groaned and bore,
Through her whole length of mountain visible:
There lay the city thick and plain with spires,
And, like a ghost disshrouded, white the sea.
So may the truth be flashed out by one blow,
And Guido see, one instant, and be saved.
Else I avert my face, nor follow him
Into that sad obscure sequestered state

Where God unmakes but to remake the soul
He else made first in vain; which must not be.
Enough, for I may die this very night
And how should I dare die, this man let live?

Carry this forthwith to the Governor!

We notice that four of the monologues are spoken by people close
to death: Pompilia's, the Pope's,[36] and the two by Guido.

Guido's second monologue reminds us of 'Mr. Sludge', as did the
first. This time the situation is even more macabre than in most of
the death-bed monologues by Mrs. Hemans and earlier poets:[37]
Guido is being visited, in the condemned cell, by the Company of
Death. The second presentation of this evil man is so lacking in
subtlety that it prompts the reflection that modern psychology
might have helped Browning to make him more interesting, if not
more sympathetic. Guido still speaks as a casuist to casuists, but
more particularly as a nobleman to noblemen, referring continually to his own 'honour' but showing no sympathy at all either for
Pompilia or for the child whom she has borne him. In the 'appropriate drunkenness of the death-hour' he exposes his own character
completely, dying boastful and unrepentant,[38] playing desperately
for time and finally crying out in terror:

Abate, Cardinal,—Christ,—Maria,—God, . .
Pompilia, will you let them murder me?

In the last part, comparatively brief as it is, we are presented
with four further accounts of the affair. The first is a letter from a
'Venetian visitor at Rome' who is astonished at the Pope's severity
(by which he himself has lost a bet), which he can only attribute to
political prejudice. He goes on to describe the scene of the execution with zest, and to give a completely false account of Guido's

---

[36] Pope Innocent XII lived two further years, dying as a very old man: in the
poem, however, he regards himself as being close to death.

[37] Cf. Fuson, pp. 37–43.

[38] Langbaum (p. 111) believes that Guido's last cry 'is his salvation', and that
'The implication is that he dies repentant'. Historical accounts of Franceschini's end
do claim that he died repentant, but as they are inspired by the Church that is not
surprising. My interpretation corresponds to that of Cook (Appendix x), with which
DeVane tentatively agrees.

allegedly penitent death. 'No, friend, this will not do!', the poet observes explicitly, before passing on to another letter, a letter addressed to Archangelis in which the writer regrets that certain points that might have assisted the defence have reached him too late to be of use. Archangelis comments characteristically on the letter, recurs to his favourite subject, his little boy—who has greatly enjoyed the execution—consoles himself with the reflection that the Pope always was stubborn, and hastens on to the preparation of his next case. The third account is a letter from the other lawyer, Bottinius: so far from being proud to have been spokesman for 'truth, at issue with a lie', he regrets that he has had, 'as usual, the plain truth to plead'. He too believes the falsehood put about by the Church, that Guido died penitent. In spite of his success, he is in no good humour, being particularly incensed by a sermon preached by an Augustinian monk on the text 'Let God be true, and every man A liar'. A passage from this sermon is the last account of all. The monk warns his congregation that truth cannot always 'look for vindication from the world', affirms that in this case God has put forth 'His right-hand recognizably', and praises the Pope as God's instrument,

> . . . an old good man
> Who happens to hate darkness and love light.
>
> (xii. 593–4)

Although the monk is not certain that he himself has done rightly in abjuring ordinary human love, he is quite certain of the unreliability of rumour, the emptiness of human fame. As fame has been Bottinius's great aim in life, reading this sermon infuriates him, and he decides to take advantage of a technical slip by which Pompilia's innocence has not been formally proclaimed by the court to plead that she must be judged guilty of adultery, so that her will should be set aside and her goods given to the 'Monastery of the Convertites'. Bottinius exclaims that this will show the meddling monk the true power of the law, whereas in fact it confirms what the monk has said, that only in exceptional cases is the truth recognized by human justice.

In the last 120 lines the poet himself addresses the 'British

Public, who may like me yet', commenting on the sequel, approving of the Pope's hope that 'doubt would do the next age good', and preaching

> This lesson, that our human speech is naught,
> Our human testimony false, our fame
> And human estimation words and wind.

He reverts to a subject broached in the first part, the importance of Art,

> . . . the one way possible,
> Of speaking truth, to mouths like mine at least.

Mere assertion of facts is unconvincing, but Art can show the truth,

> Beyond mere Imagery on the wall,—
> So, note by note, bring music from your mind,
> Deeper than ever e'en Beethoven dived,—
> So write a book shall mean beyond the facts,
> Suffice the eye and save the soul beside.

Two of the most careful students of *The Ring and the Book*, Richard D. Altick and James F. Loucks, have done well to cite a passage from Carlyle's essay 'On History':

Nay, even with regard to those occurrences which do stand recorded, which, at their origin have seemed worthy of record, and the summary of which constitutes what we now call History, is not our understanding of them altogether incomplete; is it even possible to represent them as they were? The old story of Sir Walter Raleigh's looking from his prison-window, on some street tumult, which afterwards three witnesses reported in three different ways, himself differing from them all, is still a true lesson for us. Consider how it is that historical documents and records originate; even honest records, where the reporters were unbiased by personal regard; a case which, were nothing more wanted, must ever be among the rarest. . . .[39]

---

[39] Thomas Carlyle, *Critical and Miscellaneous Essays*, ii ('Centenary Edition', vol. xxvii), 87: quoted by Altick and Loucks, pp. 26–7. Carlyle described the poem as 'a book of prodigious talent and unparalleled ingenuity', but his further comment that 'of all the strange books produced on this distracted earth, by any of the sons of Adam, this one was altogether the strangest and the most preposterous in its construction' offended Browning, who 'bade me good morning': see *Carlyle in Old Age*, by D. A. Wilson and D. W. MacArthur (1934), p. 176.

Browning's 'Roman Murder Story' was certainly far from being an example of this 'rarest' case, yet he was quite explicit about the nature of his aim in a letter to Julia Wedgwood:

The business has been . . . to explain *fact*—and the fact is what you see and, worse, are to see.[40] The question with me has never been, 'Could not one, by changing the factors, work out the sum to better result?' but declare and prove the actual result, and there an end. Before I die, I hope to purely invent something,—here my pride was concerned to invent nothing: the minutest circumstance that denotes character is *true*: the black is so much—the white, no more.[41]

By giving voices to a dozen and more people of the time (both the actors in the events described and a number of bystanders and commentators on the action) Browning attempts to provide a 'stereoscopic view'[42] which will throw the truth into bold relief.

This at once presents itself as an interesting literary experiment rather than an impressive method of testing the truth, since the gossips in Parts II, III, and IV know very few of the facts, and are completely biased, while the hired advocates are not interested in the truth, wishing merely to display their own ingenuity and win the case. Only two of the speakers can know the truth about Pompilia's chastity—Caponsacchi and Pompilia herself—and they tell the same story. Only two can know the truth about the murder— Guido and Pompilia—and one of them is a scoundrel and a liar, the other an innocent and truthful girl. In the essay just quoted, Carlyle goes on to point out that in some instances the historical truth is 'passed over unnoticed, because no Seer, but only mere Onlookers, chanced to be there!' Although there is no danger of that occurring on this occasion, Browning himself plays the 'Seer' or 'recording chief-inquisitor'[43] quite openly at a number of points in the poem, most decidedly in Part I and near the conclusion of Part XII. Browning is so open about this that it is hard to see why he was so set on periodical publication. Chesterton described *The Ring and the Book* as 'essentially speaking, a detective story',

[40] Browning was writing in November 1868, when only the first of the four volumes of the poem had been published.

[41] *Wedgwood*, pp. 158–9.

[42] Julia Wedgwood's phrase: *Wedgwood*, p. 152.

[43] 'How It Strikes A Contemporary', l. 39.

claiming that it 'has exactly the same kind of exciting quality that a detective story has';[44] but if the essential thing about a detective story is that the reader is kept guessing to the end about the identity of the criminal then Browning's poem has nothing in common with a detective story. It is true that Chesterton immediately qualifies his statement by claiming that 'its difference from the ordinary detective story is that it seeks to establish, not the centre of criminal guilt, but the centre of spiritual guilt', but even then his claim is hard to substantiate. It would be correct to state that the 'truth' that unfolds as the poem progresses is not the truth about the action, but rather the full truth about the motivation of the dramatis personæ; yet even of this we are given the essential outline near the beginning.

It would also be fair to comment that the truth as Browning saw it was extremely simple. Bishop Blougram tells Gigadibs that we are all most interested in mixed characters,

> The honest thief, the tender murderer,
> The superstitious atheist, demirep
> That loves and saves her soul in new French books,[45]

but one of the most striking things about the principal characters in *The Ring and the Book* is that they are depicted in black and white.[46] Chesterton claimed that the poem is peculiarly modern because Browning

perceived that if we wish to tell the truth about a human drama, we must not tell it merely like a melodrama, in which the villain is villainous and the comic man is comic. He saw that the truth had not been told until he had seen in the villain the pure and disinterested gentleman that most villains firmly believe themselves to be, or until he had taken the comic man as seriously as it is the custom of comic men to take themselves.[47]

---

[44] Chesterton, p. 168.

[45] ll. 396–8.

[46] Cf. Langbaum, p. 135: 'It is certainly a valid criticism of *The Ring and the Book* that good and evil are not sufficiently interfused. Our judgment is forced from the beginning, whereas it would seem to be peculiarly the genius of a poem treating different points of view toward the same story to treat each point of view impartially, allowing judgment to arise out of the utmost ambiguity.'

[47] Chesterton, pp. 174–5.

If ever a villain was villainous, we must reply, it is Guido:[48] when he portrays himself as a 'pure and disinterested gentleman' (and he comes near to that, once or twice), it is in pure cynicism, as an exercise in casuistry which he more or less expects to be taken for what it is. Browning could have made Guido a more sympathetic character, grey rather than black, but it is clear that he had no desire to do so. If ever a heroine was virtuous, equally, it is Pompilia. The character of Caponsacchi gave Browning a more obvious opportunity for subtlety of characterization, but even with it he chooses a very straightforward portrayal. The young priest is reformed by love as completely as Troilus in Chaucer's great poem, although unlike Troilus he does not aspire to the natural end of sexual love.

If we consider Browning's claim to be a faithful historian, then we are bound to conclude that he is excessively credulous, since it is hard to believe that Pompilia and Caponsacchi were technically 'innocent', harder to believe that they were altogether virtuous and Guido altogether evil. But our concern is with the poem as a work of the imagination, and on this ground we are bound to point out that it would be better, subtler, more interesting, if what we guess to have been the historical truth were (in any event) presented as the imaginative truth of the poem. Julia Wedgwood was right when she told Browning that she would 'allow [him] no advantage whatever from the fact of [his] material being history':

'Tant pis pour les faits!' if they are not artistic. Fate has no conception of the fitness of things, you must not copy her bungling sketches, full as they are of false perspective and harsh colouring, but give us some relief from her coarse picture gallery by your truer representations.[49]

If Guido were not wholly a villain, if Pompilia and Caponsacchi were lovers, the poem would be more compellingly interesting and the moral issues raised more worthy of our attention.

The same lack of subtlety appears in the characters of the two advocates and of the Pope. Browning felt the contempt for hired lawyers that is characteristic of many imaginative men of high

---

[48] 'The poet in his ancient office', Chesterton further observes, 'held a kind of terrestrial day of judgment, and gave men halters and haloes; Browning gives men neither halter nor halo, he gives them voices' (p. 171). In fact halters and haloes are only too much in evidence, in *The Ring and the Book*.   [49] *Wedgwood*, p. 191.

principles and impatient temper. In one of his letters to Julia Wedgwood he refers to his advocates as 'the buffoon lawyers', while in another he wrote explicitly:

I hate the lawyers: and confess to tasting something of the satisfaction, as I emphasize their buffoonery, which was visible (they told me at Balliol, the other day) on the sour face of one Dr Jenkins, whilom Master of the College, when, having to read prayers, he would of a sudden turn and apostrophize the obnoxious Fellows, all out of the discreet words of the Psalmist, 'As for liars, I hate and abhor them!'[50]

Browning's contempt for Archangelis is not in question, yet we notice that the merit of his monologue suggests that the poet took pleasure in depicting his character, just as Chaucer (we may conjecture) took pleasure in depicting the characters of the Monk and the Summoner. As for the Pope, he is a wholly good old man, *ex officio*, the 'office' in question not being the Papacy (indeed), for which Browning had little respect, but that of the poet's own spokesman in the poem. Julia Wedgwood noticed this at once:

I feel as if there were more of that which seems to me your special message to us in the Pope's speech than in anything else you have written—it seems to me to leave my mind full of seeds. . . . There is a sense of the great schism of life being healed in some chords of yours . . . that I have never felt equally in any one else. I can feel, as I listen to Innocent, that this poor little planet is a good inn for our souls to rest in, before they start on the long journey. . . .[51]

It is interesting to juxtapose a sentence or two from Henry James, as he reflects on the 'latent prose fiction' that might be extracted from *The Ring and the Book*:

Greatest of all the spirits exhibited, however, is that of the more than octogenarian Pope, at whose brooding, pondering, solitary vigil, by the end of a hard grey winter day in the great bleak waiting Vatican . . . we assist as intimately as at every other step of the case, and on whose grand meditation we heavily hang. But the Pope strikes us at first—though indeed perhaps only at first—as too high above the

---

[50] *Wedgwood*, pp. 167, 177.
[51] Ibid., pp. 180–1.

whole connection functionally and historically for us to place him within it dramatically.[52]

James is clearly in two minds about the Pope, for on the one hand he considers dispensing with him, while on the other he is tempted to envisage, as 'the very end and splendid climax of all', a scene in which Caponsacchi is 'sent for to the Vatican and admitted alone to the Papal presence. *There* is a scene if we will; and in the mere mutual confrontation, brief, silent, searching, recognising, consecrating, almost as august on the one part as on the other.' It would have been a strange scene, and an impressive one, if it had really been 'silent', and it is an obvious criticism that every speaker in *The Ring and the Book* goes on talking for far too long. To this criticism the Pope's monologue is particularly vulnerable, although its last 900 lines no longer seem irrelevant when we realize that Browning is not merely concerned with the truth about one particular incident, but with the whole question of man's search for truth.

In spite of all the talk about the 'stereoscopic' and 'relativist' elements in *The Ring and the Book*, one is driven to the conclusion that the complexity of its technique is more apparent than real, and that the poem is inspired by a vision of life that is simpler and more naïve than that which informs the great short poems of the 1840s and 1850s. Browning's concern with the idiosyncrasies of men and women has become less disinterested: his growing eagerness to teach is associated with a slight yet clearly perceptible waning of his dramatic skill. 'What easy work these novelists have of it!', he had written to Elizabeth Barrett more than twenty years before:

a Dramatic poet has to *make* you love or admire his men and women,— they must *do* and *say* all that you are to see and hear—really do it in your face, say it in your ears, and it is wholly for *you*, in *your* power, to *name*, characterize and so praise or blame, *what* is so said and done . . if you don't perceive of yourself, there is no standing by, for the Author, and telling you.[53]

    [52] 'The Novel in "The Ring and the Book" ', in *Notes on Novelists* (1914), pp. 315–16.
    [53] Kintner, i. 150.

In *The Ring and the Book*, as we have seen, the author does 'stand by', so anxious is he that his message should not go by default. The 'modernity' of the poem has been exaggerated, alike by Chesterton and by Langbaum,[54] and it is difficult to see it as other than a dead end in the history of English poetry. When Fielding wrote *Joseph Andrews* and *Tom Jones* the example of classical epic helped him not only to produce two books of major importance but also to prepare the novel for further development in the hands of his successors. When Browning wrote *The Ring and the Book* the example of the novel helped him to produce a poem a hundred times more readable than his wife's *Aurora Leigh*, but he neither created a masterpiece nor pointed the way to the poets who succeeded him. While *The Ring and the Book* is the most impressive long poem written in the Victorian Age, it is also a reminder that no great long poem was written in the Victorian Age.

If we compare *The Ring and the Book* with *Troilus and Criseyde*—and Browning is a poet of sufficient stature to justify such a comparison—Browning's poem is bound to look a little provincial, reminding us of the limitations of Victorian England as a seed-bed for serious poetry. No comparison that can fairly be made has a similarly reductive effect on 'My Last Duchess', 'The Bishop Orders His Tomb', and a number of the other shorter poems to which I have returned time and again throughout this study because they form the centre of a body of work which gives Browning an assured place in the major tradition of English poetry.

[54] Cf. John Killham, 'Browning's "Modernity": *The Ring and the Book*, and Relativism', in *The Major Victorian Poets*, ed. Isobel Armstrong. For Langbaum's reply, see the preface to the 1972 re-issue of *The Poetry of Experience*.

INDEX

(This index does not include the Preface)